Sutton

## ALASKA 1932

The triple promise of gold, flying fellowship and a chance to be his own boss beckoned Bob Reeve to the Far North. He had already done his pioneering in South America, flying routes that no one else dared to do. But he was stirred by stories of the Alaskan bush pilots, a hardy breed of independent, freelance flyers who were conquering Alaska in their single-engine planes, without airports, navigational aids or government subsidy. Without help from anyone, they were making history on their own, charting the wilderness by learning to "read" the nameless mountains and rivers.

## GLACIER PILOT

Over the next thirty years he carved an intrepid niche for himself in that brotherhood. This is the story of those years, the adventures and exploits of the man who became "Mr. Alaska."

# GLACIER PILOT

*The Story of Bob Reeve
and the Flyers Who
Pushed Back Alaska's Air Frontiers*

## Beth Day

A COMSTOCK EDITION

Library of Congress Catalog Card Number: 57-6761

ISBN: 0-89174-009-0

This edition published by arrangement with
Holt, Rinehart and Winston

Third Printing: May 1981
Fourth Printing: October 1986

Printed in the United States of America

Additional copies of this book may be obtained by sending a check or money order for the price of the book
plus a dollar for the first copy and 75¢ for each additional copy ordered. A free catalog of books published
by Comstock is also available.

**COMSTOCK EDITIONS, INC.**
3030 Bridgeway, Sausalito, CA 94965

*To Tillie Reeve and Donald Day,*
*who stood by with Jovian patience,*
*high good humor, and lively encouragement*
*while this book was being put together*

# Contents

# Preface

If you look down upon a world globe, you will see that Alaska and the Arctic compose the most centrally located area on earth. From the North Pole it is only 2950 miles to New York; 2300 to London; 2050 to Moscow. "If World War II should come," predicted General H. H. "Hap" Arnold, "the strategic center will be the North Pole."

A natural air theater, its cities divided by virtually insurmountable terrain, Alaska was using airpower as its means of transportation, its supply line, and its source of emergency aid, long before the rest of America was even taking aviation seriously. Today, Alaskans fly thirty times more per capita than other U.S. citizens. The growth of Alaskan aviation is without parallel; its development is the story of the courage and initiative of its individual citizens and pilots.

When you first board one of the big, comfortable Northwest Airlines Stratocruisers, out at Idlewild Airport in New York, you get your initial taste of frontier Alaska in the friendly informality of the plane's personnel. At the bustling Seattle airport, as you listen to schedules being announced in Japanese and Hawaiian, you begin to realize just how far west—as well as north—the Territory really is, but a handspring from the Orient. Flying Northwest's northbound flight to Alaska, over a wilderness of open water and forest slashed by fir-lined fjords that cut inland from the open sea, you are aware of how awesomely impenetrable much of our Far North is. But the man beside you points to those uninhabited landmarks as old friends. He is Alaskan, with the frontiersman's identity with space. As you circle over Cook Inlet approaching the city of Anchorage, he tells you proudly that Anchorage was, during World War II, the fastest-growing city in the world, its population leaping from 12,000 to

60,000 within a few hectic years; that it is the purest transportation town in America, with 98 per cent of its business in transportation, and that predominantly by air.

There is little doubt that Alaska, at long last, is on the march—its isolated, mountainous terrain connected by a network of modern airways, its skies filled with planes. It is our jumping-off point to the Orient by way of the Aleutian Islands, and to Europe by way of the North Pole.

But, until a few short years ago, Alaska was ignored both strategically and in the development of commercial aviation. Without federal aid or modern navigational equipment, Alaskan bush flyers pioneered the skies of the Far North and prepared the way for both the commercial and military flying of the future.

This is the story of one of those aerial pioneers, glacier pilot Bob Reeve. It is also the story of Alaska's coming of age, and of the other daring flyers who, along with Reeve, converted its vast wastelands into the busy air center of today. If at times it seems to be a record of forced landings, near-disasters, and crack-ups, it is because the thousands of successful, uneventful flights made by Reeve and the other pilots do not reveal the drama of their story. Those were the "routine" that they were striving to establish against tremendous physical odds. Many of those early flyers have crashed to their deaths. Fortunately, a number are left who are able to tell not only their own stories but those of the men who are gone.

I wish to thank those men who cooperated so unstintingly in the creation of this book: flyers Ray Petersen, Merle Smith, Noel and Sig Wien, and Jack Jefford; mechanic Tom Appleton; Reeve Airways Captains Borland, Kelly, and Forsythe; Wien Airline Captains Hulshizer and Friericks; and Wien's Point Barrow station manager, Forrest Solomon.

Special thanks are due to the personnel of Northwest Airlines, both at Saint Paul, Minnesota, and at Anchorage, who contributed so generously to this book: Chairman of the Board Croil Hunter; President Donald Nyrop; Vice President Frank Judd; Anchorage Manager A. B. "Cot" Hayes; George Masters and Jerry Anderson of the Public Relations office; and Northwest Captains Fairbrother and O'Neill.

I wish also to express my appreciation to the Civil Aeronautics Administration's Chief of Public Information, Mr. Charles Planck, and the other CAA and CAB personnel in Washington who took the time and had the patience to explain the various facets of aviation legislation.

Thanks, too, for their fine Alaskan hospitality, to Mr. and Mrs. Thornton Wheaton, Artists Sara and Fred Machetanz, Ellen and Harvey Goodale, Mr. and Mrs. Elmer Rasmuson, Mr. and Mrs. Noel Wien, Mrs. Helen Buckingham, and Mr. and Mrs. Clifford Cernick of the *Anchorage News*. I am also grateful to Alaskans Admiral C. E. "Squeaky" Anderson, Mr. Henry W. Clark, Bill Egan, and Owen Meals, who all provided invaluable sources of information.

Mr. Bradford Washburn, director of the Boston Museum of Science, was kind enough to give of his time, as well as the permission to use material from his private journals of the Lucania expedition. Mr. D. W. H. MacKinnon, Vice President of Northeast Airlines, was helpful in filling in background on Reeve's early life.

Finally, thanks go to the Reeve family—Richard, Roberta, Janice, David, and Whitham Reeve, and "Grandma" Morisette—as well as the Reeve Airways office personnel, who all put up so graciously with the confusion while this book was being assembled; to Clara Kent Pearce, without whose expert help this manuscript could not have been read; and to Howard Cady, for enthusiastic encouragement.

*Beth Day*

Chappaqua, New York
March 15, 1957

# 1. He looked like a tramp

As the weekly summer freighter whistled up to the wooden dock of Valdez, Alaska, one brisk, sunny day in 1932, a man slipped quietly from under a covering of tarpaulin on one side of the deck, jumped ashore, then elbowed through the mixed throng of whites, Indians, Old Russians,* and bearded sourdoughs who lined the pier, watching the boat unload. As he strode down the board walkway toward the center of town, the stranger's footsteps echoed hollowly on the planks that crossed the tidewater flats on a trestle and led to the main street, parallel to the sea and one block north of the dock. Main Street, the stranger found, was an empty slash of muddy road, lined on both sides by unpainted false-front buildings. There were two hotels, a grocery, a Chinese restaurant. At the northeast corner of the main intersection, the Pinzon opened hospitable doors to any man interested in a game of billiards, bar service, a hand of cards, or a place to sit down. But even the Pinzon appeared momentarily deserted. Valdez' four hundred-odd citizens had apparently all gone down to the dock to watch the steamer unload. The newcomer hesitated, then walked on to the edge of town, where he spied a knot of workmen mending the dike that circled the back of the little village. Beyond it a mighty range of mountains jutted from sea level up to snow-covered peaks ten thousand feet high. Each spring, at breakup time, the ring of glaciers back of Valdez, drain lines of the giant ice cap, sent down torrential streams that but for the dike, would have inundated the town. The rutted road that led north of the village to connect with the Richardson Highway, which bisects the Alaskan interior, crossed twenty-nine glacial streams before it attained solid ground.

* Descendants of Russian colonists who came to Alaska in the eighteenth century.

1

As he approached them, the stranger noticed that although the workmen remained at the site of their jobs, they were looking down at the dock below, at the scene that provided Valdez with its main weekly attraction in the summer, its monthly entertainment during the long, snow-drenched Alaskan winters. Valdez, unlike most insular, seasonally isolated Alaskan towns, enjoyed the luxury of year-round boat service. The Valdez Arm, extending from Prince William Sound in the Gulf of Alaska, stayed open throughout the year, making the little town the "farthest north year-round open port in the world." Blessed by open water and towering mountains, Valdez liked to think of itself as the "Switzerland of America." Some found it more like Norway, with its deep glacial fjords and craggy peaks.

As the newcomer drew near them, the workmen watched him with open curiosity. Tall, thin to the point of gauntness, the man walked with a pronounced limp, as at every third or fourth step his right leg seemed to refuse his body's weight and gave way beneath him. He was dressed in knee-high laced boots, dirty hiking pants, an absurdly (to Alaskan minds) long leather jacket that hung in shreds almost to his boot tops. A tight billed cap was pulled down over his dark hair. His face, shadowed by the cap, was taut and sharply molded, dominated by brilliant blue-gray eyes and a clipped dark mustache over thin, tightly drawn lips. "He looked," the Valdez group decided, "like he could use a shave and a free meal."

"You a flyer?" asked eighteen-year-old George Ashby as the stranger drew within speaking range.

"Yes," the man grunted, a slight smile relaxing the edges of his compressed mouth. "How'd you guess?"

"Your boots," grinned George, pointing to the high laced boots, which were one of the trademarks of flyers of that period. The boy eyed the man with fresh interest. Flying was the biggest thing in Alaska—and Valdez—in 1932.

"Any flying going on here?" the man asked in a low, gritty voice.

"Sure!" George said, his dark eyes lighting with pride. "Frank Pollack's got his Monocoupe based here right now. And Wien, Mirow, Gillam—all of 'em get in here, bringing in passengers for the boats."

"Any planes around here that no one's using?" pressed the

stranger. "I heard over in Seward that there was an Eaglerock——"

"Yep," the sturdy youngster nodded a quick affirmative. "That belongs to Owen Meals. He doesn't fly any more, but he has been leasing it out by the hour to other pilots. The last guy overshot the field and wrecked it."

"Where is it?" the stranger interrupted impatiently.

"Over there at our field." George pointed proudly to an area beginning just inside the dike, where a swath of ground about twelve hundred feet long had been cleared of trees and rock. It was faced at the north by the six-foot dike, and a fifty-foot high-tension wire stretched menacingly across the southern end. On the town side of the airstrip a garage building was labeled. "Owen Meals, Ford Dealer, Mechanic." Nearby stood a diminutive hangar.

"Thanks," the stranger muttered, and headed for the garage.

Valdez was justifiably proud of its short, hazardous runway. Most towns in the Territory didn't have that much. All Alaska had was need. Its cities, isolated from each other by a series of great mountain ranges and by stretches of soggy tundra over frozen subsoil, were, as General Nathan Twining was years later to call them, "but islands in a vast sea." Their one chance of intercommunication, of year-round supplies and mail, lay in the airplane. It was to become their train, bus, ambulance, and hearse. When John Barrymore's yacht lay along Alaska's southeastern shores, other flyers presented pilot Clayton Scott (now a test pilot for Boeing) with a leather medal for being the first aerial laundry driver, when he took the job of flying dirty laundry from ship to shore. (The first outboard motor introduced to Alaska was unfortunately lost when a depressed citizen of Anchorage borrowed it to tie around his neck and leap into the Knik Arm.) "My most interesting load," reported Jack Jefford (now chief pilot for CAA), "was two murderers, two insane men—and Miss Alaska!" With no federal airfields in Alaska, and no federal appropriations to build any, the ingenious Alaskans took it upon themselves to make a home for the airplanes they needed. Local businessmen pooled their cash to buy planes and hire pilots for their towns. Spurred by pioneer Alaskan aviator Ben Eielson's experiments at Fairbanks in 1923, railroad man Jimmy Rodebaugh made a trip Outside the following year, and came back with two used Army Standard trainers and a lanky blond Minnesota stunt pilot named Noel Wien. The merchants of Cordova treated young Harold Gillam—who had come to Alaska as a construction worker and learned to fly at Fairbanks—to three planes, which Gillam managed to wreck six times in six months in 1931, but Cordova needed air service badly enough to keep Gillam in planes despite his luck. Over at Juneau, fisherman Nick Bez and other businessmen had taken over a defunct Seattle-Alaska air service and its manager, A. B. "Cot" Hayes (now Anchorage manager of Northwest Airlines), and were struggling to establish the first scheduled airline in Alaska, to service the fishing industry.

When Alaskans wanted airplanes to land at their town, the citizens banded together to clear a runway that would make a landing feasible. As far back as the spring of 1923, the total population of the little railroad town of Anchorage had declared a public holiday and turned out with shovels, rakes, and scythes to clear an airstrip. They later named it Merrill Field, in honor of ex-Navy flyer Russ Merrill, who pioneered flying in the Anchorage area before his plane was lost over Cook Inlet in 1929. During spring breakup, when the airfield became unusable, the local pilots obligingly switched temporarily to the city golf course, where the turf and sod held despite the wet season. When an airstrip had been cleared, the Alaska Road Commission (founded in 1920 to look after the Richardson Highway, Alaska's "one road" from the southern coast through to the Interior) took over and willingly shoveled off acres of snow and ice.

There were no communications at Alaskan airfields, no equipment beyond the rough dirt strips. Maps of Alaska, sketched by the Road Commission, were accurate enough but incomplete. Great areas were marked "Unsurveyed." Of what was sketched in, "there was a mighty lot of difference between looking at things from the ground and the air," explains Noel Wien. "The only maps we had were made by men on the ground. When we looked down at the same scene from the air, we saw something very different."

The Alaska Communications Service, under the Army Signal Corp, helped the pilots by offering daily weather reports from its few stations. "They looked out of their window and made a report and a forecast at 8:00 A.M. and 1:00 P.M.," says Cot Hayes, with a smile. "Between and after, it was any-body's guess." There was no report of any kind at intermediate points. A pilot who became a good amateur weather forecaster saved himself a peck of trouble.

Flying was already four years old in Valdez. In 1928 Owen Meals had made the first flight up to Fairbanks, and the town had been air-minded ever since. From Valdez, the original port of entry to the Interior, supplies and people first traversed the Richardson pack trail north in 1905. Gradually expanded to a wagon road, the Richardson finally carried its first automobile in 1913. Although it was open but three months each year, with good luck a man could drive the 360 miles in three days in the summertime (but if he met another car, he had to back up as much as a mile to pass). By air, even with the slow planes necessitated by Alaska's short, rough fields, it wasn't over a three hours' ride. The only other means of getting from the coast "inside" was by the nine-teen-year-old Alaskan Railroad, which stretched 470 miles from Fairbanks to Seward, over ground so hazardous that it was common for the locomotive to jump track—and in winter there were delays of hours and sometimes days while snowslides were cleared off the track. Flying took a tenth of the time—if all went well. And Alaskans were gamblers at heart. It wasn't like the States, where, as Cot Hayes remarked sadly of his 1929 Seattle-to-Alaska air service, "a thousand folks would come down to see the ship land and take off—but no one would get in it."

When the passenger boats (the only means of getting from Alaska to the States) came up the Inside Passage to Valdez and Seward, pilots swarmed like honeybees from all over the Territory, looking for fares back to their home bases. Hans Mirow flew in to pick up passengers for Nome, Oscar Winchell for Anchorage, Noel Wien for Fairbanks. Bob Ellis and Alex Holden vied for passengers for Juneau, Ketchikan, and Sitka, in southeastern Alaska. In that area there was not enough flat land for a railroad, an auto road, or even an airstrip, but a float plane could slip you in almost to your house—if your pilot was as good a seaman as he was a flyer, which Holden and Ellis both were. After docking his float plane at Ketchikan, Bob Ellis regularly delivered his freight by bicycle, from door to door.

The stretch of sketchily cleared ground that was the Val-

dez airport boasted a "city hangar" next to Owen Meals' garage. Along the walls of both buildings were stacked the inevitable drums and cans of gasoline and oil, for all gassing up,
at this time, was still done by hand.

Although there were no planes on the field as the newcomer approached it, Pollack's Monocoupe droned above, then
banked to come in for a landing, hovered briefly over the
strip, and settled to a neat stop. A shy-faced, stockily built
teen-ager slipped out of the cockpit.

"That was a fine landing, son," murmured the stranger ap-
provingly.

"Thanks," the boy said, then added, with a burst of pride,
"I just soloed." He eyed the man's scuffed boots, dirty trou-
sers, and odd, ragged jacket with frank curiosity. "I'm Bill
Egan."

"Reeve," growled the older man, "Bob Reeve." He smiled
briefly. "Last time I flew a Monocoupe I was lucky to get
away from it."

"Oh?" Egan looked incredulous as he silently compared the
ragged stranger before him with Valdez' air heroes: trim,
neat, prosperous-looking fellows like Noel Wien, Joe Crosson,
Harold Gilliam. Of them all, it was Gilliam who played the
part best. Fastidious, trim-bodied, and broodingly handsome,
Gilliam was a hero all along the coast of Alaska. Asked to
write an essay about his favorite person, a third-grade Indian
student in Cordova had written a poem:

> *"He thrill em*
> *Chill em*
> *Spill em*
> *But no killem*
> *Gillam."*

Frugal of speech, withdrawn, but warm to his friends, swar-
thy, gypsy-eyed Harold was the favorite of children, air-crazy
boys, and especially women. "Everybody loved Harold," explained one oldtimer, then added sagely, "—except maybe a
few husbands!"

With a shave, clean clothes, and a more relaxed expression, Reeve too might have been handsome, Bill Egan decided. But he obviously wasn't making anything by it.

Reeve left the boy and walked on over to Owen Meals'

shop, where he found the tall, fair, soft-spoken man working in his garage. Yes, Meals admitted in his slow, slurred speech, he did have an Eaglerock plane. But it was pretty well bunged up. He led the way to the hangar.

The engine, Meals explained, was fine. It was a Wright J5 that had been especially designed and fitted at the Wright Company for Sir Hubert Wilkins to take on his Arctic expeditions. Wilkins and Pilot Ben Eielson had carried it on their history-making flight across the North Pole to Spitsbergen in 1928 as a spare. But the fuselage of the Eaglerock was a mess. When the pilot to whom Meals had leased it had overshot the Valdez field, he had torn off part of the lower wings on tree stumps. Both the lower fuselage and the tail surfaces of the fabric-covered plane were torn. It would need some new ribs, patching, careful realignment—at least a month's work.

"I've been leasing it out at ten dollars an hour," Meals explained.

"I'll pay you that when it's fixed," Reeve agreed. "How about hiring me to do the repair job? I've got my A&E license."

"All right," Meals said affably. "It would take me a while to get to it. I always have auto work to do in the summer months. Tell you what—I'll pay you a dollar an hour to rebuild it. Then you can lease it at the regular rate."

"It's a deal." The men shook hands.

When word went around Valdez that Owen Meals had hired the new man to repair his plane, the consensus had it that Owen was off his rocker. This ragged, down-and-out fellow a mechanic and pilot? He was nothing but a dead beat and a tramp. He'd obviously stowed away on that steamer, too broke to buy his passage. And someone said he'd even bummed medicine off the local druggist.

Valdez could barely wait till the day arrived when the Eaglerock was once more in shape to fly. In the past three or four years, as aviation had caught on in Alaska, the country had swarmed with men who claimed to be pilots. Abandoned wrecks of planes were mute testimony to their senseless, costly bragging. It surprised the citizens of Valdez that a man as substantial as Owen would be fool enough to entrust his plane to another one of these fast-talking "chee chockers." You'd think, they argued, that after that last smashup Owen would be wise enough not to let anyone but a professional touch his plane.

It was the last of July before the Eaglerock was repaired. When word came from the field that the little plane was ready, the report passed swiftly from mouth to mouth, "Owen's mechanic is going to fly that plane. Let's go watch him wreck it!"

Annoyed by their doubts and whisperings, Reeve had said no more about his flying. "I was broke and sick and feeling mean," he admits, "so I didn't communicate much. I just stayed to myself and kept my mouth shut."

The morning that Bob and Owen rolled the Eaglerock out of its hangar, Valdez gathered as if summoned by a mass alarm. In minutes the little airstrip was lined with eager spectators. "It was just like a bullfight," comments Bob. "They were gleeful and excited, just waiting for the kill."

Still dressed in his original outfit of dirty britches and long, ragged jacket, Bob snubbed out the inevitable cigarette that hung from the corner of his mouth, climbed into the pilot's position in the rear seat of the two-seated open-cockpit biplane.

"You going to take it up, son?" called a man from the crowd.

"Yeah," growled Reeve. "No experienced pilots here today, so I'll have to test it myself. I always have wanted to try to fly one of these things."

Someone whistled, the spectators tensed, watching Reeve bend over the controls.

"Why, he doesn't even have a helmet!" sniffed one lady.

"Nor goggles," added another. "He certainly doesn't look like any flyer I ever saw!"

Without comment, Reeve worked quietly, revved up the engine, taxied out into the strip, took off straight up toward the vast ring of mountains that circled the little village of Valdez. In minutes, the Eaglerock was nothing but a dark splotch against the snowcap.

It was all over so quickly that the spectators looked around at each other in disappointment. Only Owen Meals smiled. "Bob handled that little Eaglerock just like he would a big, powerful plane—nice and easy," he recalls. "But then, I wasn't worried. I'd seen his logbook."

Climbing steeply, Reeve headed directly from the tiny

coastal pocket of Valdez up into the Chugach Mountains that ringed the little town. Five miles past the town dike lay the grinding Valdez glacier, one of the twenty-odd tongue glaciers that crawled in frozen torrent down to the valley from the giant ice cap above. On he flew, up toward the ice field where an occasional nunatak appeared in startling contrast to the glistening frozen sea.

Reeve listened contentedly to the steady, sure drone of the engine as he climbed, felt the sing of air around his ears—and, for the first time since he arrived at Valdez, relaxed. It was good to be back on wings again! As craggy saw-tooth peaks and frozen rivers slid beneath him, he soon found himself in a veritable sea of ice and snow. His altimeter registered ten thousand feet. Before him swept an apparently endless horizon-to-horizon stretch of perpetual snow, broken only by the occasional sharp outcroppings of sullen black rock. Some of the mountaintops were jagged, some needlelike, some shaped in spires; but all were incredibly sharp, their knifelike edges piercing the sky as if reaching for the vulnerable belly of the fuselage. Grimmest and mightiest of Alaskan ranges, the no man's land of the Chugach, Reeve knew, stretched eastward with no perceptible break into the Saint Elias of the Canadian Yukon, the second largest ice cap in the world, next only to the Greenland. Reeve looked at his Road Commission map. These mountains were but roughly sketched in, major areas blank: Unsurveyed.

Reeve flew as low as he dared, cannily keeping his small ship away from the violent tugs of the downdraft, lee side of the mountains, while he studied the tongues of ice that leaped forth from the giant peaks. Their frosted surfaces in this summer season were pleated and crinkled by innumerable crevasses, and some—Reeve shuddered as he looked into the lethal ice caves—were large enough to house Valdez' Main Street! In winter, Reeve realized, these dangerous slits would be covered by a deceptive coating of soft snow.

An occasional spot of ground that had escaped the snow cap showed the effect of glacial action, the earth scoured and chewed by the weight of moving ice, then pushed out into giant humps and ridges like a furrowed field. Reeve whistled softly. "And I thought the Andes were tough!"

As he skimmed one knifelike peak that converged onto a glacial field, without warning a sudden violent gust of wind snatched at the plane's fragile wings. Fighting to maintain altitude in the extreme turbulence, Reeve at last managed to climb out into calmer air. So—that was a williwaw!

At each point where glacier and mountain meet, the wind splinters off in sudden, shocking violence. Cold air rushing down from the snow cap speeds toward the warmer air below, and when trapped by a peak, the pressure of the air mass builds into the velocity of a miniature tornado, then spills over with such force that it can snatch and hurtle planes, or even boats sailing along a mountainous shore, to destruction.† These are the unpredictable williwaws of the Far North, hated by men of sea and air.

Reeve flew on, studying the frozen face of the Chugach, the occasional black-watered fjord where chunks of ice lay motionless on the dead water. It was hard to realize that in such an inhospitable, nearly impassable land lay the riches of the earth: gold. The bonanza gold, the easy-to-gather ore, had long since disappeared from Alaska and the Yukon. But rich quartz lodes still lay in these inaccessible peaks, scarcely touched because of the expense and physical labor of getting at them. Reeve circled, flew down over a shelf of ice tucked against a sheer wall of rock. Somewhere along there was the Big Four Mine . . . and the Ramsay Rutherford . . . the Mayfield. . . . Valdez, Reeve knew, had been one of the richest mining centers in Alaska, and had for years boasted its own, stock exchange. But now it was a dead town. Only talk was rich any more. Talk, and a few nuggets in oldtimers' pockets. For the only way to get to the mines up here was by back pack. Men on showshoes making the laborious trek across the face of the glaciers, hauling sleds of equipment (they couldn't use dogs since they fell through the deep snow). Sometimes they used horses, but, manpower or horse, they couldn't get in enough supplies to make it worth while. Now if a man could fly in. . . . Reeve peered at the slippery ramps of ice that hugged the mountain sides. Glistening white sheets, with no distinguishing depth, no perspective. Involuntarily he tightened up. This was a land stronger and tougher than any human being.

† In 1945, a high-pressure area built up behind mountains, out in Prince William Sound, and when it finally spilled over into the town of Anchorage, winds reaching one hundred miles per hour killed twenty-two air-borne people and wrecked sixteen airplanes.

"I already had six years of flying and over three thousand hours," he says, "and my estimate of my ability was not low, but when I had a good look at those saw-tooth peaks and ice caps, and felt the wrench of one of those 'willies,' I figured if I put in ten years flying that stuff, and another ten thousand hours, *maybe* I could call myself a pilot!"

His face set in lines of sober speculation, Reeve turned the little Eaglerock back to the Valdez field.

## 2. It didn't hurt to be a little crazy

"The year I was born," says Bob with a sly grin, "the weather was so bad that not one plane got off the ground!" The year was 1902—just twenty months before the Wrights made the first successful heavier-than-air flight at Kittyhawk. Like many another aviation pioneer, Reeve's own lifetime has paralleled the meteoric strides from Jenny to jet flying. Aviation left its mark on the decade in which he was born, producing men like Lindbergh, Doolittle, Twining, Curt Le May. It was a new profession, and adventurous men were being born to meet it, among them the twin Reeve boys, Robert and Richard.

Born in Waunakee, Wisconsin, sons of the depot agent, the Reeve twins could look back, if they cared to, to an impressive list of rugged Yankee ancestors, who first settled on Long Island in 1690. Seven Reeves fought in the Revolution. The boys' grandfather had pioneered by ox team to Sauk County, Wisconsin, and had been made a captain for his gallantry during an Indian uprising. Their father, "a real old-time Yankee aristocrat" in looks and temperament, was telegrapher and depot agent for the Chicago & North-Western Railway. He stayed at Waunakee, rather than taking an advancement in a larger city, because the little town was only ten miles from the university of Madison, and he had his scholarly heart set on a college education for his sons.

After their own mother died when they were two, the boys' father remarried. There were other children to absorb their parents' interest. On the fringe of this new family, the twins found little comfort in each other. Although identical in looks and temperament, restless, curious, and belligerent, with their stubborn dark heads set on adventure, Richard and Robert each had to be the leader—which meant that each traveled alone. "We were too much alike," says Bob, "to ever

12

get along well with each other. We were both stubborn, and both went our own way."

At the age of six Bob decided to run away. But his restlessness was tempered by a shrewd Yankee instinct for survival and a realistic knack for making plans. "I knew I was too young, and I'd just be brought back home if I tried it—so I bided my time and waited till I figured I was old enough to make it on my own."

Bob bided his time reading, dreaming, hunting, and trapping. Although a voracious reader, school offered little challenge. "I had a photographic memory, and I could look at a page and remember everything on it. School was too slow." Sometimes to amuse himself he created theoretical problems, which he worked out months or a year ahead of the class. He spent many hours alone, trapping the rolling, timbered hills around Waunakee which had been contoured by glaciers thousands of years ago. "I became," he declares, "the champion skunk trapper of Dane County, Wisconsin!" He made his spending money and bought his own clothes off his trap lines from the age of ten.

But always he was troubled by a vague unnamed restlessness. "I knew there was something beyond the hills of Waunakee." The sleepy little town had for years a fixed population of 443. As in other small towns, there was a saying that whenever a baby was born, another young man left town.

When he was seven or eight years old Bob read about the Wright brothers. From then he was convinced the "future of the world lay in the air." He devoured all he could find on flying and on the expanding world, the Far North, South America, the Orient. When the Reeve twins were nine, newspapers headlined the extraordinary flight from New York to California made by Cal P. Rogers. It took the flyer over two months to travel from coast to coast, but he made it. It was enough to set imaginative young minds to thinking about what lay ahead.

When Bob was fifteen he decided "the time" he'd been waiting for had arrived. World War I was on, and he was old enough and tough enough to get along on his own. He cashed his savings account, "borrowed" his dad's railroad pass, and caught a train for Dubuque, to enlist. There the Army turned him down. But the boy had his head set, and hitched a ride

on to the next recruiting station, at Davenport, Iowa. There
the recruiting sergeant looked the teen-ager over and sighed.
"You're underage, chicken-breasted [Bob was born with
slight concavity in left lung] and underweight. But you look
like a tough kid and that's the kind we need!"

"It's a good thing he took me," twinkles Bob. "I'd hocked
my overcoat at Dubuque!"

A few months later Richard Reeve got his father's permission to enlist in the Navy.

Bob saw his first plane in 1917, when a bunch of Jennies
flew over Fort Benjamin Harrison in formation. Two years
later he took his first ride. A flyer at Camp Custer was joy-
riding customers for five dollars a throw. Bob shelled out the
precious five bucks and climbed up in the front, the pilot got
in back, and they took off in a whirl of dust. "We were up
only about five minutes, just once around the field. But I'll
never forget it. You were right out there in the open, with
the struts singing, the wings shaking, the guy wires whining
around your ears. I kept thinking, With all those wires it
would sure make a fine chicken coop. But I've never had a
flight like it. Perched out there in the open air, you really
knew you were flying! It was a thrill few people are privi-
leged to know in the airplanes of the modern age."

Discharged at the end of the war as a sergeant, Bob wanted to re-enlist, but at his father's urgent pleading went back
home to school. The few months in high school, however,
were too great a change in pace for the young infantry sergeant, and, while brother Richard kept the school lights burning, Bob ran off—this time to San Francisco, where he
shipped as ordinary seaman on a boat headed for the Orient.
At Shanghai he jumped ship and got a job in the Chinese mari-
time customs service, where he served on the Yangtze and
Taku Rivers, out of Shanghai and Tientsin. Of his couple of
years adrift in the Orient, Reeve has oddly little to say. "Almost got drowned in the Taku," he admits. "That scar on my
hand? Oh, some fool Japanese cop damn near bit my thumb
off!" Whatever he was up to, it all added to Reeve's personal
theory of self-education: "The world is tough and life is hard
and you have to be tough to survive."

The year 1921 found him again jumping ship, this time at
Vladivostok, where he was overtaken by a compelling plea
from his father that brought him straggling home once more.

This time Bob really tried to please his conscientious father. Completing his missing three years of high school in six concentrated months, he was able to enter the University of Wisconsin in the fall of 1922, where brother Richard was already enrolled as a sophomore.

"If my twin brother and I could have passed title to our reputations, we could have got a million bucks each from the rich boys who envied us our questionable prestige!" The Reeves, running with the other "big boys" who had also been in the war, managed to liven up the campus with some general hell-raising.

Of the two and a half years that he stuck out college life, Bob remarks succinctly, "I learned to make gin and not bet into a one-card draw."

There were other things. "I had two thoughts in those days: girls and flying. In the mornings I thought of flying first."

Aviation, on the national scene, had suffered a shameful letdown following the war, despite the proddings of prophet Billy Mitchell. It was a national apathy that was not to be shaken off until Lindbergh caught the mass imagination in 1927. But there were a lot of young men over the country who didn't share the country's lethargy.

In the Phi Delta Phi fraternity house at the university was the picture of a dreamy-eyed, thoughtful young man who was already a hero to the younger boys—Army Air Force Lieutenant Carl Ben Eielson, who had been at the University of Wisconsin briefly in 1916. The fall that Bob entered college, Ben Eielson, disappointed with the indifference to aviation on the home front, had headed for Alaska. There, within a year, he was able to stir up enough interest that Alaskans bought him a plane, and in February, 1924, he began the first series of air-mail flights in the Territory.

On the school campus Bob found compatriots in George Gardner, Monk MacKinnon, and Ora McMurray, "our patron saint, who had been in the Lafayette flying corps." A fellow by the name of Cash Chamberlain had an old Jenny parked out on a little field at the edge of Madison, and the air-minded quartet got in the habit of sneaking off the campus, cutting classes to "play with the Jenny." Cash was a barnstormer, and for a few bucks he would take them up and let them experiment with the controls.

Monk, George, and Bob got called into the dean's office within days—just six months short of Bob's graduation. "I find, gentlemen," said the dean soberly, "that you all have an overriding interest other than your education." It was true. And being expelled from college pushed them all a step closer to their objectives. Air was to become their business. Today, George Gardner is president of Northeast Airlines; Monk MacKinnon is his vice president in charge of maintenance.

Bob headed for Florida, where he had heard, as so many others had, that a boom was on. Perhaps there was even money enough to support flying. He got a job as a hod carrier in Winter Haven and attempted to save enough for flying lessons. Time off, he hung around the little airfield, helping gas the planes for free. But the boom burst before he had the necessary cash—and there were no more salaries for hod carriers, no more money for joy rides in an airplane. The field closed, and Bob moved on to Beaumont, Texas, in March, 1926, where he had heard that the gambling Texans were still supporting the flying machine—at least at carnivals.

In Beaumont, for the first time, Bob stumbled into "the life I'd been looking for." He joined up with a wild pair of barnstormers appropriately named Hazard and Maverick, who lived off the country by putting on a flying circus for anyone who would give them a meal. "Every day," says Bob admiringly, "they lay in bed till noon—and sometimes two and three o'clock." Then they put on a show, at a carnival, circus, or county fair. One day Bob watched them miss the cue and break the stunt man's jaw. "Folks would pay to watch flyers risk their necks," explains Bob, "but nobody would think of giving you a regular job."

America was not yet ready to take aviation seriously. The young men who had learned to fly in World War I had the choice of either barnstorming for a precarious living—or going into another profession. "They'd pay to see you get killed," commented one, "but you couldn't get 'em to take a ride—even for free!"

Noel Wien, founder of Alaska's oldest air line, and noted for his extreme caution, described stunting with Walt Bullock (Senior Captain, Northwest Airlines Great Circle route to the Orient) at a fair in Minnesota in 1921. "We made six passes before we could get our planes close enough for the stunt man to wing-walk from one to the other. Neither of us liked to risk our necks—or our airplanes—but it was the only way a flyer could make a living in those days." Lee Fairbrother, former RAF flyer, now captain for Northwest, laughingly recalled his barnstorming days: "Gosh, we thought we were rich when we had fifteen cents!"

Considered freaks by conventional society—somewhat in a class with today's hot-rodders—the barnstormers were a world unto themselves, with their own special pride. "They [the rest of the world] didn't think much of folks who could fly. We didn't think much of folks who couldn't fly!" "We gloried in missing meals." "You didn't have to be crazy to fly in those days, but it sure didn't hurt to be a little crazy!"

In exchange for two months' work around their airfield, partners Maverick and Hazard gave Bob three hours of flying instruction, called it five, and told him he was ready to solo.

"It's a good thing," comments Bob, "that I was what you could call a natural-born flyer. It took me years to get over some of the bad flying habits that rubbed off on me from those barnstormers. As far as those boys were concerned, any take-off or landing was a good one—so long as you walked away from it."

Maverick and Hazard's plane was a "half Jenny, half Canuck" ship, aptly christened the Black Bottom after the popular dance of that period, because of its sluggish, sensual way of going "round the rounds." Its instruments consisted of an oil-pressure gauge, rpm indicator, and magneto switch. Air speed was determined by watching a strip of metal on the strut, which bent out to show how fast you were going. Reeve learned the "workings" of the simple little plane, and eventually did all the tuning and overhauling. When the first federal control of commercial aviation, the Air Commerce Act of 1926, was put into effect and the government began licensing pilots and mechanics, Reeve applied for and got one of the first Engine and Aircraft Mechanic's licenses, as well as his commercial pilot's license.

After a year and a half spent doing "the rounds" in the Black Bottom, Reeve turned to a more conservative form of aviation and briefly joined the Army Air Force as a flying cadet at March Field—where he once more caught up with brother Richard, who had joined the regular Army as a cadet, and a young graduate of West Point whom Reeve had

first met in 1926 and found to be a "really good guy," named
Nathan "Nate" Twining. "He was the only one who gave me
a break," says Bob. It was a friendship that was to survive
the years.

Although brother Richard liked it, regular Army life did
not especially appeal to Bob's independent spirit, and when a
periodic physical checkup revealed the chronic high blood
pressure that he had successfully concealed at his entrance
examination, he was not unhappy to find himself a civilian
once more. Besides, he now had the chance he'd been waiting
for: an opportunity to "fly the big ones."

In 1928 the United States Post Office had offered for bids
the contract for two-way air-mail service to South America.
The bid went to the newly organized Pan American-Grace
(Panagra), controlled by Pan American Airways, which had
been operating in Central America, and the W. R. Grace interests, which served the South American coast as importers-
exporters and as steamship operators. Captain Harold R.
Harris, a former Army flyer, had been appointed operations
manager of the new project, and in December, 1928, the first
leg of the new air-mail service was inaugurated with a
weekly schedule from the United States to Lima via the
Canal Zone. The equipment for this ambitious new undertak-
ing consisted of three airplanes—a Loening Amphibian for
the tropical Central American end of the route, two Fairchild
land planes for the western coast of South America—and
two pilots with South American experience, Lloyd "Dinty"
Moore, from Nebraska, who had been an instructor in Peru,
and Henry Elliott, from Louisiana, who had gone south with
a cotton-dusting project.

Unlike timid Stateside residents, our southern cousins
snapped up the new service. Within weeks, Colombian, Ec-
uadorian, and Peruvian businessmen were vying for space for
themselves, gold, machinery, express, and even livestock. It
was soon necessary to reserve passage weeks in advance. Pan
Am-Grace quickly put in rush orders for more Fairchilds,
more pilots, and, to handle big loads of freight and passengers, a fleet of bulky trimotor Fords.

Since few pilots were trained to fly anything as big as the
multiengined ships, the Ford Motor Company began hiring
likely pilots to train in their own factory, then send down
with the planes to assemble them and check out the Pan

Am-Grace pilots in their use. During the training period the
Ford company sent out their pilots on a regular public-rela-
tions shuttle freight line between Lansing, Detroit, and Buf-
falo, to attempt to prove to wary ground-lovers that flying
could be both scheduled—and safe.

Bob joined the Ford group, hurdled the course in a short
four months due to his background in the mechanics of aircraft as well as flying, and was soon on his way to South
America to await delivery of the first Ford. While awaiting
its arrival, via ship, at Guayaquil, Ecuador, Bob stayed in the
Canal Zone and Central America familiarizing himself with
the Pan Am routes and weather. The flights in Pan Am's amphibian Sikorsky S-38's gave Bob his first taste of blind flying.
"In that country each flight was an occasion." Tropical
storms hit with sudden violence, "just like turning the Pacific
Ocean upside down." Even though the cabin of the plane was
closed, the water pushed through every seam, and when the
pilot was also forced to open a window in an attempt to see
out, "it rained about as hard in the plane as outside." Although these sudden blinding torrents might not last over fifteen minutes, it meant flying from ten to fifty feet above the
lashing waves, with a down visibility of about ten feet and a
forward visibility of fifty to one hundred. Once when Reeve
was flying copilot with a Pan Am captain, they saw a break in
the blinding cloud bank, made for it—and when they came
out, found the whole Pacific Fleet just below their wing tips,
the dirigible Shenandoah hanging in the air only yards from
them. If they hadn't taken the break in the clouds, and had
proceeded blind, as usual, they would have collided. Arriving
on secret maneuvers, the fleet had come into the area without
giving the Pan Am operations any warning of their presence.

In this tropical land of 370-inch rainfall, it was a common
occurrence for the extreme humidity to drown out the magnetos in the short space of time the plane was afloat while
unloading mail. Pilots carried blowtorches to dry them out.
But sometimes they couldn't get the engines going until the
sun came out hours, or days, later. In contrast, the southern
end of the mail run, down the west coast of South America
to Lima, was over a vast, rolling desert extending miles without sign of habitation. The first time he took the flight, Reeve
noticed that old hand "Dinty" Moore thoughtfully loaded a

case of cold beer. "You got to be mighty careful of the water in this country."

Delivery of the first Ford to Lima bordered on becoming an international incident. Captain Harris wired Reeve, at Guayaquil, in Spanish, that he had better bring the Ford on over to Lima before the official date of its reception, and take a look at the race track where he was supposed to land before attempting to bring the big, fast-landing plane into such a small area. Reeve could then land at Las Palmas, at the Pan Am field, and ferry the Ford over on the Sunday set for its arrival. Do this, advised Harris, *sin publicidad*. Obeying orders as he read them, Reeve barreled into Lima, buzzed the president's palace, made a few vertical banks over town, flew low over the race track, then came on into Las Palmas. "You came in quietly without anyone hearing you?" asked Harris. "Hell no," said Reeve, "I buzzed the place like you said. *Sin publicidad* means show it to everybody, doesn't it?"

Harris blanched. President Leguía had issued a special proclamation, announcing that the arrival of the Ford at a stated hour would be followed by a reception at the president's palace and a citizens' celebration. The archbishop of Lima would be on hand to christen the plane. The whole city would be out at the hippodrome to watch the American pilot "drop in from the skies, from Guayaquil." "And you buzzed town!" Harris shuddered. "We're finished, Reeve. They'll take the concession away from us!"

Reeve dug the telltale wire out of his pocket. He'd boned up on his Spanish before coming down, but somehow *con* sounded more negative than *sin*. "Well," he said unhappily, "maybe nobody was looking——"

On Sunday, August 1, 1928, at the moment officially designated by President Leguía for the Ford's arrival from Guayaquil, Reeve, dressed in his one suit, with copilot Raymond "Red" Williams, who had just arrived from the States, beside him, flew over from Las Palmas to the Lima race track, where the crowd was waiting. Bob looked over his "landing spot" uneasily. The track was little more than a narrow stretch of ground just inside the arena, with the crowded grandstand on one side, big trees on the other—and at the end a deep ditch. To add to the complications of landing the big, fast-landing ship in such a short, narrow field, a crosswind had risen. Reeve glided the Ford in over the spectators' heads, stalled, then sideslipped into the narrow track, setting the wheels down gently. The Ford rolled forward down the track—and, as they neared the ditch, one of the brakes failed, refusing to take hold and stop the plane. For a vivid second a sickening vision of airplane worth $67,000 piled in the ditch flashed through Reeve's mind. But "Red" Williams came to the rescue, throwing all his strength on the one working brake. The plane ground-looped sharply, stopped two feet short of the ditch.

As they taxied up to the grandstand, President Leguía came forward to welcome them. With diplomatic tact and a straight face, he enquired, "Did you have a good trip from Guayaquil today?" However, one stony-faced member of the reception committee was not to be taken in quite so easily.

"I saw you flying over town yesterday," he said accusingly to Reeve.

"Not me!" Bob gulped.

President Leguía shook his head firmly. "Not this man. You must be mistaken." He whisked Reeve over to the safety of the grandstand. An ardent aviation enthusiast, "Iron Man" Leguía was not about to have his celebration ruined. Lima had its aviation holiday. *La Prensa* got its front-page story (August 2, 1929). And Panagra kept its Lima franchise—despite newcomer Reeve's slight linguistic error!

South America, Reeve found to his delight, was years ahead of the States in its enthusiasm for aviation. With its countries and cities isolated by tremendous mountain ranges, endless pampas, dense jungle, and barren desert, it was taking an enthusiastic, realistic look at the possibilities of aviation as a means of surmounting both rough terrain and high altitudes. Necessity here, as Reeve was to find later in Alaska, overcame fear. People flew—where they had to. In the States they could take a train. But from the northern coast clear to Santiago, a vast territory over twice the length of the whole United States, there were only four latitudinal railways to the interior, two of which crossed the continent, and only one local longitudinal railway. There was no north-south transportation except by water. Before air, mail service from the States by the fastest ocean carrier took sixteen days. East of Chile, the vast Argentine and republic of Uruguay were separated from their sister republics by the mighty Andes. Except for the annoying gadfly bites of pocket-sized revolutions, South America was "wide open" to the new air age and the men who pioneered it. Here, you didn't have to get people to take a ride; they clamored to get aboard. Even the most illiterate Indian in the most isolated village would grasp Reeve's arm eagerly, ask him if he knew Lindbergh, the name that had fired the imagination of the entire world. Driven by necessity imposed by endless untenable miles, South Americans grasped wings as a special god-sent gift. They used planes to haul food, supplies, mail—even to carry corpses. Pilot Ira "Red" Smalling of Chicago came in for some good-natured ribbing when, loaded with a corpse as darkness approached, he landed on lonely desert and spent the night bedded on a sand dune—rather than continue to fly, after dark, with a dead man!

In Lima, Santiago, later in Buenos Aires, Reeve found himself in a nest of real flyers—"the kind of guys who were born with pinfeathers," aerial frontiersmen who had flocked from all over the world to take advantage of South America's hospitality to the new transportation medium. There were the American pilots: Eddie Hamilton; John Montgomery; Cherokee Indian Eddie de Larm, who was to figure in a historic hegira; Ralph O'Neill; and Bill Long. The French had a line, too, and "every take-off was like Columbus sailing for the New World." The French reveled in the glamour and formality of flying; spent two hours saying good-by at each take-off; held receptions when their flyers returned without crashing. Young Antoine de Saint-Exupéry managed, while Bob was there, to get himself lost in the Andes, giving the newspapers a two weeks' field day before he made a graceful reappearance. "The French," commented Bob, "lived for the social and the daring side of flying. The Americans mostly didn't give a damn. They were down here because they loved to fly—and this was one of the few places you could make a living at it."

In July, 1929, the successful mail run was extended by the United States postal department from Lima nineteen hundred miles south to Santiago, Chile. When Pan Am-Grace offered Bob the opportunity to pioneer this new, long leg of the mail run, he leaped at the chance to do "long-distance flying," rather than the up-and-down passenger-mail service that was the destiny of the trimotor Fords. Since the Chileans refused to allow the new southern division to carry passengers, reserving this business for their own national airline, Bob used smaller planes and flew alone with no load except mail, making only fuel stops between Lima and Santiago. He was assigned, for these long-range flights in a comparatively empty plane, a single-engine Fairchild 71 and later a Lockheed Vega. This was the beginning of a lifelong love affair. Not with the trim, speedy Lockheed, but with the slower, dependable Fairchild. "The best performer at high altitudes of any plane I've ever flown." This model Fairchild, designed in 1928, was to figure in all of Reeve's later glacier flying, even in his wartime supply run out to the fog-swept, mountainous Aleutian Chain as late as 1946.

Regular pilots in South America were getting five hundred dollars per month. For this especially long run Reeve drew one thousand dollars per month, the highest pay of any flyer in the area. "You can't drink up a thousand bucks a month," he grins, "so I began to save a little." "Besides," he adds soberly, "I didn't drink when I was due to fly the next day, so I only had a couple of days a week when I could throw money around."

Foreign Air Mail Route Number 9 was at this time the world's longest and fastest mail route, and the longest aviation route in the world. Since the nineteen-hundred-mile stretch between Lima and Santiago was too far to go without a base, Bob made his home at Arica, in the far northern end of Chile, between the two major cities.

It was in Arica that Reeve got his famous leather jacket, which later caused so much comment in Alaska. He once loaned it to a flyer friend who was headed on a dangerous trip to the headwaters of the Amazon. Before some especially hazardous flight, the pilots frequently gave, or loaned, each other some personal article for good luck. It might be a pair of gloves, a necktie—or a leather jacket. When the friend returned to Arica unscathed, Reeve decided that this particular jacket was lucky—and wore it constantly from that time on until it literally fell off his back.

A Chilean cavalry regiment was stationed at Arica, and, discovering that Bob, while in Texas, had been indoctrinated with their favorite game of polo, they made him an honorary member of their group—then gleefully set about "murdering" the newcomer. "I thought I could play polo till I started

playing with the Lanceros," sighs Bob. "But after the first
game I realized I not only wasn't as good as I thought—I
never had been. They'd ride me down, ride me off the side
lines, mop up the field with me—and always with a polite little smile and *'perdóneme.'* To help compensate in some
measure for his lack of experience, Bob eventually bought
"the two fastest polo ponies in the area," and then "I could
at least catch up with them."

The Lanceros taught bachelor Reeve how to drink rum
and ginger, gamble at "ship, captain and crew," and play one
game in which he surprisingly excelled, wrist and finger bending. In this version of our Indian wrestling, the contestants
put their elbows on the table ("being careful not to knock
over any refreshments"), clasp hands, and attempt to best the
other man by forcing his arm down to the table. Between
flying and polo, Reeve had a strong hand and wrist, and was
well on his way to becoming amateur wrist and finger bending champion of Chile, when he met his Waterloo in the
person of a slight, boyish, five-foot-four Chilean Air Force
pilot. "I hardly deigned to give the little fellow a match," reports Reeve sadly, "and then he had my arm down before I
ever got started." The Chilean modestly confessed to Bob
that he had grown up in a village where this was the favorite
sport, and had been practising it since the age of five.

Much as he enjoyed the society of the Chileans and Argen-
tinians, Reeve was not able to stomach their hot, spicy food.
The Latins loved nothing better than to wine and dine pilots,
but for Reeve "those twenty-course banquets were a nightmare." A Wisconsin meat-and-potatoes man, during his two
and a half years in South America Reeve lived principally on
bread and bananas, a sack of which was routinely tossed into
his plane each morning while it was being gassed up.

Taking after his old buddies, Maverick and Hazard, Reeve
enjoyed the barnstormers' prerogative of "laying in bed" till
the final moment, then dashing out of his quarters, crawling
into the plane, and taking off. Once when he came into Anto-
fagasta, where he occasionally remained overnight, the commanding officer of the Chilean air detachment that was based
there called him in. Would the American pilot, the C.O. asked
politely, "cooperate with the Chilean Air Force to the
extent of not furnishing a bad example for the young flyers?"

"What do you mean?" asked Reeve, genuinely puzzled.

"My flyers," said the C.O., "have recently been appearing on duty with coveralls pulled over their pajamas!"

There was more than barnstormers' bravado to Reeve's casual attire. Flying from eight to fifteen hours a day, he needed all the sleep he could get. Once a week he covered the 3800-mile round trip between Lima and Santiago. This took five full days of flying, and he never knew when he would be called on special duty during his two days off. It was nothing, in those days, to fly over 150 hours per month, mostly above 10,000 feet, without oxygen.

In addition to the exhausting hours in the air, the pilots were frequently called upon to be their own mechanics. Anywhere but at the city bases, crack-ups and engine failures had to be repaired on the spot. Colonel Homer Farris of Kentucky once performed the remarkable feat of rebuilding one of the big all-metal Ford trimotors four hundred miles in the interior of the continent. Once, when he was flying one of the Pan Am Sikorskys from Cristobal to Buenaventura, Reeve came up with an original answer to the annoying problem of engines drowned out by the tropical rains. Putting up an asbestos canopy to shield the flame, he then led a two-inch piece of pipe from the flame of the blowtorch to the magneto, thus attaining maximum heat without danger of fire. When he got one engine started, he kept it going, then started in on the second. With both working, even though the magnetos would get wet again in a matter of minutes, he could make it into the air, and they would eventually dry when he left the rain belt. His method became the standard procedure for the amphibian pilots.

In September, 1930, the mail service joined the east and west coasts of South America by extending the route from Santiago east across the continent to Montevideo on the Atlantic coast, via Buenos Aires. This meant a record eight-day airmail service from New York to Buenos Aires. It also meant conquering the 23,000-foot Andes.

First of the mail pilots to fly the new leg over the mountains was Red Williams, in one of the trimotor Fords. He found, to his horror, that the big plane's safety factor in high altitudes was practically zero. When one of the three engines failed, the other two were not able to sustain the ship in level flight in the thin, rarefied air. Rather than increasing safety, the presence of the multiengines actually increased the chance of motor failure over that of a single-engine plane. Twice, Red had one motor conk out on him, over the Andes, forcing him to sink "blind" down through a blanket of clouds— toward the mountaintops. Luckily, each time he was able to glide into a valley between peaks. But he didn't figure his luck would hold out for a third time.

A new experimental multiengined plane was hurriedly designed and rushed down from the States. But it also failed to function at the twenty-thousand-foot flight level needed to clear the Andes. Supercharged motors with high-ratio (fourteen to one) blower gears were installed in the Fairchilds. The reliable Fairchilds got across the mountains with comparative safety. But they needed a still stronger, higher-flying plane than the Fairchild, one whose wings could not be snapped off by the terrible Andean winds. After exhaustive tests a specially built Curtiss-Wright Falcon, powered by six-hundred-horsepower supercharged motors, was shipped down. It proved best in high-altitude performance, climbing with ease to almost six miles, well above the cloud banks that congested and obstructed the mountaintops.

It was not only the planes that suffered from the thin air. Unless they took oxygen, the flyers found their lips turning blue, their eyes glazed, their veins distended, and eventually their entire bodies expanded, due to the congestion of the blood and the inability of the heart to circulate to the lungs. When his heart was no longer able to bear the strain, the pilot fainted. Oddly enough, once normal altitude was reached there seemed to be no ill effects; the increase of oxygen immediately resuscitated the victim. Several times when the oxygen tanks failed to function the mail pilots fainted, their planes fell off into a spin, but a few thousand feet of change in altitude was sufficient to revive them, so they were able to regain control of the plane in time to avert a crash. The normal requirements seemed to be to begin taking oxygen at twelve thousand, although some men waited until they suffered ill effects from the altitude. Because of his narrow, thin body, Reeve found that he could hold out comfortably to twenty thousand, while men with a burlier build felt ill effects at fifteen thousand.

"Until my first crossing of the Hump, as we called the southern Andes," admits Bob, "I felt a certain amount of skepticism about the other boys' stories of deathly air pockets or downdrafts that snatched your ship out of control. They told about flying unwittingly into a downdraft [the wind follows the contour of the earth, creating updrafts on the windward side of mountains, downdrafts on the lee side] and having their planes literally thrown thousands of feet down in the space of a few seconds." One day Red Williams came in with a bit of startling evidence. Hitting an air pocket, the impact had been so violent that a steamer trunk in the baggage compartment had been thrown almost through the duralumin and steel fuselage of his plane.

A few days later Reeve came into Santiago from the nineteen-hundred-mile junket from Lima with his taste buds set on a little "refreshment" followed by a few chukkers of polo, only to find a cable awaiting him from Red Williams at Montevideo. The Ford that Williams was flying had been wrecked in a hurricane. Reeve was to proceed immediately to the Atlantic coast, across the Andes from Santiago, with the mail and repair parts for the Ford. After a false start that same afternoon, jinxed by bad weather, Reeve set out early next morning, heading for the Andes, which were completely obscured by heavy fog. Climbing blind, Reeve found that at three thousand feet the fog still spattered against the window of the plane with the intensity of heavy rain. Six thousand, ten thousand—and he had still not come out "on top." Keeping his eyes on the bank-and-turn indicator, which was his only assurance that the plane was still in level flight, he leaned the mixture for higher altitude and gave the motor full throttle. There was no turning back now, since a descent through such fog would almost certainly spell a crash on a mountain top. He could only climb. Finally, at sixteen thousand, Reeve glimpsed a spot of sun breaking through. At seventeen thousand he was at last on top.

Only the highest peaks of the Andes protruded above the fog bank; topping them all was twenty-three-thousand-foot Mount Aconcagua, the highest point in the western hemisphere. Reeve's course lay a few miles to the right of this great peak, through thirteen-thousand-foot Upsallata Pass, which led into the Argentine. By this time Bob was beginning to feel the effects of the rarefied air. All of the oxygen tanks were with Williams, the regular Andes pilot, over at Montevideo. Reeve had none. Black specks began to dance before his eyes. He soon found every motion a painful effort. He looked at his altimeter. He was already over twenty thousand, and he dared not go higher for fear of blacking out, although ahead of him lay cloud banks. He had no choice but to locate some "hole" through which to spiral down to a lower altitude, in the hope of finding a break down along the bottom of the pass through which he could fly on to the Argentine.

After cruising for about twenty minutes, Reeve located a thin, feathery break in the clouds, through which he could see ground far below, at the bottom of the pass. Throttling the motor and putting the Fairchild into a tight spiral, he started down. Five thousand feet below, he came out into clear air at the bottom of the pass. Following this, in a few moments he could see the Christ of the Andes, which marked the crest of the pass, the dividing line between the two countries. Beyond the statue the mountains fell away from a cliff, almost a sheer drop of thousands of feet down into the Argentine valley below. There was barely enough room between the low-hanging cloud bank and the immense statue for Reeve to crowd past. Once by, the valley below lay clear.

But, as the Fairchild skimmed by this final obstacle of the Andean trial, Reeve "got the surprise of my life." With no warning, the plane was suddenly whipped out of his control, caught by the downdraft on the lee side of the high peaks. Within seconds, the plane was sucked down nearly a mile. "A vision of mail, Fairchild, and Reeve scattered over those crags below flashed through my brain." But as the crags rose to meet him, the downdraft suddenly switched to an updraft a few feet from the earth, and shot the plane upward with a reverse shock so violent "that it would have torn the wings off of a less sturdily built plane."

When Reeve finally set the Fairchild safely down at the Mendoza field, no one greeted him. Eventually the Pan Am-Grace agent saw the plane out on the field and came running out, amazement written over his face.

"I never expected to see you!" he cried. "The All-American telegraph operator stationed on top of the Pass saw you hit that air pocket and a few seconds later saw a cloud of dust in the valley below. He called in to Mendoza that your plane had crashed."

While flying Foreign Air Mail Route Number 9, Reeve twice made aviation history. On one flight he established a speed record between Santiago and Lima, while at the same time making the second night flight in history up the west coast of the continent. When a storm over the Andes held up the mail twenty-four hours behind schedule from Buenos Aires, Reeve took it and flew straight through, covering nineteen hundred miles in twenty hours. Making only two stops to gas up, he flew the last eight hundred miles nonstop (the Fairchild had a range of nine hundred miles) through the night, using a flashlight to read his compass. Every couple of hundred miles along the route, stations lit bonfires to guide him. But, since fog hung low along the shore line, Reeve took a course several miles out over the Pacific, where, next to the water, the fog cleared for about a hundred feet of ceiling. Reeve flew the entire coastal run, by compass course only, in pitch darkness, at an altitude that never exceeded one hundred feet.

He made some hard and fast rules about flying in fog, which were later to hold good in Alaska and the Aleutians. Although he would climb blind to come out on top—when he knew that he would be able to land in the clear at his destination—he never let down blind through fog. Along the high plateau of the South American west coast, he never flew on top of fog, since without instruments to guide him, there would be no safe way to come down. Instead, he chose to fly his single-engine plane thirty or forty miles out at sea, where he could always find a clearance for visual flight at ten to a hundred feet, and at least ditch in the water. Forcing himself to rely on his bank-and-turn indicator and altimeter to judge the absolute altitude and level flight of the plane, he put hoods over the cockpit and taught himself to fly blind. Once, flying blind when he was caught over the Andes in a snowstorm, Reeve crossed Upsallata Pass without knowing it, which Ripley featured in *Believe It or Not*.

Reeve, Williams, and the other mail pilots learned how to cannily circumvent the daily duststorms, thunderstorms and violent winds of the Argentine pampas by hedge-hopping, flying only a few feet off the ground, where the contour of the earth modified the violence of the head winds. But their Herculean efforts to get the mail through on schedule did not impress one Argentine rancher whose herds of cattle Red Williams twice scattered with his low-flying plane. Next time Williams flew over that particular hacienda, he was greeted with a load of buckshot. Several of the shots missed his head by inches; others penetrated the oil tank of the plane, causing him to limp into Mendoza, just short of a forced landing. After that, the mail pilots elected to fly the high altitudes and buck the head winds when they reached that particular ranch.

Flyer Eddie de Larm got in the worst trouble of any of the American group with the trigger-happy Latins. Flying for NYRBA (New York-Rio-Buenos Aires line) till it folded, Eddie stayed on in Buenos Aires looking for free-lance work. Hired to fly a Fokker F-10 by a group of revolutionists, de Larm wound up at his destination, Concepción, jailed along with the others and faced with the threat of a firing squad. Back in Santiago the American ambassador called the American flyers together and reported the sad news. "They can't shoot de Larm," moaned one pilot. "He owes me one thousand pesos!"

When they asked what they could do to help their buddy, the ambassador shook his head. "Nothing that I know of. De Larm got in with the wrong bunch."

The pilots were not ready to give up so easily. Although they couldn't go into Concepción with a revolution in full swing, they pooled their wits and cash, and came up with a few likely "contacts"—usually available in Latin countries. Within forty-eight hours de Larm, armed with a file, had broken out of the cárcel, made his getaway from Concepción, and headed, on horseback, across the Andes to Buenos Aires. Riding five different horses to exhaustion on the snowbound, craggy peaks, the rugged Oklahoma-born Cherokee finished the remainder of his remarkable thirteen-day hegira on foot (the last five days without food) and finally arrived at Buenos Aires thirty pounds lighter, his face blackened by frostbite, his legs a mass of calluses from ankles to thighs from riding bareback—but very much alive.

Even the mail pilots were endangered as revolutions swept the continent like prairie fires, breaking out first in Bolivia, then Peru, then the Argentine, next Brazil, finally Chile. Pilot Tom Jardine of Madison, Wisconsin, was seized at Arequipa and forced to ferry an armed band of revolutionists to Tacna, Peru. There, upon landing, he and his party were greeted with a fusillade of shots, and Jardine managed to escape on foot to the Chilean frontier while the boys were busily shooting it out. Pilot Byron Richards of Oak Park, Illinois, was ordered, at gun point, to fly revolutionists from Pisco to Lima, refused, and somehow managed to avoid being killed—for which bravery the Peruvian government presented him with five hundred dollars in gold.

At a cocktail party in Lima, Reeve mentioned to the pretty, dark-eyed girl beside him that he was going to fly to Talara, Peru, on the following day.

"Ah," she smiled, "you'll be in time to see the fun."

"What fun?" Reeve asked, puzzled.

"There is going to be a revolution there tomorrow."

Sure enough, when Reeve flew into Talara he discovered he could not land because a revolution was going on, and he was forced to fly on to Guayaquil. Next day he had his answer to the puzzle of how the girl happened to know the plans—when her father was made the new president! He lasted about forty-eight hours before another change was made.

The mail pilots sometimes wondered, as they stumbled out of their cockpits half frozen and exhausted after their daily struggle against blinding fog, vicious storms, violent Andean winds—and revolutionists' bullets—if the folks who wrote and received all those letters ever gave a thought to the price paid for the convenience! On one flight, when Bob was overcome by a sudden violent attack of influenza as he was flying over Chile, he turned over the controls to a Chilean airman who had come along as observer (to see that no pictures were taken) and stumbled into the back of the plane, where he lay down. "The plane began flopping all over the sky, but I was too sick to care." When it came time to land, Reeve forced himself to crawl up front and execute the landing. Later he thanked the Chilean in front of some other officers. "Him?" exclaimed one in surprise. "Why, he's only been in the air once before in his life. He's never had any flying instruction!" Reeve has never since turned over the controls to anyone.

Flying the treacherous Andean run, Reeve learned a cardinal rule of survival in the air: "Never get into anything where you don't have an 'out.'" Finding himself trapped by fog once in a canyon near Copiapó, Chile, Reeve discovered to his horror that he had gone in too far, and that there was no way to turn around. His only chance lay in pulling up straight ahead on instruments and attempting to spiral up out of the mountains that rose six and seven thousand feet around him.

Boxed in the clutch of the tightest fix of his life, Reeve tried to climb too fast in the thin air, had almost made it to the top when he suddenly noticed his compass going round and round and realized he was in a spin. Fixing his gaze on the bank-and-turn indicator, he sticked and ruddered the Fairchild until he saw the ball and needle centered. This was his first experience pulling out of a spin in the blind. The compass was so placed that he had to watch it in a mirror. "It turned opposite from what I was accustomed to." Once righted, he again climbed, and again, in his tense effort to climb out of the narrow trap, he pushed too fast, and, just as he saw the clouds breaking ahead, slipped into a second spin. "When I pulled out of that one, the mountains weren't ten feet from my wings." This time he got the compass orientated in the mirror, climbed slowly and evenly—and made it to the top. He had climbed from one hundred to ten thousand feet. He'd also learned that, rather than just watch the bank-and-turn, he must also more closely watch his air speed in relation to the high altitude. The turbulent air caused great fluctutation in the air speed, and the plane stalled easily in the thin air.

Having an "out" meant not only not sticking your nose anywhere unless you could get out, but always having a spot to make a forced landing. "As I flew along I learned to keep an eye out for likely emergency landing fields." Although the big cities boasted good airfields, they lay far between. There was only one field, at Mendoza, between Santiago and Buenos Aires. When overtaken by storm, fog, darkness, or just plain loss of his way, Reeve learned to set his Fairchild down smoothly onto plowed fields, along a sandy beach, or on the nitrate beds of the Atacama desert in Chile. These old sea beds, pushed out by the ocean and then shriveled by the sun into irregular choppy shapes, had, Reeve found, an occasional smooth spot among the upheavings, just as you could find a smooth area between crevasses on a glacier. The nitrate beds were a light yellowish brown in color, with enough shadows to judge depths from the air and get a perspective. A sharp eye coupled with a photographic memory for landscapes enabled Reeve to set his plane down for a smooth landing on rough terrains in the middle of nowhere, to wait out storms, or, if lost, get his bearings, then take off and fly on.

Any tendency Reeve had to a "big head" or overconfidence, which his youth might inspire, was thoroughly and forever squelched by the inexplicable hazards of the type of flying he was doing. "I learned," he says simply, "to always fly a little scared."

"Everything can be going great. You think you're really a pretty hot pilot, you've got all the answers to everything, plenty of experience, everything going fine—you're just terrific—then, all at once, GRRR WHAM BANG—you're in the greatest trouble in your life."

There were times, Reeve found, when it was even wise to throw away the rulebook. The first time he flew into Arequipa from Lima, he landed downhill into the wind on the short (two-thousand-foot) steep field that had been built at eight thousand feet altitude alongside a dormant volcano. At the bottom of the steep downhill grade was soft sand. When it was time to take off, Reeve found that it was necessary to taxi the plane uphill through the drag of soft sand, all of which, his mechanic's mind told him, put a tremendous strain on the engine, abusing the power so important for take-off. Reeve made up his mind that the next time he landed at Arequipa, hell or high water, he'd land uphill so he wouldn't have to taxi so far through the sand.

On his next flight Reeve did it his way—landing uphill but downwind—thus breaking a cardinal rule of flying. "When my wheels touched I was doing a hundred mph in the soft sand—but within two thousand feet I was at a dead stop, right at the top of the field, ready for take-off."

An order came through to Reeve from the Pan Am-Grace office: "Land into the wind at Arequipa field according to normal procedure." Reeve refused. "As long as I'm flying, I'll use my own judgment." They said no more, and within months Reeve's theory was grimly verified when several pilots were killed at Arequipa when their engines burned out under the strain of plowing up through the soft sand, failed to develop sufficient power for take-off—and crashed at the end of the runway.

In 1930 Reeve flew 1476 hours of straight mail flying—setting another world's record. He never failed to complete a schedule. In his many hours alone in his plane, Reeve got in the habit of keeping a supply of magazines and newspapers on hand, and when things were going right and the plane "flying itself," he caught up on some of his reading. "It was while flying twenty thousand feet over the Andes," he will tell you, "that Reeve Airways was born."

Stateside newspapers in November, 1929, headlined a story that rocked Reeve's memories: Carl Ben Eielson, pioneer of Far North aviation, and his young Alaskan mechanic, Earl Borland, had disappeared over Siberia, on a flight to recover furs from the ice-bound American freighter *Nanuk*. For the next three months (Alaska's worst winter in ten years) flyers from Canada, Russia, Alaska, and the States flocked through the hazardous blizzards to join the search. A handful of Alaskan bush pilots, based at the Teller roadhouse on the Arctic coast, weathered the terrible winter and scoured the skies in their single-engine, open-cockpit planes, whenever the violent weather gave them a few minutes' break. For months, newspapers carried the story of the Eielson search. Reeve, flying the Andes, read the week-old Chicago *Tribune* that his father sent him with growing excitement. Once he became so absorbed in an account that he flew fifty miles off course. "If they'd had CAA in those days they'd have murdered me!"

His fascination was twofold. Having met Eielson when the flyer once visited the University of Wisconsin, Reeve had followed his career ever since. Beyond that, he was stirred by the stories of the conclave of flyers who had gathered to hunt for Eielson: the Alaskan bush pilots, a hardy breed of independent, free-lance flyers who were conquering the Far North in their single-engine planes, without airports, navigational aids, or government subsidy. Without help from anyone or anybody, they were making history on their own, charting the wilderness by learning to "read" the "nameless mountains and rivers that run God knows where." Men like Ed Young, Joe Crosson, S. E. Robbins, Frank Dorbrandt, Noel Wien, Matt Nieminen, Harvey Barnhill—and a youngster by the name of Harold Gillam, who had only a few hours in the air when he begged an open-cockpit Stearman from Eielson's newly formed airline in Fairbanks and flew north, to become, with Crosson, one of the two flyers who actually made the discovery the world had been waiting for: the shattered wingtip of Eielson's Hamilton sticking out of the snow. Weeks later, the bodies of Eielson and his plucky young mechanic, Earl Borland, were finally recovered from their snowy graves.

"From the time I was twenty, I had had three ambitions,"

says Reeve. "To have a ten-goal handicap at polo, fly around the world in twenty-four hours—and make a million dollars. It occurred to me that I was not getting there—fast. I'd met my masters at polo, I couldn't get any backers to fly around the world—but that millionaire business was wide open. And, with it, a chance to be my own boss."

Reeve had recently run into a pair of sourdoughs from the Far North who had excited him with tales of wealth still left in Alaska and the Canadian Yukon. Old "Swiftwater Bill" Gates—who had won his nickname walking to escape the Whitehorse Rapids, and who had come to Arequipa to prospect—told Reeves tales of the Dawson gold rush and of "hills full of gold" still waiting to be cleaned up. Eddie Craig, general manager of Anaconda Copper at Santiago, had been a young mining engineer at Kennicott. He told Bob about that initial strike near the Chitina River. "They sent a kid fresh out of college to look it over, and he reported to the company, 'I can see five million dollars in sight.' Doubting the new boy's analysis as overoptimistic, they sent an older man to check. He came back: 'The kid's wrong. There's thirty million in sight.'" Over two hundred and fifty million dollars of ore had actually been taken out of Kennicott.

The triple promise of gold, flying fellowship, and a chance to be his own boss beckoned Bob to the Far North. He had already done his pioneering in South America; there was little left now but routine, exhausting flying. His decision to go to Alaska was clinched in January, 1932, when he smashed a Lockheed by hitting a rock on a newly graded runway at Santiago, blowing a tire and wrecking the plane. "Pilot's error" was the verdict, and "pilot error had no part in Pan Am's employment. I figured the Panagra boys in New York might be a little stuffy, so I beat them to the draw and resigned."

"I had made money like a horse down there," Reeve reports cheerfully of his two and a half years in South America, "and I spent it like a jackass." Back in the States, Reeve dropped $17,000 on the stock market. ("I was a bull when I should have been a bear.") At home in Wisconsin on a visit, he went hunting, fell through the ice, walked dripping wet for four miles to his father's house, and soon found himself in bed with what appeared to be a violent case of chills and fever. For a month he lay flat on his back, too ill to move. Noticing that his right leg seemed to be shrinking in size, Bob decided that his icy dunking had resulted in "muscular rheumatism." He figured out a rugged schedule of exercise and hard work to "toughen up" when he got out of bed. What he had actually suffered, he discovered years later, was an attack of polio.

In an effort to regain his strength, Reeve beat his way across the country, stowed away to Alaska. Arriving at Anchorage "with twenty cents in my pocket," he found that "great bunch of free-lance flyers" he'd read about. They were there all right—and they had the Territory pretty well sewed up. Anchorage had more flyers than its business called for. "The best-situated pilot there," mused Reeve, "was a fellow named Charlie Ruttan, who had married the baker's daughter and was eating regular."

A classic story about bush pilots was making the rounds of the Territory. A woman, so the story went, had called down from her hotel room in Fairbanks, saying that a bush pilot was molesting her.

"How do you know it's a bush pilot?" asked the proprietor.

"He's got high boots, a watch with sevenhands, and a nickel in his pants pocket."

With little active flying going on in the States, many another pilot had had the same notion as Reeve, and beat his way to Alaska. Despite the Territory's vigorous acceptance of aviation, there were more flyers than business in these depression years. "The only way a guy could make money in Alaska in those days was to open a still or find a gold mine."

Oscar Winchell, who was running a one-man line out of Anchorage, loaned Bob twenty-five dollars to get on south to the coastal towns where the passenger boats came in. Reeve went to Seward, only to decide that no opportunity existed there. From Seward, he had stowed away to Valdez.

# 3. Getting a stake

Reeve settled the Eaglerock smoothly on the little Valdez strip. It was hardly his choice of planes, but it would fly, and it was his chance to get in business again. The crowd of spectators had dispersed; only a handful of little boys had stayed to watch Reeve land. "After they saw you take off," smiled Owen, "they knew there'd be no excitement around here."

It was true. After the initial take-off Reeve found that his position in the town had already undergone a subtle change. Broke as before, he was no longer considered a transient but was, without doubt, a pilot, one of that special breed that Alaska calls its favorite citizens.

That night at the Pinzon, the old-timers included Reeve with a new courtesy. "You see the mines up there?" they wanted to know. "The Ramsay Rutherford, the Big Four?"

"Yes, I spotted some of them," Reeve admitted.

"We were surprised to see you heading up into the Chugach—none of the flyers around here go in there at all except through Thompson Pass into the Interior. They don't fool with the mountains over where the mines are." "Anything going on up there?" Reeve asked casually, a growing idea taking hold in his mind, making his scalp tingle with excitement.

"Them hills are full of gold," grunted one old miner, reaching into his pocket. "But it may as well stay there, as hard's it is to get out. Look here," he held out a dully gleaming nugget the size of a pigeon's egg. "I knocked that out myself, just this spring. But it kills you—trying to get back and forth across them glaciers——' '

Bob moistened his lips. "Ever get anybody to fly anything in for you?"

"Naw," the group of men grunted in unison. "None of the

boys around here will carry anything except passengers—and they won't carry them into the mountains."

"Ever hear of any of them trying it—to land on a glacier, I mean?" Bob persisted.

One of the men scratched his head, then said, "I heard that Joe Crosson landed on a glacier last year some time, to carry out a sick man. Had an awful time getting off. Swore he'd never do it again."

Bob thought of the nitrate beds of the Atacama Desert in Chile. They had always had smooth spots, big enough to bring in a plane. He'd bet the glaciers had too. The main trouble—those nitrate beds had been yellow, the best color you could want, from the sky. Glaciers were white, a flat white blur with no reference points, no perspective.

"There are some mighty rich lodes up there," the man with the nugget said slowly. "Think you could haul me in?"

"I don't know," Reeve said. "But it's worth thinking about."

The room suddenly came alive, as though an electric shock had passed through the twenty or thirty tired old bodies seated around.

"Could you haul in supplies?" asked one, his pale eyes brightening.

"Take in a crew?"

"Carry grub?"

Reeve looked around at the old-timers, their craggy faces lighting with excitement and hope. Here was a hand-made business—if he had the courage to try.

"If you'll charter my plane and my time," he said slowly, "I'll haul you into the mountains—and set you down close to your mine, you and your supplies."

Rather than the excited answers he expected, the roomful of men sank back into their chairs, as one man.

"Nobody's got any money," one of them explained to Bob. "We don't live on anything but jawbone credit around here."

Money in Alaska, and especially in the broke little town of Valdez, Reeve was to learn, was a "once-a-year" proposition, when the results of the trapping and mining season came in. Then debts were paid, money changed hands for a brief flurry of time, and everyone went back to credit again until the next year. Workers who came in for seasonal jobs with the Alaska Road Commission returned to Seattle for the winter, taking their cash with them. "Their contribution to the economy of the Territory was a couple of bucks' worth of beer on the Fourth of July." This was also basically true of many of the miners, who came up from the States to work their claims during the short summer season and then returned to their homes with their earnings. It was also true of the fishermen who came up seasonally from Seattle. Little cash stayed in the Territory. What payments were made out of season were generally handled in gold dust. In the old says "sweepers" had worked in stores for free sweeping up the gold that sifted to the floors. In some groceries the customer had a chance to throw dice, "double or nothing" for his bill.

"Probably crash your plane if you did try to land up near the mines," predicted tall, hawk-nosed old Ed Wood, who had once cowboyed on Teddy Roosevelt's ranch in the Dakotas. "Nothing can get up in there except horses."

"Just wait, though," a man named Cook spoke up. "I think we might get Clarence Poy interested in coming up from San Francisco, if you could promise to get supplies in to the Big Four. He's got the money and owns stock in the mine. I know he'd put up some money to see it opened up again."

"Why don't you write him?" Bob suggested. "You tell him, if he'll put up the cash, I'll fly you in—and all your gear—or break my neck trying."

Cook strode over to one of the game tables, grabbed a sheet of paper, and sat down. "I'll write him tonight."

A pair of strange men, who had been sitting silently along the wall listening, walked up to Reeve.

One put a hand on his shoulder. "How about taking us out to Middleton Island, son?"

"Middleton?" Reeve was puzzled.

" 'Bout 100, 130 miles south of here," explained one man. "Past the Sound, right out in the Gulf."

"What's the chances of landing out there?" Bob asked. "Do you know the place?"

"I was out in a boat," said one of the strangers. "It's got a fine smooth wide-open beach. It'd be easy to set a plane down there."

"What's out there?" asked Reeve.

"Gold in the beach sands—just like over at Nome," said the prospector.

"All right," Reeve agreed, "I'll take you out in the morning."

Next morning Reeve started out on his first charter, loaded the prospectors into the front seat of the Eaglerock, climbed in the back, and headed south—toward Middleton Island. A hundred and forty miles due south of Valdez over open water, he sighted the island. The "fine beach" was steep and strewn with rocks. Bringing the Eaglerock down on the only smooth spit he could find, Reeve landed axle-deep in "fluffy pea sand." He was stuck.

While the three men struggled to move the plane up to higher land for protection from the surf, the tide started coming in. Yards away from them, ten-foot combers broke across the beach. "I figured," said Reeve, "that right about then the only transportation between Middleton Island and the mainland was about to go back to the original silicon and magnesium from which it derived!"

Hurriedly flattening the prop for increased power, Reeve attempted to take off from the sand, and "all that that did was made the prop blades spread out like the horns of a moose," while the wheels remained stuck in the soft sand.

"I wasn't about to swim 140 miles, so I started running around looking for something to help." Luckily Reeve unearthed an old block and tackle, with some rope still on it, washed in from a shipwreck. He hastily sunk a "deadman" log twenty feet in front of the plane to secure the block and tackle and then fastened it to the plane, and by alternately digging up and reburying the dead man, slowly inched the plane up to higher ground, only feet ahead of the tide. By the time they had hauled the plane up to dry land, the waves were breaking over the Eaglerock's tail and the men were working ankle deep in swirling water.

While the prospectors staked their claim, Reeve scurried over the bleak, storm-lashed shore till he found more shipwreck remnants—an old carpenter's vise and rusted sledge hammer. Putting the prop blades in the vise, he beat them out one at a time with the hammer till they gradually resumed their former shape.

When the men had staked their claim, Bob took off—only to find a storm that obliterated the town hanging over Valdez. He turned toward Seward, an hour's flight away. When he set the Eaglerock down at the Seward strip he had five minutes' gas left in his tank. Although a sample that he brought back from Middleton and had assayed showed the island was high in gold and other minerals, "that was my first and last flight to Middleton Island!"*

"I didn't even get paid," reports Reeve, "but that trip was worth thousands of dollars in experience. It taught me to beware of booby traps—and landing fields described by enthusiastic prospectors. They thought a plane could come down anywhere—where there was a little gold."

"Nice little landing field" were to become fighting words to bush pilots all over Alaska and constitute one of their biggest headaches. Not only prospectors, but trappers, Indians, Eskimos, anyone who wanted to get somewhere, would promise faithfully that there was "a fine level landing field" at their destination. Partly through ignorance of a plane's landing requirements, partly through foolhardy enthusiasm, they caused pilots many minor wrecks and some casualties. One of the classic Alaskan versions of this happened when cautious Noel Wien finally agreed, after much reassurance, to take an Eskimo to a village north of the Arctic Circle, where the Eskimo told Wien he *knew* the landing facilities were good since John Cross (another veteran Alaskan bush pilot) had landed there the week before. Noel flew in and came down on the "nice smooth" beach—only to nose over in the treacherous sand. At that moment he felt a tap on his shoulder, looked around into his passenger's smiling face. "That's just the way John Cross did!" the Eskimo assured him.

Reeve's first paid charter was, oddly enough, from women. "The kind of girls," smiles Bob, "who had no enemies!" and some of the few Alaskan citizens who ever had any cash. The shady ladies offered Bob five hundred dollars to take them from Valdez over to Nome, on the west coast of Alaska,

* Reeve always intended to do some prospecting on Middleton, but the island was turned into a range station during the war. As it was perfectly located for getting advance weather reports, CAA put two weather men on Middleton in 1944. Wanting some access to civilization, the lonely weather men cleared off a twelve-hundred foot runway and called CAA Chief Pilot Jack Jefford to come in. Jefford flew over in a Fairchild, buzzed the strip, and went away. The nonairminded radio men had built their strip so that it ran right into the CAA buildings! The federal government later tarviated the airfield and withdrew the entire island from private entry.

which lies along the Bering Sea. Reeve made the long cross-country flight without incident and was able to pick up another customer at Nome, an old-timer named Charlie Fromm, who wanted to be flown a short hop to Council, in the interior of the Seward Peninsula. Needing gas, Reeve went out to the Nome field, where he met a "competitor" pilot, who asked him where he was going. When Reeve told about his charter, the flyer obviously figured newcomer Reeve was horning in on his territory. Reeve paid for his gasoline, picked up one of the unlabeled barrels, and took off. What he actually had taken was not gasoline but a distillate—low-grade kerosene. The other flyer, figuring he'd be better off without Reeve's competition, didn't tell him the difference. Only a short way out of Golovin, Reeve's engine quit. He glided in for a landing on a hard spot on the beach, checked the magneto, spark plugs, and carburetor, but found nothing wrong. Then he recognized the kerosene odor in the carburetor. He drained it, bought gas from a nearby trader, and flew on. When he reached Council, a thirty-five-miles-per-hour crosswind had come up, and he was unable to land. He followed the Nukluk River looking for a likely spot of beach, tried for a landing on a two-hundred-foot patch of river bend—and overshot, dragging the plane's wheels through the water "like pontoons." When he finally got his plane down again on dry land, his passenger climbed out of the cockpit and stalked off—without a word. "He didn't even say good-by."

Walking the rest of the way into Council, Reeve's passenger, Charlie Fromm, spread the story of the wild trip, and told how glad he was to get away alive from a fool flyer who burned kerosene in his engine and used half water and half beach for a landing field! It was a story that took Reeve years to live down.

Flying back into Nome to look for a fare for the long flight home to Valdez, Reeve stumbled into his first taste of Alaskan justice. The townsfolk told him by all means to come down and witness a trial being held the following day. "It's bound to be good."

Water, in the isolated coast town, was often more precious than the gold along its beaches. Nome was situated on a bed of solid permafrost that eliminated the possibility of an underground water system, and the city's water supply was carried from house to house by wagon and the citizens limited as to its use. A scavenger wagon, locally called "the honey wagon," took care of the lack of indoor plumbing. (In 1955 a public funeral was held in Nome for "the only horse in (Arctic) Alaska," who had spent his lifetime hauling the honey wagon.) During the mining season, when the population of Nome was at its annual height, water rights became especially precious. The case that was due in court that summer of 1932 concerned one Dirty Dick Charles, who had tapped water from the flume belonging to miner Charlie Newhauser and had been caught in this antisocial act.

The case was further jeweled by the first appearance of a new district attorney, who was representing the Territory and out to win his initial case as well as impress the local citizens.

Dirty Dick chose to appear in his own defense.

The D.A., cutting loose in a flight of oratory, made a lengthy, impassioned speech depicting poor old Dick as the worst type of character in God's province—a man so low that he would actually steal his neighbor's *water*, that precious necessity of this far-flung province of the great North. When he had used up all the invectives at his command, the D.A. turned to the sourdough jury and demanded that Dirty Dick be given the limit of the penalty.

Dirty Dick, too, had been swept by this magnificent appeal. With tears in his eyes, he rose, spread his hands in a gesture of defeat. "The country's sure gone to hell when a poor man can't take a little water to make an honest living. But if it's bad as he says, you better send me to the pen."

The jury retired. All of them sourdoughs who had, during a lifetime of prospecting around waterless Nome, stolen a little water at some stage of their careers, they took five minutes to reach their verdict:

"We find Dirty Dick not guilty of breaking into Charlie Newhauser's dam and stealing his water."

At this unexpected reprise, Dirty Dick jumped up from his chair. "The water's mine, huh!" he shouted. "I can get all I want, huh?" Waving his arms in excitement, he started running out of the courtroom.

"Hey Dick, you come back here!" roared the foreman of the jury. "We found you not guilty this time of breaking into Charlie Newhauser's dam. *But don't you ever do it again!*"

There were other Alaskan customs Reeve was to run into

on this trip. Hearing that the post office paid twenty-five cents a pound for flying air mail, Reeve called on the Nome postmaster, Billy Arthur, to see if he could fly the Nome mail down to Anchorage to catch the boat.

Arthur looked at Reeve with an odd expression and said, "You don't look fit to fly the mail. The back end's out of your pants. Don't know if I could trust you with the U.S. mail or not."

Bristling, Reeve said, "I'll bet you I've flown more mail more miles over more rough country than anyone in this whole damn Territory—and I haven't lost a letter yet."

"Where was that?" asked Arthur.

"Foreign Air Mail Route Number 9 in South and Central America."

"Hmm," Arthur scratched his head. "I don't know about your plane——"

"Plane's in good shape. I'll show it to you."

"You haven't been up here long. Doubt that you know the country."

"I've got just as good maps as anyone else, and I can find my way anywhere——"

Arthur dredged up a couple more reasons why Reeve wasn't qualified to fly the mail, then finally, when Reeve kept pressing him, quit stalling and blurted out the truth: "Listen here, young fellow, you may have flown mail in every country in the world and be the best darn mail pilot there is. But as far as I'm concerned there's only one man who gets to fly air mail out of Nome—and that's my son-in-law, Noel Wien!"

Leaving the post-office business to the "family," Reeve hustled for passengers on the Nome street and eventually uncovered a pair of boys who wanted to catch a boat to take them out to the States and college. Heading out with his load, over the unfamiliar country, Reeve got a grim lesson in Alaskan topography. When he reached the mountains between McGrath and Anchorage he found them obscured by a high overcast. Starting at the bottom, he followed the mountain passes up to seven or eight thousand feet and then invariably hit an impenetrable bank of clouds. For three hours he fought to get through the passes, following each one up to the inevitable point where he couldn't get through. Finally, running short of gas, he turned back to McGrath. There, taking on a hundred gallons of $1.50-per-gallon gas, to replace the gas that he had bought for 25 cents per gallon at Nome and wasted on the mountains, he told his predicament to old-timer Charlie Koenig, who did the gassing.

Koenig listened, his eyes bugging in amazement. "No wonder you didn't get through! You've been trying to fly through the highest pass on North America—right next to Mount McKinley!" Reeve knew now why "paying the gas bill" was the biggest worry of the Alaskan bush pilots. The mistake he had just made ate up all the profits from the trip.

When he finally got back to his Valdez base, a little wiser though by no means richer, Reeve decided the first thing on the agenda was to "do something about that leg." It had given him constant trouble since he arrived in Alaska, giving way unexpectedly, so that more than once he had pitched forward ignominiously on his face. A good look at the vast stretches of unpopulated country between Valdez and Nome convinced Reeve that flying Alaska would require a maximum of physical fitness. If a man were forced down out in the mountains or on the tundra, he would need all his strength to mush out. When Reeve found that one of his Pinzon pals, prospector Charlie De Witt, was planning a search for a lost mine on the side of Mount Sanford, 170 miles from Valdez, he joined the party. It was the sort of project that both stirred his latent interest in mining and promised a "kill-or-cure" treatment for his bad leg. Only the first 100 miles could be taken by car, then the remaining 70 miles from the Copper River on would have to be traveled on foot.

The first day out, Reeve could make only about three miles across the boggy, rough tundra. The second day, he made over four. Since he couldn't keep up with De Witt and the two Indian guides, the miner and one guide went ahead, one Indian stayed behind with Bob. It took nine days to reach the site, but by then Bob's leg was perceptibly building in size and strength. Setting up a camp at the base of Mount Sanford, the party spent ten days climbing up and down the mountain searching for the mine. They never found it. But Bob found something infinitely more priceless—the use of his leg. Within three weeks, the muscles had rebuilt to the point that he could walk without difficulty.

It was on this trip that Bob had his first experience with an

Alaskan bear. While climbing along with De Witt, the two men spotted a fine grizzly bear with two cubs.

"Let's let those bears know we're here," said De Witt, and fired his rifle in the air a couple of times.

His eye on a trophy, Bob borrowed the 30-30 and went in after the grizzly. De Witt had a prospector's "respect" for bears, and wanted no part of them. Bob trailed for a while, eventually lost track of the bear, and turned back for camp. Walking in quietly in his shoepacs, unheard and unseen Reeve saw De Witt bending over, his back to Bob, mixing bannock for supper. Bob slipped up behind him and growled "Wooof!"

De Witt took off "like a Roman candle," fleeing down the canyon without a backward look. Bob yelled after him to tell him it was a joke. When he discovered that it was only a gag, De Witt was furious. He slunk back to camp, glowered at Reeve, and refused to speak to him for two days. Finally, on the third day, De Witt turned to Reeve and spoke:

"DON'T YOU EVER DO THAT AGAIN!"

By the time they had returned to Valdez, Bob was feeling more fit than he had in over a year, and he plunged energetically into plans for fall and winter work. Although there was still nothing going on around Valdez, he found that the mining town of Chisana (they call it Shoe-shana) which lay three hundred miles to the east of Valdez on the eastern slope of the volcanic Wrangell mountains, near the Canadian border, survived on a community basis the year around. The Chisana mine had been shipping in its winter supplies over the mountains by horse and sled. When Reeve offered to fly in the supplies at twenty cents per pound, which was about a quarter of the former cost, the mine-owners quite naturally leaped at the chance. Since he had only the little open Eaglerock to work with, Bob had to do some close figuring. The only space for freight was in the passenger cockpit. Another problem was the long three-hundred-mile run from Valdez to Chicana, with no weather reports and no radio. He estimated that his best bet lay in shipping both the gas he would need for his plane and the mine supplies to the nearest point reached by the highway, then flying them the last leg over the mountains to the camp, a short range that he could judge visually for weather conditions. Trucks carried the supplies from Valdez up to Chestochina, a trading post and roadhouse along the highway one hundred miles west of Chisana. Basing there, Bob began making the short freight hauls the last hundred miles over the mountains to the Chisana mines. Despite his trucking bills, he was able to net fifteen cents per pound.

Like most other Alaskan fields, the Chestochina airstrip had been privately built by nonflyers. There was a tall pole at one end of the field with a high radio antenna, and tall timber at the opposite end. "An Alaskan pilot," Reeve commented drily, "is supposed to be half bird."

Many of the roadhouses, which had originally been built at intervals dictated by how far sled dogs could travel in a day, had converted to the new air age by building an airstrip to entice pilots to stop over. "They never put the field in the open," reports Bob, "but always so that you had to clear some obstacles. More than one radio antenna has been carried away on the tail fork of a plane at take-off."

Unlike the Stateside version, Alaskan roadhouses are hotels or inns, wayside stops that provide sleeping quarters, homelike atmosphere, and home cooking for travelers. Usually run by a couple or a widow, they generally have a big comfortable living room with a fireplace or a hundred-gallon oildrum stove fired by cordwood, a few animal heads on the walls, skins on the floor, comfortable chairs, and books or magazines lying around. There is a clublike atmosphere, and most of the guests know each other. At night, as twenty or thirty flyers, truckers, trappers, and miners gather round, "The first liar has no chance."

The roadhouses that bid for flyers found their worst problem was in collection. Holed in by weather for days at a time, it was generally hard for the pilots to cough up the standard $1.00 for breakfast, $1.50 for lunch, and $2.00 for dinner, as well as the price of their room, when they left. But flyers brought business to the roadhouses in the form of paying passengers, and they were often forgiven their lack of funds. Although high-priced, as was everything in Alaska, roadhouse food was generally excellent: home-cooked, filling meals of moose, sheep, or caribou, home-baked bread and pastries at each meal. There was no bar service during these prohibition years, but if a man felt in need of some cheer, he could always stir up a local "woods chemist" such as the venerable

Doc Blalock at Tazlina, a favorite of all the flyers in the area.

"The first time I paid my bill at a roadhouse, I was shocked," admits Reeve. "I was used to paying thirty-five cents instead of a dollar for my ham and eggs. All set to squawk, I suddenly realized nobody was making a fortune out of the roadhouses either, and I held my peace. Food and supplies were hard to come by. And I learned to put up my own prices, like everyone else, to pay the high cost of Alaskan living."

The Copper Center roadhouse, a hundred miles north of Valdez, off the Richardson Highway, was one of the favorite bases for flyers from Seward, Juneau, Cordova, McCarthy; and it was there that Reeve first met Gillam. Run by tall, strapping "Ma" Barnes, who had come to the Territory during the gold rush, Copper was a special favorite in that it boasted the only telephone along the line, and the flyers could call in for weather reports. The party line extended over a four-hundred-mile area, and there "were no secrets." Everyone along the line lifted their receiver, and the power decreased accordingly, so that the man making the call could hear only about half the conversation. One day Reeve, desperate to hear the information he had requested, suddenly rattled off a few lines in Spanish, and the power promptly came back as everyone hung up.

Beginning his flights out of his Chestochina roadhouse base on November 15, Bob soon discovered just how fast winter descends in Alaska. It was already forty below zero in the Copper River area and getting colder. Before he had begun the Chisana contract, Bob had gotten a thorough briefing from Owen on the winter flying techniques that had been developed by the Alaskan pilots to care for their planes and themselves. Owen and Bob prepared the Eaglerock for cold-weather work by lagging the oil tank and the oil line with asbestos, to keep the oil hot in flight and to prevent its freezing the instant the engine was turned off. But that precaution didn't eliminate some furious moments' work for the pilot the second he brought his plane down in subzero weather. "You had to land with an oil can in one hand and a piece of wire in the other."

First job on landing was to ream out the oil valve hastily with a wire and start the flow of hot oil down into the lowest part of the system before it had frozen over. (Oil in subzero weather freezes like water.) Once the lower spigot had been reamed out, the hot oil from the upper area drained out into a can. The pilot then carried his oil can into the roadhouse and begged a space for it in the kitchen, near the cookstove. "Alaskan roadhouses all smelled the same—a mixture of warm oil and boiling coffee."

When the oil had been safely stashed in the warm interior of the roadhouse, the pilot next fitted his plane with wing covers made out of a light cotton mattress ticking, to prevent the accumulation of heavy frost which would have to be scraped off before take-off.

"Then," says Bob, "you get hold of four oil drums (the national landmark in Alaska, no habitation is without them) and roll them under the wings and rope the plane to them—so it'll be 'somewhere in the vicinity' when you come out next morning."

There was also a daily inspection for oil leaks and damage to the fabric. A rip was an easy job in the winter—"you just cut a piece of fabric, put it on with one coat of hot dope, and it stayed frozen all winter."

"If you found a leak in the gas tank which couldn't be fixed by a sliver of rag or a whittled twig, you turned your back on it."

Occasionally metal crystallized on the engine. If it couldn't be refastened with baling wire, as a last resort the pilot could look for somebody within a hundred miles who had an acetylene torch and knew how to weld. When the throttle stuck, due to a shrinkage of the combination of brass, aluminum, and steel in the frigid temperatures, it could be adjusted by shooting hot kerosene into it until it once more assumed proper flexibility.

Reeve had already learned down in South America, that "graves are full of pilots who didn't warm their engines." Before taking off in subzero weather, there was a good two hours' work for the pilot, with his fire pot, engine cover, and fire extinguisher. Covering the motor to keep wind from extinguishing the flame, the plumber's pot was lighted and set below to thaw the engine. The extinguisher had to be at arm's reach, since you never knew when the flame would contact grease or gas and set fire to the cover. You could, Bob found, load your plane while the engine was being warmed—if you looked at the fire pot every thirty seconds. In sixty-below-zero temperature, the engine took a full two hours to thaw out; at thirty below, it thawed in an hour. Your engine was thawed when the propeller shaft was free of frost.

Although there were heavy snows on the ground, Bob did not have skis on the Eaglerock, since it had old-fashioned narrow wheels, which were adapted to snow landings. Later, when he used planes with skis, examining the skis—and possibly blowtorching ice from underneath them—was still another chore of winter flying.

Inside the plane, even for the short hundred-mile haul, Bob carried his fire pot, extinguisher, motor and wing covers, sleeping bag, emergency food, 30-30 rifle, ax, shovel, and, following an old custom, an armful of magazines and a deck of cards. "You run out of hamburger and newsstands mighty fast in Alaska."

During that first winter flying in Alaska, in the fall of 1932, Bob developed his own technique for maximum engine efficiency in cold weather. He soon discovered that no amount of heating by fire pot could warm up the engine to really safe take-off power. "The most you could get was from one-half to two-thirds normal horsepower." To increase the safety factor of the flight and lessen strain on the engine, Bob warmed up the engine as best he could, then took off *empty*, flew around the field for a few minutes, landed, put the engine cover back over the engine, and let the plane sit a period, with the heat generated from the brief flight spreading and diffusing over all the parts, while he loaded the plane. This allowed all parts of the engine to acquire the normal metal expansion required for efficient operation. He was then able to take off on his trip with normal horsepower. This method was especially effective on the engines of that period, since they contained a mixed assortment of metals—aluminum, steel, and bronze—all of which had different coefficients of expansion.

An engine that had been thoroughly preheated, Bob found, was much less apt to develop dangerous carburetor ice during its operation. As air and fuel were metered through the carburetor jets of the float-type carburetor, a forty-degree temperature (Fahrenheit) drop occurred, that under certain atmospheric conditions and temperatures formed ice in the carburetor throat from the moisture content of the air. This ice restricted the flow of the mixture to the diffuser section and choked off the engine power. Since cold air was denser and gave more boost to the engine's power, Bob learned to start his take-off with the carburetor heat partially applied to guard against internal engine icing (the heater was controlled in the cockpit by a push-pull control connected to the spill valve). Then, as the take-off run progressed, he shut off the hot air and shoved it on full cold to obtain the added power boost. Clearing obstacles with this extra spurt of power, he once more applied the carburetor heat during level flight.

Although few pilots, Reeve found, paid quite as much attention to these problems of winter flying as he, a higher percentage of take-off accidents was averted because of the "kindly qualities" of subzero air. Sixty-below-zero air was so dense, and had so much lift to it, that "it forgave many deficiencies in both engine and human performance." Yet its attendant frost was a constant enemy. Only a fraction of an inch of newly laid frost, the amount which could be gotten in a few minutes' unloading time on the ground, was sufficient to destroy the lift of the plane's airfoil. In the mornings, Bob found, a small layer of frost had almost always formed between the time he removed the wing covers and was ready to take off. "The last thing you did before take-off was to take a rope and slide it back and forth along the wing and remove the last coating of frost." The "tail feathers" (stabilizer) as well had to be cleared.

To cut down fire hazard, Bob made sure that the carburetor was thoroughly drained of gasoline at night, and dry when the torch was put under it the next morning. After the engine was properly thawed, he added the gas and preheated oil. In pouring oil from the can back into the engine, some always spilled outside the tank—which became to Bob a sign of good luck. If he didn't accidentally spill some oil as he poured it in, he deliberately splashed a little over the engine cowling. The roadhouse cooks, almost as planewise as the flyers, set the oil can next to the stove when they first went in to put the hot cakes on in the morning, so it would be good and hot by take-off time. Cooperative to a marked degree, the one warning they gave their flyers was, "Clean the bottoms of your cans before you bring them into my kitchen!"

Bob found to his surprise that the oil can had an innocent

enemy. Forced to make an emergency landing when his oil pressure dropped in flight one morning, he examined the oil pump relief valve and found that a hair from his caribou parka had gotten into the valve and kept it from seating properly, which resulted in the plane's loss of oil pressure. From then on, he took extreme care of the oil can, making sure he didn't get fleece from his gloves or parka in it when he was draining the plane. A man couldn't work long at fifty or sixty below without mittens and parka, but they could give him trouble. "Particularly caribou or reindeer. You could hang it in the front hall of a house, go back to the kitchen—and find it in the soup! It really gets around."

That first winter, fresh from a warm country and having active circulation, Bob wore lightweight underwear and clothes, then heavy wool, and a fur parka over that. By the next winter, however, he was into traditional Alaskan longjohns and wool clothes under the inevitable "parky." Flying into Chisana one day, his goggles fogged over just as he was coming in for a landing. Blinded, he slipped the goggles back and stuck his head out to see what he was doing. In the open air, at sixty below zero, his eyes promptly "frosted." He barely made it to the ground, then cradled his head in his warm hands till the pain died down and he could see again. "There was no more flying that day!"

A year later, flying a cabin plane into Chisana, Bob ran into another serious round of eye trouble. He had laid his fire extinguisher, loaded with pyrene, on top of some freight behind his seat. Flying through a narrow canyon, he felt something spray his cheek, and turned around to receive the full spray of pyrene directly in his eyes, which blinded him. The fire extinguisher had shaken down, landed on the handle, and set itself off. "I'll never know," sighs Bob, "how I made it through that canyon. I was completely blinded. But there was nowhere to sit down, and I couldn't do anything but keep flying." Eventually the natural fluid in his eyes washed out the pyrene to the extent that he could see a little, and he flew on to his Chisana landing.

"During my first year of flying in Alaska," Bob recalls, "I used to worry all the time about doing the right thing at the critical moment. There were so many unknown factors, and I worried about what I'd do when the chips were down. I spent many a sleepless night planning the next day's work. But after that first winter's flying in the mountains, I found that experience had taught me the right reactions. I automatically made correct decisions in crucial moments. So—I quit worrying."

Although his contract was to haul mining supplies to Chisana, Bob soon found that, like other bush pilots who serviced isolated regions, he was expected to serve also as mailman, message-carrier, and purchasing agent for the men who stayed the year round at the mine sites. Each trip they gathered round to see what he had brought them, and gave him special orders to fill. Although there was no pay for this service, Bob did his best, but, not familiar with Alaskan tradition, had his mind more on his job than on special favors. One day, when he flew into Chisana and the miners, as usual, crowded around the plane, an old Swede came up eagerly, clutched Bob's arm. "Got my snoose?" Reeve thought a second, puzzled, then remembered. Just as he was taking off for his previous flight, this man had asked him to haul in a supply of Copenhagen snuff.

"Sorry," Reeve said, "I forgot it."

The expression of disappointment and disgust that crossed the miner's face seemed to Reeve beyond the emotional requirements of the situation! Without a word, the man turned his back and stalked off. When Reeve had gone, the old Swede went around the camp spreading the verdict, "That Reeve no good! He forgot my snoose!"

It didn't take much more time around Alaska for Reeve to grasp the vital importance of the pilot to the folks who lived in isolated communities. This was their lifeline with the rest of the world, their chance at communication and comforts. It was traditional that every time a plane landed the flyer must greet every person who came out, omitting no one. He must bring every item they had asked for, no matter how trivial or how difficult it was to procure. It was much more than a packet of needles or a can of snuff. It was their assurance that they were still a part of the outside world, and it was a tradition of Alaskan fellowship. When they put in a request, it was generally for some luxury on which they set their hearts; then they counted the days till its arrival, as children do at Christmas. To then be disappointed was a crushing and often humiliating blow.

"In these tiny communities," explains Reeve, "it was important to have everyone on your side. I soon learned to shake hands with everyone who came near the plane, whether I'd met them or not. Have a word for everyone; mail and packages for anyone expecting them. When I forgot that old fellow's snoose, I had let him down terribly—before all the others. He talked about it for years. And, so help me, I never knowingly neglected anyone again. I learned how to get along in Alaska. In the States, one could make an enemy, but his sentiments would be lost among 150,000,000 people. In Alaska, the population is so small that the people you see today you are going to see the rest of your life. If one person is down on you, the whole Territory will know about it in a week!"

The following year, when he again serviced Chisana, Bob made a point of buying up fresh fruits from the freight boats at Valdez and hauling them into the camp. "When those old fellows looked at a fresh peach, you should have seen their mouths water! It meant more than diamonds—or gold dust. For some of them it was the first fruit they'd had in fifteen or twenty years!" Hauling such luxuries in on speculation, Reeve found the men were glad to pay. He charged what he had paid the boat, the extra time and work going under the label of "service" that Alaska expected of its flyers.

When he finished his first Chisana contract, in the winter of 1932, Bob found that he had taken in $2800 and cleared about $2000. The money was paid to him in gold dust, carefully weighed out to the fraction of a dollar, at the going rate of sixteen dollars per ounce, less the silver and basemetal content of the gold. Chisana gold was high grade and refined out to $15.50 per ounce, and the price was used in trade. Later, Bob was to discover how lucky it was that he was actually paid at the termination of the work. It was fall, after "cleanup," and the miners were in the chips. Most jobs, Bob soon found, were never paid at the time, but only at the cleanup season when people had money. Through the rest of the year, the whole Territory lived on credit, running charge accounts with their supply outfitters, air lines, grocers, and landlords until cleanup time, when they all cheerfully paid each other till the money was once more all gone and credit again in force. Many merchants carried miners for years. Most eventually paid—if the gold was there. Although lacking in a cash crop, Alaskans proved to be singularly responsible for their long-standing debts. Merle "Mudhole" Smith (now president of Cordova Airlines) described being stopped on the streets of Anchorage, Fairbanks, and Cordova by old-timers that he had hauled somewhere ten or fifteen years earlier who, at long last, had the money to pay their bills. "They wouldn't mail it in, nor give it to the accounting department, or even my secretary," smiled Smith. "But they'd pay it to me."

Pilots felt the pinch with oil companies who, not as casual as other Alaskans, wanted cash settlements for their gas bills. One of the classics of the bush pilots—credited to big genial Ray Petersen, president of Northern Consolidated Airlines, who first came to Alaska as a bush pilot in 1934—concerns the time when the manager of the Northern Commercial Company at Bethel cornered Ray and demanded to know when he was going to make a payment on his gas bill.

With a grieved look, Petersen said, "Mister, this is the way I work it. Things going like they are now, I take in about two thousand dollars a month, and I have about three thousand dollars a month in bills. The first of each month I put all my creditors' names in a hat and start drawing out names until my two thousand dollars is exhausted." He frowned at the man warningly. "Now you get me down on you, and next month I won't even put your name in the hat!"

The two thousand dollars that he had cleared on the Chisana job meant that Reeve, for the first time since he hit Alaska, had a "stake" and a chance to get a plane of his own. The open-cockpit Eaglerock had done its part, but he was ready for a bigger cabin plane, with which he could haul freight the year round. With most of the other pilots specializing in passengers, Bob figured he could carve out his own territory by sticking strictly with freight. Harold Gillam, on the contrary, told Bob that he wanted his freight "on two legs so it could walk itself on and off the plane." But Bob wasn't interested in an admiring flock of passengers. He was interested in making a living. Besides, freight didn't ask him a dozen times a day, "How's the weather? When are we going to take off?"—queries that Gillam avoided by going into hiding until the weather cleared.

Reeve went to Fairbanks, where had heard there was a surplus Fairchild 51 for sale by Pacific Alaska Airways, the Pan Am subsidiary that was planning to inaugurate regularly scheduled service in Alaska. The price of the Fairchild was

$3500. Bob paid $1,500 down, promising the rest in the next two years. It was fortunate there was a Fairchild available in the Territory. For, after his experiences in the Andes, Bob had his heart set on this slow, dependable workhorse. If it could fly the Andes, it could fly the wild and surly Chugach back of Valdez, where the mines lay.

With no mining operations till spring and no passenger boats coming in, Bob took his new plane to Anchorage, where he tried to pick up a little free-lancing till the mines opened. There he found Oscar Winchell, Steve Mills, Harry Blunt, Art Woodley, Matt Nieminen, and Lon Cope all at their home base and "a little stiff-necked about a competitor."

But "it was get some business or starve."

Although no passengers were coming in and out of Valdez at this time of year, they were still departing and arriving from Seward. Most pilots didn't like to go into Seward because of its exceptionally short runway and turbulent winds. "But after flying in and out of Valdez and Chisana, Seward was just up my alley." While the other boys raided the trains at Anchorage, as they arrived from Seward, to pick up travelers and fly them on to their homes "in the bush," Reeve left that sport to the Anchorage flyers and flew down to Seward to pick up passengers fresh off the boat, before they took the train to Anchorage.

The first people off the boat that he met were a couple named Mr. and Mrs. Ole Hay and their two children, bound for their home at Nome.

# 4. Making the headlines

Reeve loaded his passengers, Mr. and Mrs. Ole Hay, four-year-old Johnnie and baby Olga, just four months old, into his new Fairchild and headed northwest for Nome. He reached McGrath, the crossroads of many of the air routes in the Territory, that same evening, without difficulty despite the intense subzero cold and the threat of drifting ice fog* in the air. The little river town of McGrath, finding itself on the main air line from Anchorage to Nome and from Fairbanks to Bethem, had hospitably built its airstrip along the main street, so that incoming planes could taxi right up to the gas supply and gas up while passengers walked into the road-house next door for coffee or food. It was not unusual for seven or eight different lines to be weathered in at McGrath at one time, and it was known as a good spot to "practice up on your poker." Although Valdez, according to Reeve's claim, was the "poker headquarters of Alaska," McGrath often ran it a close second. And woe to the pilot who turned up at this popular crossroads without his short-snorter dollar bill signed by the other pilots. If a man owned a short-snorter and was caught without it, he had the choice of paying the other men a dollar apiece or buying everyone a drink. One of Reeve's short-snorters, dating back to 1932, is signed by Joe Crosson, Ed Young, C. E. Robbins, Frank Dorbrandt, Al Munson, and Harold Gillam. A form of amusement, when the flyers were fogged in, was to try to catch a man without his short-snorter by trailing him into the bathroom. "A fellow was never safe," sighs Reeve. "He could be called upon at any moment to produce his short-snorter. And the rules were

---

* Ice fog is a peculiarly Alaskan phenomenon. It occurs when the particles of water suspended in the air, which make fog, freeze, so that ice particles, rather than droplets of water, hang in the air.

57

that he had to have it on his person." The men learned to roll up the bill and stick it back of an ear, or in their mouths, while they bathed. If they weren't going to get into a tub of water, they put the bills under their watch bands.

Reeve and his passengers spent the night at the McGrath roadhouse, and took off next morning for the last leg of their journey in sullen gray skies, with rapidly falling barometer and temperatures reading fifty degrees below zero. But the cabin of the Fairchild remained reasonably warm, the sullen sky offered medium visibility, and all went well till they hit the Yukon River. There the ceiling perceptibly lowered, just as they reached the mountain barrier to the western coast. Unable to get through the pass at Unalakleet, Reeve set a course to detour up the Koyukuk River, then northwest down the headwaters of the Kateel River, and thus beat a course west of Norton Sound. Anticipating the possible magnetization of his fuselage and compass at a time when he needed them, Reeve had demagnetized the fuselage of his new plane, had his compass newly swung, and felt confident that he could chart an accurate course without getting lost.

But knowing where he was did not answer all his problems that day. Halfway down the Kateel River he ran into 0-0 ice fog, a complete "white-out," with the wings icing up rapidly. The canyon was too narrow to turn around—even if he could see. He elected to land straight ahead, down through the towering spruce trees, onto the river ice.

There was no alternative but to make camp—fast. While Bob drained the oil and put on the wing covers, Ole Hay hustled out, dragged in a dead spruce tree, and quickly got a roaring fire going. It was now fifty-five degrees below zero.

When he had his plane drained and tied down, Reeve pulled out his two sleeping bags and got Mrs. Hay, her baby, and son safely wrapped up in them, near the fire. Worried about the baby, Bob decided to sacrifice frost prevention, and took off the plane's wing covers so that he could fashion a canvas shelter over the sleeping bags. His emergency rations consisted primarily of dried beans, which take a long time to cook. Instead, Bob got water on for tea, then raided his freight load and pulled out two roasted chickens he was carrying to one man's sweetheart as a special Valentine gift. Privately, Bob thanked the practical lover, who had sent food instead of flowers or a book.

With chicken and hot tea and hardtack to warm them, Mrs. Hay looked a little less grim, her eyes less accusing as she silently watched the pilot. Though she said nothing to him, Bob felt that she was certain he had lost his way and brought them to sure disaster.

While Bob and Ole Hay chopped wood all night and kept the fire blazing, the woman and children dozed fitfully. Of them all, the tiny baby seemed least concerned about the exposure, and slept most of the night, snugly bound up in the warm sleeping bag.

When morning came, Bob and Ole Hay had cut fifty-three spruce trees averaging eight inches in diameter, chopped them into eight-foot lengths, and dragged them to the fire through three feet of snow. Greatest handicap was the ax blade, which kept flying off the short handle. At one point Bob had had to dig in the snow for forty minutes to recover it. "In the morning that camp site resembled the winter quarters of a milling herd of moose."

The coldest temperature was reached between five and eight in the morning, when hot tea three feet away from the fire froze within minutes.

At three o'clock the next afternoon, after twenty-five hours in camp, the dense ice fog showed signs of lifting. Bob chopped a hole in the ice to make sure which direction was downstream. He estimated that, even if he were confused about which river they had hit, downstream on any river there was bound to be habitation of some kind. When the weather lifted to two-hundred-foot visibility, Bob heated the engine, scraped frost off his wings, loaded his passengers, and headed downstream. Within half an hour they reached the village of Shaktoolik on Norton Sound. He was, Bob was pleased to discover, exactly where he had thought. He landed safely on a narrow creek in front of the small Eskimo village and herded the Hays and their children to the house of the schoolteachers, Mr. and Mrs. David Mazen, who greeted them with delight. "We heard you were lost somewhere around here," the Mazens told them. "The whole Territory is in an uproar about you!"

Shaktoolik, Bob found, had a radio—but no transmitter. Hourly broadcasts were carrying the report of the lost plane and its passengers, but there was no way of notifying anyone that they were safe. The Mazens dispatched a native runner fifteen miles to the nearest phone, but he was soon back with word that the high winds had suspended all phone service.

The lost plane's arrival in Shaktoolik was a godsend to the isolated village. Mrs. Mazen, out on a dog-sled trek a few weeks before, had suffered frosted lungs and was badly in need of hospitalization. Trader Frank Beeson was suffering from a combination of heart trouble and dropsy, and needed to be carried to a hospital. Unable to communicate with the rest of the Territory during stormbound winters, both the school teacher and the trader had expected to die for lack of treatment.

When he left for Nome three days later, when the weather cleared, Reeve took Mrs. Mazen along with the Hays, and promised to return for Beeson when he could get back. Safe at Nome at last, the Hay children were examined and pronounced sound, with no ill effects from the harrowing trip. Mrs. Mazen was immediately operated upon, "which," announced the Nome, Seward, and Anchorage papers, "probably saved her life."

Weathered in at Nome for ten days, with a storm over the mountains that led to the Interior, Reeve spent his time picking up a little cash, flying for Hollywood director "Woody" Van Dyke, who was on location in Nome making *Eskimo*. Reeve's job was to make a series of flights out over the Bering Sea, searching for polar bears to work as extras in the movie. The bears had enough sense to stay hidden, and as soon as the weather cleared Reeve quit the movie business and flew back to Shaktoolik to pick up trader Beeson.

As he was suffering from severe dropsy, fluid had accumulated in Beeson's body until he weighed over three hundred pounds and was completely incapacitated. The villagers brought him out to the plane on a sled. With Reeve's help, they literally stuffed the sick man into the Fairchild, and Reeve set out for Anchorage. He made it into McGrath with no difficulty, spent the night, then flew on toward Anchorage the next day. Within miles of Anchorage's Merrill Field, while flying over on the west side of Cook Inlet, Reeve ran into blinding ice fog, making it impossible to go in for a landing. He turned back, looking for some safe place to land with his sick passenger. Finally he spied a cabin along the Skwetna River about sixty miles out of Anchorage, and set down gently on the river ice. "It was murder, trying to carry that man across the river ice to the cabin!" But Reeve finally dragged his passenger into the camp. Finding no one there, he got a fire going, put his passenger to bed, then went back to tend to the plane. The trapper whose cabin they occupied never showed up, but Reeve fed Beeson and kept a warm fire going all night. Next morning he found the remains of an old sled and was able to load Beeson on it and slide him down to the plane. "But that narrow door!" Bob sighs. "For a while I didn't see how I could make it!"

Once loaded, Reeve took off for Seward, where he delivered his patient to the Seward hospital. There, when they drained off the accumulation of fluid, Beeson lost 150 pounds in one month! The next time Reeve saw him, Beeson was ambulatory.

Back home at Valdez, Reeve discovered that he had been initiated into the ranks of "Heroic bush pilots." Newspapers all over the Territory, and several in the States, had lapped up the lost-plane story, happily headlined, PILOT BOB REEVE, FOUR PASSENGERS LOST, and the like. The Seward *Daily Gateway* (February 14, 1933) apparently in need of a good yarn, rhapsodized: "The saga of Pilot Bob Reeve and his plane passengers, Mr. and Mrs. Ole Hay and children, is another epic of the North; another glorious chapter to be enscribed on the pages of history of Alaska's airmen who have charted Northern Skies and won the admiration of the world for their record of achievement. . . . Pilot Bob Reeve, hero of the battle with a blizzard . . . *etc.*"

There was no doubt about it; Alaska was proud of its pilots. And the folks back in the States were impressed. The home-town papers of Waunakee and Madison began featuring the saga of Reeve, who had joined that incredible daredevil bunch up north. Bob's father, to whom he wrote regularly, furnished material for the papers. Alaskan bush pilots were a good subject for news in the thirties; they and their adventures had an aura of romance, much as the doings of movie and TV stars do today.† Soon after the much-publicized Nome trip, Bob began getting his first fan letters.

The winter of 1932-1933 Bob described as "the greatest

† In 1927, *Variety* reported that the popular acclaim accorded Lindbergh was "one of the most astounding demonstrations ever given a citizen in American history"; that "a new sort of hero worship" had taken hold in America.

winter of my life." He was doing what he wanted most to do—giving service and building up a profession. What's more, Valdez was beginning to feel like home. When he had bought his Fairchild, Bob had insisted on "everything," and had both wheels and skis for his plane, as well as extra motor parts. "I even had spare wings." Whatever he lacked he "scrounged around the Territory" and picked up from wrecked Fairchilds. Although he had no hangar at the little Valdez strip, "I had the largest hangar in the world—the wide open spaces!" He built a little wooden shop for his parts and tools, and loved nothing better than to putter around, working on his plane in his spare time. "One of the sights in Valdez," smiles Noel Wien, "was Bob out there on the field in his greasy coveralls, with airplane parts and tools spread all over the ground."

Bob always rented a cabin close to his plane's pasture, and when the wind howled off the glaciers at night his sense of ownership gave him little sleep. Many a night he pulled on his trousers and parka and hurried out to the field to see how his pride and joy was weathering the high winds. He learned to "quarter" the airplane at least two-thirds angled from the wind, to destroy the lift of air so the wind wouldn't tip the plane over. "I had enough ropes on that Fairchild to have held the steamship *Yukon* to the docks at Valdez!" he laughs. And yet the williwaws that sped down off the ice cap at the head of Valdez glacier could defeat the most careful plans. Once, when he had just landed and stepped out of the cockpit, a sudden burst of wind lifted the plane and it started to fly. Bob jumped on one ski, as it sailed past him, and was carried up with it "just like a balloon," 50 feet into the air. It flew along about 250 feet, then let down, gently, without injuring the plane. One night, when we went out to check his plane in a fifty-mile glacial wind, Reeve heard a "swish" through the air, and looked around to see a piece of sheet metal, which had torn loose from someone's roof, whip by his head, missing decapitating him by inches. It actually came so close it tore the edge off his parka.

The winter winds of Valdez were hard on any but the staunchest sourdough. During Bob's first winter, the Department of Commerce inspector,‡ Hugh Brewster, came up for

‡ Civil aviation regulation was under the Department of Commerce until the Civil Aeronautics Act of 1938.

his annual inspection of the planes in the Territory. When Brewster flew from Anchorage to Valdez, with Reeve, the old Valdez wind was doing its best. "If we're going to get this ship out of this wind," Reeve explained to Brewster, "you're going to have to push the tail around."

After a few pushes, Reeve looked out of the cockpit to see Brewster high-tailing down the field. When he eventually caught up with him, hours later, Reeve asked Brewster what had happened.

"I started pushing the tail," said Brewster, "and you blasted the gun. The first blast blew off my helmet and my mittens. The second blast, I started freezing to death—so I left. I ran till I got to first house I could find, and I broke into it. A nice old lady gave me tea and cookies."

The "nice old lady" Reeve knew would be Grandma Meals, Owen's mother, whose house bordered the airstrip. Grandma laughed.

"That was certainly funny. I had my front room blocked off since I couldn't heat it in this weather. The only fire I had was in my kitchen where I was sitting. I heard that door slam and thought it was the grandchildren. But when nobody appeared I opened the door to the front room and saw this stranger standing there, shivering, holding his hands over the stove. 'Lady, I apologize,' he said, 'but I'm freezing to death.' I told him that was fine, but if he really wanted to get warm he better come back in the kitchen. There's no fire in that stove!"

By now Reeve had been around Alaska long enough, and had performed well enough, to have weathered the ignominy of being a "chee choker." He was almost a sourdough.** Chee chokers were greenhorns, in contrast to the sourdoughs who had proved they could put up with Alaskan weather and privations with good sense—and good humor.

Alaskan communities faced their snowed-in winter season by turning inward, for mutual enjoyment and mutual entertainment. Knowing they could not go anywhere nor see anything, they made their own pleasures—with weekly bridge

---

** The Alaskan definition of a sourdough is "a man who has shot a bear, slept with a squaw, and peed in the Yukon"; a sourdoughess is "a woman who has peed in the Yukon, shot a squaw, and slept with a bear." Explaining this, Reeve sighed thoughtfully. "For years I thought it mean you had to pee *across* the Yukon!"

parties, poker sessions, dinner invitations, and a Saturday night dance "for everyone in town." The Tilicum Club of Valdez, a mixed social group of men and women, held a "feed" and bridge party every week. "The ladies," says Reeve appreciatively, "took a maternal look at my lean stomach— and set out to fatten me up." He was regularly invited out, ate well with the permanent residents: bank president Gilson, his cashier Robbins, Judge Cecil Clegg (district court was held each summer in Valdez, providing the highlight of the social season), the United States marshal Stanley Nichols, Minnie and Harry Whitley, George Fawcett. . . . There were no single women in Valdez—except one, and she was "spoken for." But the family fellowship appealed to bachelor Reeve. "I was a stranger and they took me in. The Alaskan community proved to be what I had always hoped—kind, good-natured, interdependent."

Down at the Pinzon, the oldsters talked of the gold "back in the hills"; black-haired Ed Wood reminisced of the days when the horse was king. One night when a college boy joined the old-timers and talked bravely of what he'd do at school with a girl, a car, a quart of moon, and five gallons of gas, Ed Wood turned to him with a look of genuine surprise. "Son," he said, "haven't you got that backwards? Don't you mean a quart of gas and five gallons of moon?"

They were real "he-men," the old-timers. It made Bob a little sad to see them sitting around the oil-drum stove, talking of the past—with so little hope for the future. No one had heard yet from Clarence Poy in San Francisco, or other moneyed interests they had tried to contact, after Bob's proposal of flying in supplies. But, maybe, come spring, they would hear. They felt sure there were some men who would put up the necessary backing—on the prospect of seeing the mines open again.

In late March Bob got an order to take some more supplies into Chisana. There he unloaded, picked up miner Charlie Hawkins, and started back for Valdez. Flying high (in South America Reeve had developed the practice of flying as high as possible over mountains, on the theory that if he had to come down he would at least have a choice of landing spots) over fourteen-thousand-foot Mount Wrangell, Reeve's engine quit. There was no place beneath to land. The only place anywhere near was back at the Nabesan mine. Reeve turned the plane and headed back, but the turbulent air over the mountain range destroyed the length of his glide, and he soon realized he'd never make it back to the field. Instead, as he steadily lost altitude in the downdrafts, he headed the Fairchild straight ahead, down the vertical walls of the Jacksina Canyon. He brought the plane down smoothly on skis on the snowy bottom of the canyon, twenty miles short of the Nabesna mine. Charlie Hawkins, who had never been in a forced landing, stuck his feet into the familiar snow with a sigh of relief. "Sure feels good, this solid ground."

Reeve was not so happy about their situation. He checked the wires, magneto, and accessories of the plane, and then opened the valve caps and cylinder to see if the valves were functioning. As he turned the prop, the valve overhead remained stationary. This meant trouble in the accessory gear section—probably the timing gear. Whatever it was, there was nothing he could do about it where they were. Tying down the ship by chopping holes and freezing ropes into the river ice, the two men started out on showshoes for Nabesna. The engine failure had occurred at five in the afternoon; they started out for the mine at seven o'clock. Climbing up and down hills with the wind "blowing like hell" was no picnic for Reeve, although his miner friend trudged easily along, accustomed to "mushing out." At one in the morning they at last reached Nabesna, and Reeve pounded on the door of his friend Carl Whitham, president and founder of the Nabesna Mine. Wakened from a sound sleep, Carl nonetheless "greeted me like an old friend," reports Reeve happily, and promptly pulled out a jug of Doc Blalock's mountain dew to warm the weary travelers. A friend of action as well as hospitality, Whitham sent out a four-horse team to pull the plane up the river ice to the shelter of the Nabesna River bar, and ordered a dog team to carry Reeve from Nabesna to Whitham's nearest neighbor, at Salina, fifty miles west. After a heartening warming, Reeve boarded the sled; and at Salina trader and wolf-trapper Lawrence de Witt relayed him on to Chestochina, where there was a landing field. Reeve ducked into Chestochina at the moment when old-time Alaskan pilot Nat Browne was passing through en route from Fairbanks to Valdez. Reeve flagged him down and hitched a ride to Valdez. Within thirty-six hours from the time his engine quit, he was at the source of supply for spare parts. He had also tasted the miraculous competence and speed with which isolated Alaskans help out in emergency.

After a conference with Owen, Reeve decided the basic cause must be, as he had suspected, failure in the timing gear. The Wright Whirlwind engine, which he had in his Fairchild, was notorious for its weakness in this respect. To meet this and any other emergency, they loaded a complete inventory of spare parts into Owen's Eaglerock, and, enlisting the services of "Kirk" Kirkpatrick to ferry the Eaglerock back home, they took off for Nabesna.

There they found a sawmill operator who had cut off his finger, waiting to flag them down to take him to the doctor. Dumping Meals, Kirkpatrick, and the spare parts, Reeve hastily loaded the injured man and started back to Valdez. On the way they ran into heavy snow while following Richardson Highway, and Bob realized he would have to make a forced landing when he reached Thompson Pass (the lowest pass through the Chugach) and found it "pure white." He set the Eaglerock down for "the only landing ever made in four-thousand-foot Thompson Pass," waited a few hours till the weather broke, then carried the man back into Valdez, turned around, and came back to Nabesna.

The three men pushed the Fairchild up in front of a tree, removed the engine, and hauled it up to the mine, where they tore it down for inspection. The timing gear was the answer. But within another twenty-four hours the engine was repaired and remounted by being swung up through a crotch in the tree, and the Fairchild was air-borne once more. Kirkpatrick flew the Eaglerock back to Valdez.

A few weeks later, with the first warmth of spring, came the word that the Pinzon group had been waiting for. "I heard from Clarence Poy!" Jack Cook told Bob excitedly. "He says that if you will prove you can land on Brevier Glacier, he will buy the mine!"

"I can land on any of these peaks—if they've got a flat space five hundred feet long," Reeve repeated his claim. Privately, a vision of those frightening saw-tooth peaks flashed through his mind's eye. "I realized," he says, "that the innate egotism of a six-months' Alaskan expert was about to be put to a test! For the first time since I hit Alaska, I began to wonder just what I had for a hole card."

# 5. First glacier landing

Jack Cook's Big Four mine was only about thirty miles out of Valdez, up on the Brevier Glacier. It was, however, one of the highest of all the mine sites in the Chugach range, a record six thousand feet above sea level. Reeve was not certain just where the mine was located, but Cook assured him that it had a "fine, flat shelf of ice, over a thousand feet long," which would make a perfect landing field. The Big Four, like many of the other Chugach mines, was known to contain large bodies of low-grade quartz; it required full-scale mill equipment, which the local owners could not afford to install. As one old prospector put it, "Alaska is a treasure house— but someone's thrown away the key." the key was the capital needed to develop the mines, but with the going rate of freighting heavy equipment by horse at thirty and thirty-five cents per pound, it was hard to attract men with capital into Alaskan investment. They could put their money elsewhere with a greater return on the dollar. But when Cook wrote mining engineer Clarence Poy in San Francisco, who represented Chinese capital, that Reeve had agreed to fly in the mining supplies at four or five cents per pound, Poy snapped up the opportunity and offered to buy the mine from Cook, then operate it with Cook's help.

The first clear day after Cook received his answer from Poy, Cook and Bob crawled into Reeve's Fairchild and flew up to the Brevier Glacier. Like the Middleton Island booby trap, Reeve quickly saw that the "thousand-foot fine flat surface" he had been promised was actually a steep, cup-shaped snow shelf, about a hundred feet wide and not much over five hundred long, lying at a twenty-five-degree incline with a curled ridge on the outside. "There was no horizon to judge by, no perspective. It all looked flat white. There was no way of telling how close you were to the snow." Finding no refer-

ence point to judge his altitude by, Reeve decided to skim up
the snow wallow to observe the snow conditions before he attempted to land. But as he came in on his trial run, "things
happened fast. I ran out of perspective and altitude all at the
same instant." Coming in low at normal power, the plane
stalled on the steep slope and smashed into the mountain side
at the top of the incline. Reeve, with fastened seat belt, remained in his seat when the plane hit the snow bank. Cook,
with no seat belt, ended up half in the cockpit, half on the
cabin floor, his legs and arms dangling in the air.

"The propeller was picking up the whole side of the mountain," says Bob. "It was just like an Arctic blizzard outside. I
had to shut off my motor quick, so we could see what shape
we were in."

After congratulating themselves that they were still alive,
Cook and Reeve made a quick survey of their position.
Crashing into the endless depths of soft snow, the plane had
actually done little more than bury itself. There was no
mechanical damage. The two men spent the remainder of the
day digging the Fairchild out of the snow bank; then they
packed down a flat shelf and got the plane turned around and
headed downhill. When they took off, down the steep incline,
they became air-borne within fifty feet.

"I didn't like the looks of it," Reeve admits, "but I had
committed myself. Besides, I'd found that if you turn back
that first time, it's liable to become a habit."

To ensure his good faith in the project, while he took a little time to study the possibilities for a safe landing, next day
Reeve hired Gillam to fly over the mine, while Bob pushed
some gunny sacks for landing markers out to the shelf below.
Gillam, busy at the controls, suddenly heard a bumping and
thumping from the back of his plane just as they flew over
the mine. He looked around to find that Bob hadn't thrown
a thing out—but was beating on the side of the plane to
attract his attention. "For Christ's sake, Harold," Bob
shouted, "keep up your air speed or you'll do just what happened to me!"

After scattering the landing markers Reeve then made a
flight up, alone, to see if he could execute a safe landing along
the slippery incline. This time he approached the ramp in a
steep climb at full power, touched the skis of his plane at the
foot of the slope, cut the gun; and let the grade serve as a

built-in brake—enabling him to land within five hundred feet after cutting the power. The take-off, he already knew, would be immediate, requiring no more than a few feet, since the plane literally tobogganed downhill off the slope into the air. To prevent the plane from sliding back downhill when he landed, Bob hastily turned it at a ninety-degree angle before cutting the engine off, shifting it over to the right side, so that the full gas tank in the left wing would counterbalance the plane on its precarious axis.

While at the mine, Reeve put up a series of black marking flags along the left side of the slope at fifty-foot intervals, so that he would have something to judge by in future landings. Then he went back to Valdez, took Cook up with him, flew back to the glacier and pointed out his flags—proof that he had been back. "Now," he said, "we're ready to start bringing in the stuff."

Miners, Reeve found, had been trying to get Gillam to land up there for years. When Gillam found that Reeve intended to make regular landings at the Big Four, the fearless bad-weather pilot shook his head. "I thought Reeve was 90 per cent pilot and 10 per cent nuts. But now I know damn well he's 10 per cent pilot and 90 per cent nuts!" Gillam preferred to line out on a long straight run, rather than fly the short, perilous hops which were to become Reeve's special province.

After his marking flags were set up, Reeve found he had little trouble with landings at the Big Four. Take-offs were a cinch. Even with a downwind, the empty plane, racing downhill, attained one hundred miles per hour within a space of three hundred feet. "All you had to do," explains Bob, "was hold the stick back and keep the tail skid digging into the snow to eliminate the ground-looping you would normally get in a downwind take-off." To facilitate this operation, he enlarged the surface of the tail skid on his plane.

The success of Reeve's Big Four operation was a brisk, heady potion for the dead little town of Valdez. The day Bob and Cook made that first flight into the mountains, the Valdez *Miner* had reported:

For the first time in the history of Valdez an airplane was used today as an aid to opening up the vast treasure vaults in the hills in the immediate vicinity of Valdez, when Robert Reeve, accompanied by John Cook Sr. made a flight to the Big Four Mine on Mineral Creek. . . . A landing was made on a glacier a few feet from the mine. . . Mr. Cook . . . said that although he did not have the usual christening fluid with him he had named the glacier upon which the landing was made Reeve Glacier, in honor of the intrepid pilot who was first to blaze his way by plane into the realms of the Valdez Treasure Chest, an honor, Reeve says, he considers equivalent to that of his ambition of having his name and picture as a trade mark on a cigar box. . . .

Everyone who had a claim began contacting outside capital to subsidize the revitalization of the rich mining properties. Now they had conclusive proof that it could be done—on minimum investment. Within .the first week that he began supplying the Big Four, Reeve hauled in over 40,000 pounds of equipment, which included the complete milling unit. Within one month, sixty flights, he had landed nearly thirty tons of supplies at the mine site, literally hauling in the entire mine, nail by nail and board by board. He was able, in a matter of hours, to deliver material that would have taken months to bring in by sled over the tortuous glaciers.

Old Cowboy Ed Wood dourly watched Bob come into the Pinzon bar following one of these glacier flights and order an ice cream cone. "Ten, twenty years ago," said Ed slowly, "we did all the packing out of Valdez with two hundred horses and one hundred packers. Every Saturday night the packers came into town and blew it in. Now, one man hauls the same amount of freight in one day with one airplane—and comes in and buys an ice cream cone!"

With the incontrovertible proof that a renaissance could, and would, come to the mining business through the airplane, Reeve's services were suddenly in demand. While still flying his initial Big Four contract, he also signed up to haul supplies in for the Ramsay Rutherford mine on Valdez Glacier and the Mayfield mine on Shoup Glacier. An old Pinzon pal Charlie Elwood told Bob about a Black Hills prospect, right in the middle of Columbia Glacier—if Bob was interested. He was. "I had to fly to eat," he says, "and I'd finally found how I could eat regular—by doing the kind of flying that no one else wanted."

Although he had no more trouble landing at Big Four, Bob

realized that each new job would be like his first trial run there—the first dive you took, without perspective, without horizon to judge by, "had to be it." There was no way to overshoot. "On that first run, you had to cut the gun at just the right split second—or you were likely a goner."

The Ramsay Rutherford mine, only about fifteen miles back of Valdez, on the Valdez Glacier, gave Bob his toughest test. A few days before he was scheduled to make his first trial run to the Ramsay site, several prospectors and young air-minded Bill Egan hiked into the mine and set up marking flags for Bob to use.

The day of the test run, Bob took Bill along with him to point out the site. A few minutes after their Valdez take-off, as they flew over the glacier, Bill looked puzzled. "There," Bill said, pointing to a speck on the snow below them. "There's the Ramsay building—but something's happened to the row of flags we put up!"

Reeve aimed at the speck on the snow, flew down toward the tiny snow shelf alongside the grinding glacier. "There was," he says grimly, "no place to land!" But the test run had already turned into a "one-way deal." Once down alongside the shelf there was no way out but straight ahead. "Just aim, cut your gun, and there you are."

"There" turned out to be, as it had at Big Four, the snow-covered side of the mountain. The prop and skis ground into the snowdrift. Reeve hastily turned off the engine. Shaken but unhurt, Reeve and Egan climbed out to take a look. Flying head first into the snowshelf, the plane was three-fourths buried. Bob and Bill started shoveling. Hours later they had the Fairchild dug out—surprisingly, without a bent prop, despite its determined headlong charge into the side of the steep snow shelf. "Flying in there, with nothing to judge by, was just like sticking your head into an enamel pail. It all looked flat white. But by now that was old stuff to me!"

When they had the plane shoveled out and pulled around for take-off, they looked for the missing flags. Placed three and four feet above the snow only days before, the flags had been completely obliterated by a fresh snowfall.

When he made initial landings on glaciers, Bob found that frequently one ski of his plane would break through a crevasse, with no serious damage to the airplane. But after repeated landings on the frozen rivers he began to "sense" the presence of these hidden foes. "A slight undulation in the snow," "not quite as bluish in cast as the surrounding snow." As the snow got older and wetter from compacting, it took on a bluish tinge, but the thin snow crust or shelf over a crevasse did not retain the moisture and was subsequently dryer in texture and paler in color than the older snow.

Snow, Bob discovered, might have a different character in adjoining areas. That on the south side of the Chugach Mountains, next to the coast, maintained a heavy, set character due to the moisture coming up from the ocean. It provided an excellent medium for landing, and the skis of the plane sank no more than a foot into the heavy surface. But the snow on the north side of the mountains was dry, weightless, more like frost, and a plane landing on it "sank to its belly," then had to be dug out and a ramp packed down three or four feet before take-off. Air and sun changed the form of the snow by glazing it, making it slick. After a fresh fall in the interior, Bob learned to wait a day or so till the snow had been glazed over by the sun and air. Newly fallen snow on the south side of the mountains was wet and sticky and piled up over the top of the skis. "If you had to take off in it, you first taxied up and down three or four times, packing down the snow, glazing it by pressing out the water so it had less drag on the plane's skis."

Wherever he landed, one of Bob's immediate chores was to keep the plane's skis from freezing fast. If he were to make a stay of any length he cut a pole and jacked the skis up on it, then scraped off what snow and ice was already frozen on. When it came time for take-off, if the skis couldn't be cleared by scraping them with his fur mittens, then Bob got out his fire pot and melted them free. In the winter, many of Alaska's air-minded citizens kept long poles out on their local landing strips so that ski planes could taxi right up on them when they first landed.

Reeve learned to carry a supply of black-dyed gunny sacks in the back of his plane, so that he could throw them out over any area where he wished to land, and mark a runway. Miners who were expecting him to come in to their sites sometimes scattered lampblack along the snow to mark out a landing field. The lampblack, however, was not a reliable landing aid, since, wherever the sun hit it, it melted down into the deep snow, forming great potholes. Black flags were perfect for sunless winter days, orange flags most effective in bright spring sunlight.

But even after he had made several landings at a particular site and had his landing field well marked with a row of flags, Reeve found that the glacier landings never ceased to have a strange, eerie quality. Making a gliding approach to one of his glistening, cloudland fields, Reeve could see all his flags. "When they looked like one straight ahead, you were down." (The lighted slope line used on approaches to modern airports is the present-day version of this homely landing aid.) "But the only way I ever really knew I was down for sure was after the motor had idled for awhile." When the plane sank onto its feather-soft cushion of deep snow, it was often difficult for Bob to convince himself that he was really down, and he sat in the cockpit for minutes with the engine running before he could make himself open the door and get out. The day Reeve hauled Charlie Elwood into his claim on the Columbia Glacier, Charlie was lying on his belly on top of a load of freight when Reeve glided gently down onto a blanket of fresh snow, opened the cockpit door, and started to climb out of the plane.

"Don't leave me!" Charlie screamed, clutching Reeve's shoulder.

"But we're here, Charlie," grinned Bob. "This is your claim and we've got to unload."

"Holy smoke!" Charlie grunted in awe. "You sure gave me a scare. I thought we were still in the air and you were baling out and leaving me up here all by myself!"

Wherever he flew, Bob kept on a lookout for likely-looking quartz showings on the mountain peaks. Often he made lonely landings just to pick up a sample to carry back to town. When the mining business flourished, so did his. When he had the cash, he often grubstaked prospectors to go into the mountains and open up new claims.

Starting out at the five cents per pound charged Big Four, Bob learned to adjust his rates according to the risk, distance, and cost of gasoline. For short hauls out of Valdez he could afford to supply the mines at a nickel per pound, since he could carry an eight-hundred-pound load and make the round trip in twenty minutes, which grossed him about $120 per hour. To far-off Chisana, on the other hand, for a round trip averaging four hours, he charged twenty cents per pound, which was both considerably cheaper and infinitely speedier than the mines could get their supplies by any other means. Due to the distance and lack of weather information, Bob frequently had the supplies relayed to Copper Center or Chestochina, on the Highway, by truck, as he had done on his first Chisana contract, then flew them in over the mountains.

Although his business was flying mine supplies, Bob soon found, as he had on his first Chisana job, that there was a human element to his work. On each trip he had a long list of personal items to bring out to the isolated miners. "There was always some radio parts. Radio was the big thing then—and those old boys out at those camps knew more about what was going on in the world than we did in town." Each trip meant a load of dry-cell batteries, and a last-minute run by the post office to pick up the mail and carry it out. Then there were the packages of dried fruit, granulated potatoes, dehydrated soups "which didn't weigh much but meant a lot to their diet." When the Fairchild settled to a stop at the mine sites, it was almost instantaneously surrounded by a bevy of eager men. "They'd say Hello, then peer into the plane to see if I'd brought their order." Hearing the motor reverberating through the mountain passes miles away, the whole mine force had time to assemble and was invariably out to welcome the plane. After Bob had passed out the precious mail and packages, the men would ask politely if he'd had a good trip. "Their second question always was, 'Any news?'—but there wasn't much I could ever tell them. They'd heard it all on their radios."

Of all the things he could bring into mines, the cause for greatest delight was fresh fruit. "A crate of peaches wouldn't last out the day." The first time he brought in grapes to Chisana, the men ate so many there was a campwide attack of acute indigestion. When they were in season, Bob hauled in watermelons along with compressors, pipes, crushers, and dynamite—"everything from dog biscuits to steel riffles." Once, on speculation, he bought a thirty-pound head of cheese—and an old fellow at Chisana bawled him out for not letting him buy the whole head for himself!

The one load Reeve tried to avoid was passengers. ("Freight don't talk back!") Sourdoughs were generally good company and helpful in emergency, but Reeve didn't like to have to haul Outsiders—or women. When Mrs. Billy James, the young wife of the sourdough discoverer of Chisana, finally overcame her terror of airplanes sufficiently to request a flight from Valdez into the mine site, Reeve knew he was in for trouble. Cagily, he invited his friend Father Timothy O'Ryan, a Jesuit priest stationed at Valdez, to go along "for the ride." A few miles out of Valdez, when they hit their first turbulent air over the mountains, Mrs. James (as Reeve had anticipated) screamed, "Go back to Valdez!" Reeve refused. "What do you think I got this priest along for?" he asked her. "I take care of you going down, and he's here to take care of you on the way up!" With her future provided for, Mrs. James shut up, hung on, and arrived safely at Chisana.

In late spring, when the snow had melted back sufficiently to expose the crevasses, Bob made a number of flights over the mining area he served, to study and memorize their locations. One way to avoid them, he noticed, was to land as close as possible to the moraine, the upheavings of rock and gravel pushed up in the center of the glacier. If you could miss hitting the moraine itself, the nearby snow contained solid substance, pounded-up gravel, which gave a landing base, and the crevasses were smaller and narrower close to the moraine.

On his last landing at Big Four that season, Reeve had a sobering shock. The snows had begun to melt, and his runway, he noticed from the air, was two hundred feet shorter. Once down, he examined the spot and found to his horror that the place where he had been regularly landing was nothing more than a snow bridge over a yawning crevasse, which was now exposed to view! With his landing field cut practically in half, Reeve realized he could make no more landings there that season with any safety, and he made plans for dropping in supplies during the summer months.

As soon as the snow had melted off the Valdez field, Bob changed from skis to wheels for his summer airlift.

# 6. Airdrops, mud flats, and romance

Back on wheels for the short summer months, Bob gave up any more glacier landings until the following fall when he would be able to take off from Valdez on skis. He made a deal with the mines he had been servicing that, when they needed fresh supplies, they send a man, on foot, down to the town with the order. Soon Bob was dropping everything from canned beans to dynamite, and he had, as usual, developed his own techniques.

"Skip bombing may have worked in World War II—but I found it was mighty hard on the groceries!" Rather than skim low, to push out the supplies, Bob found his highest percentage of "salvage" lay in flying high—from 250 to 300 feet—which was sufficient altitude so that the cargo fell straight down, rather than ricocheting and splattering the contents. He watched to see if the boxes and barrels smashed, and if they did, he simply duplicated the order and tried again: that was his understanding with the mines he served. "The lure of gold made them all indifferent to the cost of things. They were happy so long as they got the tools to work with, the food they needed"—even when they paid double.

He took the door off the Fiarchild and carried a boy helper ("the air-crazy ones liked to go along for the joy ride; they'd work for nothing") to push out the supplies. Gas and oil were dropped in their original drums. (Half broke, half didn't.) Food was packed, with sawdust and papers around each item, into oil barrels. Once, when he carried in a load of food and bad weather forced a low drop, the results looked, according to Bob, "like the trash can of a Piggly Wiggly store."

Bob loaded boxes of dynamite in gunny sacks and then dropped the sacks. The boxes broke on landing, but the sacks caught and held the sticks. The miners then dumped the contents of the sacks, sorted the sticks out from all the splintered wood and sawdust—and they were ready to use. Once when Bob was loaded with twenty boxes of dynamite, flying out over Valdez Bay, his engine conked out. Since he had both dynamite and "a kid" aboard, he decided not to risk a rough beach landing, but stretched his glide to Valdez, and was able to reach the edge of the field in safety. Although much was made in newspapers and magazine reports of his harrowing incident, Bob does not count it as one of his narrow escapes. "A good dynamite box is harmless," he insists. "That 40 per cent mine stuff won't easily explode. It's the caps that give you trouble." The danger he anticipated was that, if the dynamite got warm and the nitroglycerine seeped through the box, nails from another box might scratch it, setting up a friction which would ignite the sticks. Reeve inspected each box carefully for leaks, and if he found any, reboxed the sticks before loading them. Then he was careful not to either shove the boxes around or subject them to sharp blows. It was a precaution that paid off. Although he dropped dynamite regularly over a period of eight years, he never had trouble with it.

"Fledgling airman" Bill Egan, the most regular of Bob's helpers (Egan later switched from aviation to grocery business, is now in Territorial politics), described what it was like to make an air drop. They would load the plane, take off with the door off the plane and a rope around Bill which was secured to the interior of the cabin so he wouldn't slip out with the barrels. Then Bob would fly in over the mine site and bank the plane so that the wing and stabilizer were up and out of the slip stream and the floor of the cabin was almost centered over the mine site. When Bob was satisfied with the position of the plane, he yelled "Now," and Bill either shoved or kicked the stuff out the open door. If the plane was not in perfect aiming position, Bob yelled "Hold it," and made another run. Reeve kept his attention on aiming his airplane, and never turned around to watch or instruct his helper. "If Bob ever once put faith in you," explained Bill Egan, "he never questioned what you did."

Once, when they had an order for a load of timbers, the lumber was so long that it actually extended over Reeve's shoulder, up into the cockpit, so that he had to hunch down in his seat to avoid hitting the planks with his head. Egan was terrified that, when the time came to shove the timber out, he would accidentally hit Reeve's head in so doing and shear an ear or give him a knock-out blow. "But all the time I was handling that stuff, Bob never even turned around."

Bob took pride in his aim—was able to plunk down the stuff just about where his customers wanted it. (Unlike some flyers who landed supplies that it took three days' digging in the snow to uncover!) He dropped a Diesel engine, dismantled and wrapped in a bed mattress, by parachute, into the Big Four—and the engine was running within four hours' time! When miner Ted Johnson ordered a fifty-pound sack of flour, Bob obligingly flew over his mine, looked down, saw where Ted had placed a stick in the snow for Bob to aim by, and let her go. The sack of flour plummeted down on top of the stick and split open, and flour spilled out all over the snow. Next time Johnson saw Bob he remarked, rather wryly, "I knew you were good, Bob. But I'm damned if I thought you were *that* good!"

As winter came on, Bob changed back to skis and put the door back on his plane. Despite the success of the summer airdrops, he preferred regular landings, with proper loadings and unloadings, to the hit-or-miss method of firing from the air. Making a run to Chisana with miner Jim Elmer, he took along a Christmas turkey to drop over Teikel roadhouse, in gratitude for weather information they had supplied him in the past via their trail telephone. When they flew over Teikel, Bob told Elmer to open the door and toss out the turkey. The door, which had been put on and off so much in the past year, came loose as Elmer opened it. Elmer stayed with it, soon found himself hanging in suspension clutching the door—and keeping a precarious grip with one hand on his seat. While Reeve kept banking, Elmer finally hauled the broken door inside the cabin and kicked out the bird.

By the following spring the price of gold had approximately doubled under the New Deal Gold Reserve Act, and the boom was on in Valdez. Bob found himself with full-time jobs servicing the Big Four, the Ramsay Rutherford, the Mayfield, and the Little Giant. Valdez had come to life, and prospectors came into town daily with "cleanups" of gold bricks. The gold fever was catching, and Bob decided it was high time he picked off a claim of his own. Flying over the Chugach, he had spotted a number of unclaimed strata of quartz running through the mountains, which interested him. But in winter, when he could make a ski landing, the lodes were covered with snow and he couldn't find them. In summer, when they were visible, he was on wheels and couldn't land.

He turned his inventive imagination to figuring out a way to make a landing when he could see the quartz. It resolved itself into a problem of how to take off down at Valdez with skis in the summer time when snow was gone from the field.

Studying the possibilities around the town, Reeve discovered an area two miles west of town, a part of Valdez Bay, which was covered by tidewater, but between tides offered a slick surface of fine clay silt and wet goose grass. Except for the problem of nightly tides, he felt it would provide a good medium for ski take-offs and landings. "While other pilots were operating by clock and calendar," smiles Bob, "I began using a tidebook for a manual of operations."

The little bay provided a clear stretch of slick mud about six hundred feet long, with tall timber at one end, a deep gulch at the other; but, Bob philosophized, "a roost is a roost." When he brought the Fairchild over from the Valdez field, fitted it with skis, and attempted a take-off from the mud flats, Bob found it even better than he had anticipated. He skimmed along the slick clay smoothly, the only point to watch being the final "shaking loose" as the plane became air-borne. "Mud is a little more critical than snow," he explains, "but that can be easily rectified by yanking the stick back faster."

The mud-flat field for ski landings was original with Reeve—and a novelty for Valdez and all its visitors. It became a 'must' for tourists, and people traveled from as far away as Fairbanks to watch the unique operations. "If I could have charged admission," sighs Bob, "I really would have had it made."

Rex Beach, hearing of this strange new method, made a trip up from Florida and stayed around Valdez a week, took a few flights with Bob, and watched him work. The Valdez boom Beach credited to Reeve's one-man efforts—which he felt could be duplicated in other parts of his beloved Alaska and start a real boom in the mining industry. Beach wrote a series of articles for *Cosmopolitan* and *American Magazine* on Alaskan mining and Reeve's work, and a novel, *Valley of*

*Thunder,* in which he patterned his hero on Reeve—glacier flights, mud-flat landings, and all. "They call him the human ptarmigan," wrote Beach, "because of his practice of diving in and out of snow banks."

Since Reeve's field was always wet—with attendant rust—Bob switched from iron skis to ones of stainless steel, "a marvelous new metal" that did not rust in the ravages of the salt tide. When the spring tide was due about once a month, he jacked up his plane and lifted the tail onto an oil barrel. If the tide threatened to come up more than three feet on the plane, he changed back to wheels and took it over to the dry Valdez airfield.

After several seasons of using his tide flats, Reeve became so familiar with water conditions he didn't take so much trouble with the tide. He found that he could both take off and land in a foot and more of water. "You'd splash at first, then skid along on top of the water—like water skis." If he were delayed up at the mines and didn't get back in time to beat the evening tide, he just went ahead and landed in the water—with no ill effects.

The other pilots watched Reeve's unique operations with interest, but were glad to stick to their old game of picking up passengers and to leave the glaciers and the mines, "Reeve's Roost" as Gillam called them, to their pioneer. Later, Haakon Christenson and Merle Smith serviced some of the mining areas and adopted the mud-flat technique for ski landings. But in 1934, to quote Harold Gillam, "Reeve can have it!" "Harold and I were good friends," says Bob, "so long as my operations were confined to the 'boondocks'—as he called the wilds—and I wasn't competing in his territory!"

Christmas morning, 1934, found bachelors Reeve and Gillam sharing a room at the Copper Center Roadhouse, and sound asleep on the bleak, sixty-three-blow-zero winter morning, when "Ma" Barnes came in and shook them awake.

"Get up boys," Ma ordered. "An Indian boy's been seriously burned over at Chestochina, Jack Hayes has frozen feet at Chisana, and Doc Blalock, at Tazlina, fell and broke his hip."

Reeve and Gillam wiped the sleep out of their eyes and looked outside. Sixty-three below and it looked like another storm brewing—verifying the bush pilot's truism that "folks only get sick or hurt in bad weather."

"Guess I'm it," Bob said slowly. "I've got the only heated cabin plane."

"Want me to go along?"

"No. Not enough room if I pick 'em all up." Reeve pulled on his wool clothes, parka, and gloves, and strode out. It was already late morning—nearly eleven, and due to get dark by two. He hied down to the Copper landing strip, about a quarter of a mile from the roadhouse, and got two fire pots going under the engine. He had only three hours of daylight in which to warm up his engine, pick up the emergency cases at three different villages, and get back, which, all told, equaled four hundred miles of flying. Since Doc Blalock was only ten miles from Copper, Bob left him till last and headed first for the Indian boy at Chestochina. The eleven-year-old child had been carrying an open can of gasoline into his house; he stumbled, the gasoline spilled, and a spark from the open fire set it off. The flames had swept over the boy, burning his chest, arms, sides, and face. He had been given first aid when Bob arrived, and Reeve hurriedly loaded the child into his plane, then flew on to Chisana to pick up prospector Jack Hayes. Loading Hayes in with his Indian patient, Bob took off fast in the growing dusk, settled down briefly at Tazlina, where Doc Blalock was waiting for him. Then he flew the last ten miles of the circuit back into Copper Center in darkness. It was already too late to try to make it on to Cordova, where the hospital was located. They would all have to wait till morning.

As he flew in toward Copper, feeling his way through the inky late-winter darkness (there were no landing lights on the planes of this period) Reeve looked out with relief. There was a well-spaced line of bonfires marking the Copper strip. Gillam was out waiting for him to come in. The two flyers unloaded the patients and carried them up to the roadhouse. Ma Barnes smeared more Unguentine over the child's badly burned arms and face and gave him aspirin to deaden the pain. A stoic, the Indian child never murmured. They made Hayes as comfortable as possible, but Blalock was in pain with his broken hip. Gillam and Reeve scrounged around in their belongings and came up with a gallon of Doc's own "painkiller," which they administered in large doses. Soon Doc was "singing and shouting and having a fine old time."

Next morning, with the first streaks of daylight, Reeve loaded his emergency cases and flew them on to the hospital. Poor old Doc recovered from his hip injury, but while at the hospital contracted pneumonia and died. Hayes had to have both feet amputated. The Indian boy came through in fine shape with only a few scars, although, according to the Anchorage *Daily Times,* "but for the timely action and good services of pilot Reeve the little fellow's life probably would have been lost."

Emergencies were routine for all the bush pilots. The sad part was they were so often a one-way trip. Most frontier Alaskans knew how to tend to the ordinary run of illnesses and accidents at their home base. It was only when they were dying that they went out by plane. Rex Beach was fascinated with the operation of Anchorage station KFQD, which, he wrote in an article in *American Magazine,* "is forever picking up cries for help, snatching aviators off their jobs, and sending them out into the wilds." It was true for all the transmitting stations in Alaska—whether they were in towns or out at isolated roadhouses. When a man was hurt, the mine or community would send a dog team to the nearest point of communication—a telephone or radio transmitting station—and the nearest pilot would be paged for help.

One night when Reeve was eating dinner at the Merchant's Cafe in Valdez, a prospector named Tipton staggered into the room, babbling incoherently, his hands and feet frozen. When they could get the story out of him, Reeve, Owen Meals, and Paddy Fitzpatrick found that Tipton and another man, named Martin, had been caught out on Valdez Glacier, afoot, in a storm. Tipton had made it down into town. But Martin was still up there somewhere, "about three miles above the face of the glacier." Although dinner time, it was in the spring when there were still a couple of hours of daylight left. The three men hurried to Reeve's Fairchild and took off. Bob had never landed on Valdez Glacier, and a quick survey showed that there was no place to land. Finally, he made a landing in a pile of boulders and moraine at the foot of the frozen river. "An unthinkable landing—except in an emergency like that," explains Bob. "Somehow I managed to sneak the plane in between boulders the size of a house without cracking it up."

The men hastily headed up the glacier on foot, following Tipton's trail. When they at last reached Martin, it was obvious death was near. The man's hands, feet, arms, and legs were frozen. "But," says Bob, "I discovered there were worse fates than freezing to death. He evidently felt no pain, and he was voluble, happy, babbling about his boyhood experiences."

The trio made slings out of their coats, began the painful process of hauling the victim down to the plane. Within a mile they heard the death rattle. There was no hope for him—and the pressing question now was what hope was there for the three of them. They left the body and hurried to the plane in the growing dark. Reeve still pales when he tells of what happened next. "I took a step—and dropped down into a crevasse." Grabbing wildly, he managed to catch hold of a rock on the inside of the crevasse and hang on till the other two men could pull him out. They eventually made it to the plane, and back into Valdez, and sent a dog team for Martin's body the following morning. But the shock of that fall is almost as sickeningly vivid to Reeve today as it was then. For years afterward, he had to force himself to walk down an ordinary sidewalk in the dark.

Normal injuries such as ax cuts were treated at the mines, rather than calling for a doctor. "They'd sew up a cut with a regular needle and thread," reports Bob. Some of their first-aid work was somewhat on the casual side. An old-time miner at Chisana gave Bob something of a shock, the first time he saw him, since his crop of bushy red hair grew in several different directions! Red Hirst had been out on horse-back one day when a bear charged him. The bear caught up with him, knocked him off the horse, reached up, and in a single swipe of its mighty paw scalped Hirst. Other men, there with him, shot the bear, then grabbed up the loose scalp from the forest floor and quickly slapped it on Hirst's head while it was still "fresh" and would grow back. The scalp stuck fast. And the other men carried Hirst into the hospital at Kennicott. "I looked at myself in the mirror," said Hirst, "and there was moss, pine needles, and broken twigs hanging in a fringe from my scalp!" The doctors got the moss out as best they could, but took no chances about fooling with the scalp, which had taken hold and begun to grow back, despite the fact that "it had been slapped on with indifferent aim" and the hair grew in all directions.

Bob regularly hauled in accident cases from the mine sites, men who had been hurt by dynamite, fallen down shafts, or been shot—accidentally or not. The oddest emergency he ever hauled was a man who had become constipated and attempted to relieve himself with a tuning fork, which pierced the lower bowel, causing internal injury.

Occasionally Bob hauled in a corpse. But, unlike Alex Holden and some of the other bush pilots, Reeve never fastened a corpse to the wing, which he claims "is one of the reasons I'm alive today."

Had he been in Holden's shoes, however, Reeve might have been tempted to waive his safety rules. An old bachelor fisherman had died out on Dutch Harbor, in the Aleutians, following emergency surgery. His will left an estate valued at $75.000 to a niece in Seattle, who promptly wired every carrier in Alaska to bring in the body of her uncle "at all cost." The flight was a plum for anyone who could get it, because of the promise of a healthy cash payment, and Cot Hayes hastily dispatched Alex Holden in a Loening amphibian from Alaskan Southern Airways at Cordova. The trip meant about $2000 to the hard-pressed company if Alex could get to Dutch and collect the corpse before another flyer beat him to it. Alex was the first flyer to reach Dutch—only to find that his corpse had been given immediate burial, due to the facts that they had no embalming facilities and that he had died of complicated internal conditions which resulted in foul odors. Alex wired Cot that his man was already under ground. Cot, with his heart set on the $2000 for his company, wired back to "get the body." They got a release from the niece in Seattle; the Coast Guard dug up the corpse, packed it in canvas, then shellacked the surface, so that it shrank down like a mummy and somewhat disguised the smell. But Alex found that he couldn't get the "stiff" into his little amphibian plane—nor, he decided, could he endure such a stench for long. Finally he strapped his mummy to a wing—and took off. On the way back he met a competitor flying out for the body. But first come was first served, and Holden delivered the corpse safely to Seward, where he turned it over to an undertaker who fixed it up for shipment. Then they sent it on, express collect, to Seattle, and Alaskan Southern got its $2000.

Which didn't keep it afloat for long. The company sold out to Pan Am's Alaskan subsidiary in 1934. When Pan Am eventually washed its hands of the treacherous southeastern coastal flying and folded up the company, pilot Bob Ellis started Ellis Airline out of Ketchikan, ex-RCAF pilot Holden organized Marine Airways out of Juneau, and company-trained Shell Simmons began flying for himself. In 1939 Holden and Simmons merged into Alaska Coastal—which with Ellis Airlines provides southeast residents with three and a half flights per person per year.

Reeve feels the most sensationally brave job of rescue work was performed by Harold Gillam. Reeve and Bill Egan were in Fairbanks, where Reeve's plane was laid up for engine repair, when word came through that Bob's old friend Carl Whitham, founder of the Nabesna mine, had fallen down a mine shaft and was severely injured. His legs, arms, and ribs were broken, and he had internal injuries as well. Reeve was helpless without a plane, but Gillam, down at Cordova, also heard the report—and went to work. A blinding snowstorm was raging from Cordova clear through to Nabesna (near the international boundary, later the site of Northway Airfield), but Gillam went on out to the airstrip and started warming the engine of his open-cockpit Zenith. The blizzard winds were so violent that it took twenty men to hold down Gillam's plane while he warmed the engine. He took off, reached Nabesna, landed after dark on an ice overflow, picked up Whitham, and headed for the hospital at Fairbanks. In their hotel room in Fairbanks, Reeve and Egan heard a faint roar above the howl of the storm, looked out of the window. It was pitch dark and ceiling zero. Bob moistened his lips. "That could be only one man in this world—Gillam." It was. With the "cat eyes" for which he was famous, Gillam managed to execute a safe landing, without landing lights, and delivered his patient to the hospital. "If he hadn't got him there that night," says Bob, "Carl would have died. As it was, he recovered."

Bob's "closest haul" in the summer of 1934 was a brush with one of the rarest of Far North inhabitants—a horse. On a charter flight to pick up Senator Alex MacRae of British Columbia and Dean (now President) Ernest Patty of the

University of Alaska at Dawson, to fly them into Fairbanks,
Reeve made a landing in a hayfield ten miles up the Klon-
dike, since there was no airfield at Dawson. His landing stampeded the "only horse team in Dawson," which the farmer
had hitched to a wagon out in the field where he was putting
up his hay. The frightened team lunged out of control and
smashed into the farmer's barn. Reeve hurried to the
farmer's aid, and as the men worked to unhitch the horses
and free them from the tangled line and smashed wagon, the
one horse that had fallen kicked the horse that was standing—which in turn kicked Reeve, knocking him a good
twenty feet. Reeve came to a half-hour later, staggered into
town for his passengers, loaded them, and started out for
Fairbanks. "I was flying by instinct only," he says. By the
time they reached Circle Hot Springs, even his instinct had
played out, and he made an emergency landing. One eye was
swollen shut, and his head was swollen to nearly twice its
normal size. His passengers switched over to a car which they
rented to take them on to their destination. Reeve "sat" at
Circle until his head resumed normal size, then went on into
Fairbanks, where a doctor stiched up the cut.

By now Reeve's glacier flights, mining activities, and frequent emergency trips had made him a source of steady copy
for the newspapers. Frank Cotter, feature writer on the
*Alaska Weekly*, and a friend of Reeve's, did frequent syndi-
cated stories on "the glacier pilot's" doings, which found their
way into Stateside journals. The floor of the cabin where
bachelor Reeve lived was soon littered with a pile of newspapers (read) and fan mail (mostly unread) that reached a
depth of one foot. The glamour boys of the thirties, the bush-
pilots were deluged with fan mail—mostly from young ladies
of matrimonial intent. "I was a happy bachelor," claims
Reeve, "and I intended to stay that way."

One letter, however, caught his fancy. "Do you," it asked
with sprightly humor, "need a secretary, bookkeeper, or extra
mine hand?" It was, Bob noticed, from a little town in Wisconsin only about thirty miles from where he was born.
"Of all the letters I'd gotten, I think this is the only one I really read through. It was gay, funny. It sparkled with personality." It was the only one he ever answered. Miss Janice
Morisette, it seemed, was bored with her secretarial job in
the States and eager for a little excitement. She had her eyes

on Alaska and wanted to know what jobs were open. Bob wrote her a report of the business going on in Juneau, and Fairbanks, what chances there were for a secretary in the Territory.

They corresponded for three or four months. Then Bob received a letter stating briefly, "I've booked passage to Alaska. Will arrive Valdez June 19."

Terrified, Reeve fled to Canada, ostensibly on a prospecting trip. He had told the girl about business prospects in the big towns, Fairbanks, Anchorage, Juneau—but it hadn't occurred to him she'd come to Valdez. It was a little town, and he didn't want the home-folks thinking he'd brought her up there. It was bad enough for a single girl to get along in a small community—without appearing under a man's auspices. Before leaving town, Reeve confided his predicament to bachelor friend, "Doc" Earl Wise, and asked him to keep an eye on her and see she got off to a good start. He also asked Owen Meals to meet the boat.

When the steamer pulled up to the Valdez dock, Miss Morisette looked out eagerly, saw darkly handsome Harold Gillam smiling politely, looking for passengers. Fair-haired Noel Wien was asking for fares to Fairbanks. Tall Owen Meals came forward, took her bag, and said he'd see her to the hotel. Of slender, black-thatched pilot Reeve there was not a glimpse. Miss Morisette sighed with disappointment and turned to Owen. A couple with whom she had become friends on the boat, discovering she meant to settle in Valdez, had offered to rent her a room in their own house. She would stay with them.

A month later Bob's curiosity, spiced by a snippet of guilt at deserting the strange girl when she most needed assistance, got the better of him, and he flew back into Valdez. When Doc Wise heard Bob's plane coming in, he hustled out to the mud flats to meet him. "She sure is cute, Bob," Doc said admiringly. "Knows how to take care of herself, too. She went to work the day after she got here, as secretary for the Road Commission." The bachelors slipped down to Valdez' Main Street, walked past the glassed front of the Road Commission office, and peeked in. Miss Morisette, small, trim, efficient, her smooth dark head bent busily over a typewriter, was hard at work. "Punching that ole typewriter, with her black hair and all," muses Bob, "she reminded me of Tillie the Toiler."

He was a little sorry he'd stayed away so long—particularly with so many solid, dependable, eligible bachelors in town!

Bob made money—sporadically. But a free-lance bush pilot had no regular income, in contrast to those fellows with steady jobs. Although his spectacular mud-flat technique, his perilous glacier landings, had attracted a great deal of attention, they had done little to further his quest for that "million bucks." "I really had gold fever," he admits. "I broke up hundreds and hundreds of chunks of ore and washed out the gold. But somehow I never made much at it."

Bob and Tillie had a formal introduction at Owen Meals' house at dinner the night Bob returned to Valdez—although they had to demand it, since the Mealses, along with the rest of the town, were convinced that the couple had known each other back in Wisconsin, and that Tillie was Bob's hometown sweetheart, come to claim him.

Bob went at courtship with the same implacable realism with which he attacked all of life's problems. His intentions, from the beginning, were serious, but he frankly did not consider himself a good matrimonial prospect. He redoubled his efforts to find a "bonanza" mine and get hold of some marrying money. In the meantime, he remained aloof from Tillie until, in his own estimation, he "had something to offer."

Finding a streak of gold that looked good up on Columbia Glacier, Bob went up to it, made camp, slept in his plane, and spent two weeks "knocking out gold." When he had fifty pounds of high-grade ore in a sack, he flew back to town on a Saturday afternoon, bursting with excitement.

His first stop was a visit with Alex Singletary, an old Montana gunman who had reformed and gone into business as a "woods chemist," succeeding Doc Blalock. From Alec, Bob procured several quarts of "moon." From there he marched over to the Pinzon, where he pulled the ore out of his sack to show the old miners, and also dispensed—without urging—a sampling of Singletary's product to further enjoy the "fellowship of discovery." "Oh, that was a great afternoon," sighs Bob. "We were all great fellows, great miners, and believed in the brotherhood of man!"

By the time he got around to his "real mission" of paying a call on his "intended" and divulging the exciting news of his new wealth, the afternoon had slipped away; evening had arrived, and with it the weekly Saturday night dance at the Moose Hall.

Reeve, still clutching his sack of gold and what was left of his last bottle of moon, arrived at the dance in high fettle, soon located his girl, elbowed his way through the ring of bachelors surrounding her ("Only in Alaska," giggles Tillie with charming honesty, "can a plain girl be the belle of the ball!") and bowing low, announced in a rich, rumbling voice that rocked the rafters, "Forget these grocery clerks, young lady. If you choose any of them, you'll have a half a dozen kids and wash dishes the rest of your life. I have just struck it rich on Columbia Glacier. And I would like you to dance with the next millionaire in Valdez."

For some reason, Bob's news was not nearly so appealing to Miss Morisette as it had been to his miner friends. "I'm sorry, Mr. Reeve," she said coolly, "but all my dances are taken."

Befuddled by such lack of enthusiasm, Reeve went out for more "moon," then, an hour later, came back to the dance and tried again. This time all he did was snatch her arm and say, "I want a word with you. Come here." She came. He led her to a corner of the room and once more regaled her with the exciting prospects in his life. Tillie let him ramble till he ran down, then fixed him with a cool eye. "I know all about you, Mr. Millioniare," she said acidly. "I've been given a reading on you, and I happen to know that you haven't paid your meal ticket at the Chinaman's for eleven months, nor your gas bill at Standard Oil for a year. Goodnight, Mr. Millionaire!"

"Well," said Reeve haughtily, as he bowed good-by, "you can't deny I've got good credit."

Rev persisted with the mine, if not Tillie, and formed a partnership with old-time prospector Andy Thompson. When a powder and grocery order was being put up for the new partners at the Mercantile Company, a local wag, noting the markings "R & T" for Reeve and Thompson, commented, "If it belongs to those two characters it must be the Rough & Tough!" And Ruff & Tuff it became. The partners staked the claim and then left it for the season, in the hopes of building up enough capital to begin the actual development of the property the following year.

That winter, his heart still set on "quick gold," Bob flew

off on another prospecting trip to Canada, looking for ore that could be placer-mined. The Ruff & Tuff was hard rock that required heavy equipment.

Billy James, the discoverer of Chisana, had seen a creek with placer gold in it on a trip to Canada in 1905. He had never been back—but always intended to go. He, Reeve, and Red Hirst (of the strange hairline) loaded camping equipment into the Fairchild and flew over to the White River in Canada. They found some fine placer gold along the river, at the grass roots, and they were able to thaw the sod and pan it out. But the real gold was down at bedrock, with masses of heavy boulders on top.

While they were out panning gold in the river, Bob heard a plane fly over, then circle around, apparently looking for something. His conscience pricked him, since on the first scouting trip they had cleared with customs at Dawson, Yukon Territory, but they had regarded a second clearance as stuffy. The men were out at the creek several miles from the Fairchild, and they watched uneasily as the strange plane landed about five miles from them, then took off. It must be the Mounties out looking for them. They decided they had better "get the hell out of the country," and hurried back to camp, threw the motor cover on, heated the engine, packed up, and took off. They had flown about ten miles from their prospecting sight when Bob noticed a small piece of paper stuck in his throttle quadrant.

Fearing an official request to report to the Mounties at Dawson, he flew on a few miles, finally opened it, and read:

> On way to Whitehorse I recognized our old Fairchild N5364 and thought you might be in trouble. See you have plenty of grub and nothing wrong with airplane that I can find. Will be back from Whitehorse tomorrow and if you are in trouble, make fire, and I will land.

It was signed "Joe Crosson."

With a smile of pleasure, Bob slipped the note in his pocket, turned around, and flew back to camp. Reeve had met Joe Crosson—Alaska's famous mercy pilot—in Detroit in 1929, when Crosson took delivery of a plane for one of Sir Hubert Wilkins' polar flights. But Bob had seen Crosson only once, in Fairbanks, since he had come to Alaska. And he had not pressed the friendship. For Crosson was a favorite in Alaska, one of the best-liked citizens; he had married the "prettiest girl"; he was the sort of well-loved man for whom everyone had a good word. Except for innate modesty, big, handsome, likable Joe could have been called the "big shot" of aviation in those days. He was currently manager and chief pilot for Pan Am's subsidiary, Pacific Alaska Airways, from whom Bob had purchased his Fairchild. This was the first sign of real friendliness that Bob had had from any of the real old-timers of Alaskan aviation. They were a clannish bunch, and apt to be jealous of newcomers. As Ray Petersen, who came up in 1934, put it, "those old-timers always made me feel like a young punk." But for Petersen and the flyers of his era, Reeve was one of the "old-timers."

When the placer mining paid for little more than the gas bills to the Yukon and back, the partners abandoned their claim. Bob settled in for a winter's work, flying passengers and supplies up to the mines. He came out with enough money to buy a compressor, drill, powder, lumber, and food for his own site at the Ruff & Tuff. He and Thompson hauled the supplies in, with Reeve's Fairchild, then "necked" them up from the landing shelf to the mine site at the top of the hill, pulling the supplies on a toboggan by manpower.

When they got the property in shape, with buildings up and equipment installed, the partners had an offer to sell out. Grasping the chance to become "temporarily solvent," Reeve sold out, for some cash, some stock, and a freighting contract to service the mine—and then turned to the serious business of courting Tillie. That winter the romance progressed favorably. When the village was completely snowed in, time was consumed with card parties, dinner parties, dances. "I'd sleep till noon, then shovel snow in the afternoon, spend a few hours making general overhauls and repairs on the plane, then party at night."

When the Road Commission office closed down for the winter season, Tillie got a job in the telephone office running the switchboard with a hand buzzer. It was a gay winter, but Tillie had little hope that Bob would ever get around to talking marriage. "He was a confirmed bachelor, just as everyone said." Cagily she had put enough money in the bank, when she first arrived at Valdez, so that she could always buy passage home, and after the long winter, with marriage apparently no nearer than before, the strain began to tell. Tillie wrote for and secured a job in San Francisco, left the land and the man she had come to love, and spent a miserable few months in California, suffering "my first real case of homesickness."

By April, 1936, she was back, however, taking a job in Chitina roadhouse for the touriest season. When Bob saw her serving beer to construction workers, he gruffly ordered her away—and she obligingly took a secretarial job in Fairbanks, which lasted two months. By then, spooky bachelor Reeve had decided marriage would be better than all this "worrying"—and his sporadic income better than their both being miserable apart. He flew Tillie back to Valdez, where they made plans for a wedding at Fairbanks, to be celebrated by Bob's purchase of a second airplane, a Fairchild 71 owned by Pacific Alaska Airways, so that he would be able to continue his flights when one plane was being repaired. Bob and Doc Wise drove to Fairbanks, where Bob collected his new plane. Tillie followed a day later, in a car driven by the dean of the School of Mines. The dean had two flats, which resulted in an enforced stopover at a roadhouse for three days until a tire was shipped to him, since they did not dare risk the isolated Richardson Highway without a spare. For those three days Tillie listened distractedly to lectures on geology, while she saw her wedding date come—and pass. When the tire arrived, and she eventually reached Fairbanks, the delayed wedding took place, and the next day the newlyweds flew back to Valdez in the new plane, on a three-and-a-half-hour aerial honeymoon.

Planning to renovate a shell of a house in Valdez which Bob had won in a poker game, the Reeves put in orders for the necessary supplies—just before a boat strike broke out, which held up delivery until the following spring. They spent their first winter living in one room of the Seattle Hotel in Valdez "with the wedding presents stacked under the bed." Whenever Tillie pulled out the gramophone and played "Way Out on the Mountain," all the miners up and down the halls of the paper-thin-walled hotel burst into a delighted chorus.

When Bob and Tillie finally married, all Valdez breathed a relieved sigh. The courtship had received lively interest, but most were glad to see it successfully concluded. The local field was now narrowed to two eligible women—and fifty men.

For the first time in his independent, nomadic life, Bob faced up to the problem of making a living. Now it mattered whether he ate or not.

# 7. "I was pushing my luck"

The first emergency freighter arrived in Valdez in February. The major portion of the cargo turned out to be a shipment of whisky, but the Reeves gratefully took what supplies had come to them—paint, wiring, and plumbing fixtures—and began putting their house in shape. Although none of their furniture had arrived, they hastily fixed up the house, repaired it against the ravages of the glacial winds, partially furnished it with grocery boxes, crates, and lumber, and moved in. Within a month after they left their hotel home, Tillie was due to make a trip to the hospital at Seward to have her first child. Because of the unpredictability of March weather, Bob refused to fly Tillie to Seward, since a forced landing might well prove fatal. She took the boat over and arrived just three days before the birth of Richard Reeve, whom they christened for Bob's brother. Back home in Valdez, Bob was standing on the wing of his Fairchild, gassing up for a trip, when the Alaska Communications messenger brought a wire out to the field and handed it to him. Bob absent-mindedly stuck the paper in his hip pocket and went on with his work. "Better read it, Bob," grinned the messenger. Bob opened the wire and read: "Congratulations on new son. Everyone fine. Dr. Williams."

"I pretty near fell off that airplane!" Bob recalls with a grin. When he got his balance he looked around wildly. "I gotta get to Seward. How can I get to Seward?"

"You're standing on the only possible transportation from Valdez to Seward!" laughed the messenger.

Bob fired up his plane and beat it over to Seward. That night the Valdez *Miner* reported:

A future airplane pilot arrived in Alaska today. He is the new born son of Pilot and Mrs. Bob Reeve . . . which, incidentally, was the reason for the hasty trip of Pilot Reeve to Seward today. . . . *Mr. Reeve* and the child were reported getting along nicely.

By the time Tillie was back home with her baby, the furniture had trickled in, and the Reeves spent their free time busily turning the shell into a snug, comfortable home. Since Bob had won the house in a poker game, they sentimentally furnished one room as a poker den for weekly gatherings, and christened it "in perpetual memory of the generosity and good fellowship" of Bob's comrades from whom he had won the house. So long as the snow stayed on the ground and blizzard winds blew, Bob was grounded at home for long stretches at a time. Winter days in Valdez were filled with the simple tasks of survival: cooking, washing, baking, and trips to the store when walking was possible (groceries were pulled on hand sleds; prosperous citizens kept a dog or two to pull them). Milk and vegetables were bought canned or dried; meat arrived from the freighters in frozen chunks, then was cut to order by the grocer. Once a year the freighter *North Star* arrived from the Eskimo village of Kotzebue on the western coast of Alaska, above the Arctic Circle, with a load of reindeer meat. "We'd all buy a good-sized chunk," says Tillie, "then keep it frozen out on the back porch."

Periodically the power went off in Valdez, and Tillie learned to have everything ready to make use of it the moment it came on. Then there was a mad flurry of activity as the pans of homemade bread and roasts were popped into the oven, pails of water drawn to do the baby's washing, the toilet flushed, the tub filled. And then it went off again, and they ate the food that had been cooked ahead, and played cards by the light of a kerosene lamp. With daily washings to do by hand, Tillie solved one problem by buying herself a BB gun, with which she pinged the local horses when they chose to graze in her yard and knock down the clean clothes.

Through the long winters, despite its open port, Valdez was isolated, its population limited to permanent residents. In the summer, tourists flooded the board sidewalks; in the fall, Alaskans from all over the Territory convened for the annual court session, "the main event of the year." Then Valdez buzzed with social activity, as the local citizens provided entertainment for their visitors. Home-talent shows were popular. In the first one in which she was asked to participate, pint-sized Tillie was given the role of the bee who stung Ferdinand the Bull. At the end of the skit, she turned her back so that they could all read what was written in lipstick across the flour-sack drawers:

RIDE REEVE AIRWAYS, THE BEST

Out at the Valdez field, Bob had his own version of advertising painted on the side of his tool shack: ALWAYS USE REEVE AIRWAYS, SLOW UNRELIABLE UNFAIR CROOKED SCARED UNLICENSED AND NUTS. Another roughly lettered sign over the door warned competitors: OPPORTUNITY MAKES RASCALS OF US ALL. HANDS OFF OUR TOOLS.

As soon as the weather cleared for flying, Bob tackled his work with an intensity that was to prove, at moments, nearly fatal. With a wife and now a small son to support, his Yankee sense of responsibility drove him into a hectic schedule. The purchase of the second plane enabled him to stay in the air whenever the weather permitted, and he grasped eagerly for any and all jobs: flying for mines, mountain climbers, photographers, anyone with the cash, or promise of potential cash, to pay.

He had learned to be a cagey prophet of weather. "My middle name is Campbell, which makes me half Scotch," explains Bob, "and I'd already learned that if you misjudged your weather and had to refuel in the Interior, where gas cost a dollar a gallon, it resulted in red ink for the trip. A few such experiences were good practical lessons for backward bookkeepers!"

Cutthroat competition was rampant over the Territory, gasoline both scarce and expensive. Many a pilot, not accurately estimating his over-all expenses, failed to adjust his prices to the break-even point, let alone to show a profit. There was, at this time, no federal legislation of routes or rates, and a pilot charged what he hoped he could get. Standard procedure in dickering for the price of a trip was not "It is so much," but "How much you got?" Debts were often settled for a fractional payment, just to get one's hands on a little precious cash. If a round trip from Valdez to Cordova cost fifty dollars and a passenger showed up with a twenty-dollar bill, "I'd haul him," explains Bob, "just to get my hands on that cash so I could buy some of the necessities of life."

Casual in his collections as a bachelor, Reeve learned to collect his bills, occasionally even by the threat of physical violence when he knew his debtor had the ability to pay. Prospector "Cousin Jack" Carrol of Chisana owed Bob four hundred dollars for several years. Carrol was never around Chisana when Reeve landed, although when Bob went to see him he found the stove still warm in his cabin. Reeve discovered that as soon as Carrol heard the plane's motor reverberating through Cooper's Pass he would take the trail out to his diggings ten miles away. Reeve made plans to get him, and the next time he landed at Chisana he headed straight over the mountains through several feet of snow, pushing hard, so that he beat Carrol into his camp and had the beans cooking for supper by the time the miner appeared. Carrol agreed to pay, and weighed out twelve ounces of gold dust. "The bill is four hundred dollars," protested Reeve, "and you owe me twenty-six ounces." "Oh no," Carrol said slyly. "Didn't you hear the news? Gold has gone from sixteen dollars to thirty-five an ounce. I'm paying you in thirty-five-dollar gold."

His head set on collecting in line with the price that had been in effect when the debt was incurred, Reeve searched his brain for a way, had an inspiration. Remembering that in the game of calling coins, the majority of betters say heads in preferences to tails, Bob placed a coin under a teacup and said, "If you can call that coin correctly I'll accept the payment at the new price; otherwise, I get the old price." "Okay," said Carrol, "it's heads."

A good loser, Carrol paid the twenty-six ounces of gold dust.

Alaskans, accustomed to once-a-year payments, often registered hurt surprise when Reeve pressed them for cash on the line. After flying newspaperman Frank Cotter and his partner Adams into a Nabesna mine site, in sixty-below-zero weather, Reeve announced flatly, "Now let's square up." Cotter and Adams registered genuine amazement. "But we sliced you in on our claim!" they protested. "Fine," said Reeve, "but how about my gas money?" Cotter and Adams dug down and came up with a dozen post-dated checks for Reeve. The checks did not bounce. "All of those guys meant well," explains Bob, "but it didn't occur to them to pay bills more than once a year, during cleanup season. But the pilots had to pay for their gas year around."

One man owed Bob two hundred dollars. When Bob found that the fellow had several Liberty bonds in the safe at the Pinzon, he cornered him on the street and forced him to go into the bar, open the safe, get the bonds, take them to the post office, and cash them!

When he couldn't scare up the cash he needed, Bob took pay in gold dust, mining interests, furs, meat, fish. One man who owed money and refused to pay was the owner, Bob found, of a fine stack of firewood. Bob loaded his plane with the wood, left a note, "Now we're even," and flew it to his own home. As other Alaskans, the man was amused rather than angered by such tactics. "There goes the kindling wood kid," he'd yell cheerfully whenever he saw Reeve.

Bob figured closely, cannily invented the most efficient devices to improve his flying operations. Although there were no weather forecasts by radio, he learned to judge weather visually. Interior weather, he found, fairly well coincided with that of the coast, after allowing a period for the storms to move eastward. When headed for camp or roadhouse with a telephone, he called ahead for weather information. Violent winds were a daily part of the game, but storms and low ceilings that blocked the mountain passes were "as much of a dead end as a stone wall." The flyer's choice was either to land in the passes and wait out the ceiling or backtrack to the first available civilization and dollar-a-gallon return gas. "Gillam bored through," says Reeve, "but there was only one Gillam." After his initial series of crashes and bad luck, Harold Gillam had developed into the finest bad-weather pilot in the Territory, flew contact through incredible hazards that left the other pilots open-mouthed with awe. On Jack Jefford's second flight into Cordova, when he first came to Alaska, he was trailing Gillam when they ran into a heavy snow storm. "I would have turned back if I could," explains Jack, "but I didn't know the country well enough—so I just plowed along after Gillam." Gillam made it safely into his home base at Cordova; pretty soon Jefford appeared behind him. Gillam was so impressed with Jefford's pluck that he offered him a job on the spot, saying happily, "You're my kind of man!" Jefford disagreed. "I would have stopped—if I'd just known where or how!" A man of iron nerve and experimental mind, Gillam was developing home radio and air navigational aid devices before they were generally introduced.

Reeve's forte was terrain—not weather. He shunned bad weather and darkness as the devil does holy water. He taught himself to judge and forecast it. He soon learned that strong winds aloft at Valdez were a sure omen of weather in the making. A moderate south wind usually meant a remotely approaching storm. A shift to southeast promised wind and snow, rain, or sleet within a matter of hours. From the pothole at Valdez Reeve studied the clouds for indications of winds and weather. Laterally he could see several miles, but vertically the visibility ranged from one hundred feet to unlimited ceiling. A southerly wind gave him a couple of days' working range; southeasterly, only a few hours. West and northwest winds were a sure omen of good weather—although they often built up into such high-pressure areas that by the time they spilled over into Valdez they were so fierce that he had no alternative but to stay tied down.

With a ceiling of 3500 feet in Valdez, Reeve found he had a fair chance of making it through Thompson Pass (the lowest pass from Valdez over the Chugach range to the Interior). Some winds, he discovered, were of local origin only, with a sure chance of decreasing at his destination. His final criterion for judging them was the presence or absence of long plumes of snow stretching from the surrounding peaks. If he saw the plumes, he could be sure that violent gusts and strong head winds lay in wait in the mountains.

There was no way of mastering the williwaw. Although you could know in general that these savage gusts would be encountered on the lee of the mountain, a climactic pressure build-up might create a sudden series of unpredictable blasts that would be encountered anywhere. They were simply a part of the game. Once, when Reeve had just landed on one of his regular supply trips to the Big Four and had not yet shut off his engine, a violent blast of air swept down on the plane without warning, lifted it up, and tossed it off the peak of the mountain as a child might toss a toy. "The instant the williwaw hit the Fairchild I gave it the gun—in an effort to get airborne. From then on things happened so fast that I have no clear recollection."

The Fairchild went tumbling into a flat spin, whirring and twirling down the side of the mountain, the wings grazing the ledges in a shower of snow. "I don't know how long it went like that, but I must have tumbled about three thousand feet. I had no concept of time. Don't remember anything much until all at once I found myself in normal flight, at about one thousand feet altitude, heading down Mineral Creek Pass."

As in his first experience flying over Upsallata Pass in the Andes, Reeve had somehow met an updraft close to the ground, with the plane fortunately headed down the canyon, which left the plane in level flight. In a daze, mechanically going through the motions of flying, which were by now second nature to him, Reeve made a landing at Valdez—then sat in the plane for twenty minutes trying to gather his wits. "I knew by all rights I should have been dead. To this day I don't know how that plane ever came out of the spin. It must have been luck. If it was—I'd used up all my luck for twenty years in advance!"

Back at the Big Four, miners Jack Cook and his son, who had come out to meet the plane and seen it go tumbling over the side of the mountain, gave Reeve up for dead, but put off a search till next day, since it was dusk. When Bob flew in the following day, Cook and his son stared at him with disbelieving eyes. "It took them a few moments to realize I wasn't a ghost."

When he deviated from his own rules about weather, Bob was headed for trouble. He had a request one day to take some emergency mine equipment into Brenner Mine, just as a southerly wind at Valdez began to shift to the southeast. Figuring he had a few hours leeway before the storm hit, and, as usual, needing the cash, Bob decided to risk a "dive into the Hanagita," and make it home before the storm. This time his too-close figuring might have worked, but he was caught short by his humanity. An accident case at Bremner Mine needed transportation to Chitina, where there was a registered nurse who could dress the injury. There was no question of refusing, although it meant a delay of nearly two hours in his return flight. By the time he got back from Chitina to the Tasnuna Divide, fifty miles out of Valdez, the storm was boiling in to meet him. There was nothing to do but "sit down" on the Tasnuna snow flats and wait.

Within hours, one of the worst blizzards of the year had broken. A trumpeter swan, also trapped by the storm, circled over Bob's plane, blaring balefully. (Later, when Reeve reported seeing this rare bird, everyone doubted it. But twenty years later the Fish and Wildlife Service discovered a trumpeter swan nesting ground at approximately the point where Reeve was grounded in the pass.)

For five days Reeve stayed in the cabin of his plane. He had his sleeping bag and emergency rations, and spent most of his time catching up on his sleep. "Every time I see corned beef or Ry-Krisp, I remember those five days!" On the fourth day he livened up his diet with rice and raisins boiled over the fire pot inside the cabin. To kill the tedious hours he got out a tool box and made complete interior inspection and tune-up of the controls, "from the instrument panel to the stabilizer worm gear assembly."

On the sixth day the ceiling rose a little, and Bob noticed that it would occasionally lift to good visibility, stay open a few minutes, then close down. Restless at the long delay, impatient to get home to Tillie and the baby, Bob decided to risk one of those few-moments' "breaks" and see if he could make it into Valdez. He got his plane warmed up and ready to go, and waited with the motor running. The instant the next clear-up occurred he gave it the gun and took off. He was half way through the pass when the ceiling "came tumbling down" again. "I found myself flying blind in a pass so narrow that I couldn't turn around. I knew I was in bad trouble." With no possibility of back-tracking, Bob kept flying ahead, using his altimeter and bank-and-turn to maintain level flight, but it was "dead blind," and "I knew that I wouldn't see to make the next bend." Suddenly Reese made out, to his left, the outline of a tongue of a glacier that flowed into the canyon. The winds blowing down off the tongue agitated the fog enough to form a thirty- to forty-foot ceiling that Bob could see stretched a short distance up the face of the glacier. Making a lightning decision, Bob swerved left out of the blind fog—"the fastest left turn I ever made in my life"—and with a few hundred feet visibility, followed the glacier up the steep slope, throttle wide open. He climbed from two thousand feet altitude to seven thousand feet at ten to twenty feet off the face of the snow, "the steepest climb I was ever in." Fortunately, the plane was empty. At seven thousand feet he broke out on top onto the mother ice cap—in the clear. "Jesus, that was a miracle."

But coming out on top of the solid overcast didn't solve

more than temporary problems. With less than an hour's gas left in the tanks of the Fairchild, Bob realized he couldn't "float around indefinitely like a balloon." Somehow he had to get down through the solid cloud bank to Valdez. "I figured if it was okay going up it should be okay going down." He picked up the next glacier toward Valdez, cut the gun, and glided down the glacier, using the same technique with which he'd come up from the pass. Finally he broke out in the open on Dutch flats, about three hundred feet above sea level. Now only one small canyon blocked his way. But it was socked in, zero-zero visibility. Circling in an effort to scheme a way through it, Reeve finally gave up, landed on a little snow field. At that moment he heard an ominous rumbling, looked up to see a snowslide tumbling down the precipice before the canyon, damming the river below. "I think I'm the only pilot who ever set off a major snowslide!" But with the normal course cut off, the river water backed up, and soon threatened to inundate the Fairchild, "my bread and butter." Reeve hastily took off again, flew around in the pothole half a mile wide and two miles long, and eventually found a shelf above the high-water mark. Next day the ceiling lifted, and Bob made it in to Valdez.

"That taught me a couple of things," says Bob. "First, never to stampede out into the sky. And second, to stick to what should have been an ironbound rule: never fly through a pass obscured by fog. Even though you might, at a distance, see through it, once you get into the midst of the fog your visibility becomes nil."

The sort of flying to which Reeve subjected his planes required super equipment as well as super flying. The strain on the plane's engine due to constant climbing to high altitudes, and the strain on the wings and fuselage induced by the violent winds, meant continual checking of the wings' internal bracing, continual danger of engine and structural failures. Once when he was flying along the Columbia Glacier a downdraft smashed the Fairchild into a fifty-foot-high moraine. The rugged Fairchild ricocheted off the rocks like a billiard ball but managed to hold together. Back at Valdez, the plane went into dry dock for an extensive welding job, as the impact had partly sheared the landing gear cluster from the fuselage, and pilot Reeve suffered a violently sore neck.

"It almost snapped my head off. But," he adds, with a shrug, "any injuries that left you walking were taken for granted."

One of Reeve's near-crashes during this fateful year of numerous accidents had little to do with factors of decision or ability. Making a landing at the Bremner Mine in blowing snow, in a thirty-mile downwind, Reeve could barely see the snow-shelf runway, nor, as it happened, could those below see him coming into land. He had just touched the runway and was moving along at about sixty miles per hour when a miner driving a caterpillar tractor suddenly crossed directly in front of the plane. "Only thing I could do was give it a hard left rudder and ground-loop off the shelf into a gully."

Reese dove twenty feet off side into the soft snow of the gully, emerged without injury to himself or plane. But it took a day's work to dig the Fairchild out of the snow and make a runway up out of the gully. Then the cat (fitted with "snow-shoes"—boards bolted onto the treads, for snow work) was hitched onto the plane by a rope, and pulled it up onto the landing shelf.

"While the average pilot spent his life on wheels," explains Reeve, "my flying was almost completely with skis on snow and ice." It was a special type of flying, with no known rules nor special equipment—and it received a great deal of attention. Actually, one of Bob's problems was how not to allow the interest and admiration his flying received to influence his good judgment. "I kept warning myself: 'Don't get overconfident. You may think you're good but you're not. Never forget that the country is stronger than you are. Luck is stronger than you are.' It is easy," he says soberly, "to become a victim of your reputation." Reeve attributes Gillam's eventual death to the fact that he had built up a reputation, and he couldn't back down, although its demands were past human ability. "One time," says Bob, "I was flying along, thinking I was pretty good, believing what folks had been saying, and I became so hypnotized by my thoughts that I looked up to find I was about to crash into a mountain! It was a good lesson. It reminded me that anything can happen—any time."

To abet his luck and ability, Reeve constantly worked out modifications for his special type of flying. A sound mechanical knowledge coupled with an experimental frame of mind enabled him to come up with some original "Rube Goldberg

devices," which aided the efficiency of his unique operations
and sometimes spelled the difference between life and death.

Although the conventional position of the ski pedestal on
Alaskan ski planes worked sufficiently well for the Interior
and far northern Alaska, which had a comparatively light
snowfall, Reeve found that in coastal Valdez, with its mois-
ture-drenched atmosphere and three and four feet of fluffy
snowfall each night, the skis were unfit for constant winter
use. When taking off and attempting to climb out of deep
snow, this conventional placement canted the forward part of
the ski down into the snow, which acted as an effective drag
to the forward movement of the plane. Thinking back to his
experience with the flying boats and amphibians in South
America, Reeve concluded that the performance of a plane's
skis was analagous to that of a flying boat's hull on water.
The position of a ski pedestal was in direct relation to the
"step" of the hull of a flying boat. When the step was too far
forward, you just "plowed water." Set far enough back, you
attained the climb-out performance to become air-borne.

Reeve removed the ski pedestal and set it back a foot.
With ample frontal area, the ski thrust upward rather than
downward, and the Fairchild "climbed like a scared cat" and
shot up out of the deep snow. To aid the upward thrust of
the skis he added a double thickness of shock cord to the
front of his skis.

When Hugh Brewster came through on his annual inspection for the government, he objected to Reeve's moving his
ski pedestals. It was contrary to the book. "Have you flown
deep snow?" Owen Meals asked him. "Five inches in Montana," Brewster told him.

"Our local snow is twelve feet deep, and you have to get
out on top or you won't get enough speed to get any lift,"
mechanic Meals explained. "You ought to see Gillam's plane
land here with his Interior-type skis. It's a biplane, but you'd
think it was a monoplane, the way it sinks down with only
the upper wings showing. Take a flight with Bob and see how
his works."

Although alterations of any kind other than those specifi-
cally approved by factory tests were frowned upon, Brewster
took Owen's suggestion, had a demonstration flight with Bob,
and approved the change.

One of Bob's pet innovations was never seen—much less

approved—by an inspector, for the simple reason that Bob knew beforehand that it would never pass. To counteract the increased speed of landings and take-offs in the rarefied air at high altitudes, Bob warped the wings of his Fairchild to attain a greater angle of attack and greater consequent lift, by lengthening the front struts and shortening the plane's rear wing struts. This resulted in the angle of attack being considerably in excess of that called for by factory blueprints. But Reeve compensated for the greater stress on the wing by a complete realignment of the internal wire bracing.

Performance at all altitudes was considerably increased. Take-offs were faster and landings shorter. However, what he had gained in their performance he lost in a decrease of several miles per hour in cruising speed, as a result of the drag created by the increased angle of the wing. His next problem was to figure some control of the stabilizer of the aircraft that would boost the tail up and realign the plane to its factory-designed attitude in level flight. Reeve began experimental test flights, and soon discovered that he could make the correction by a slight forward pressure on the control stick without loss of altitude. He reasoned that the depressed elevator had created a more stable flow of air over the stabilizer and that, as a parallel phenomenon, the curve in the flow of the air over the stabilizer and down the drooped elevator had created an effective airfoil with far more lift than had been originally engineered into the stabilizer.

With a pair of tin snips and a piece of aluminum, he fashioned a six-inch-wide extension from the trailing edge of each elevator, "a sort of flentner." Fastening them to the rib sections for strength, he then secured them with bolts and bent them slightly upward, forming a "booster" to deflect the elevators downward in a fixed position in flight. By test flights he determined their most efficient position for maximum lift and minimum drag.

The results of these private modifications fulfilled Reeve's expectations. The Fairchild's tail feathers literally became "tail wings." "That airplane actually leaped off the ground," says Reeve. "It was so obvious that some wag christened it Leaping Lena, and the name stuck."

Now that the tail of the plane was a modified lifting wing surface, the next problem was to keep the elevators safely secured to the stabilizer under the increased stress. This was resolved by doubling the number of hinges that secured the elevators.

It took all of Reeve's wit and talent for evasion to keep up with the questions put to him by both inspectors and other airmen about this strange device on his plane. But, odd as it appeared to the curious eye, it made the difference between a good performer and a superperformer for his type of work. That this odd-looking device was not merely screwball tinkering was proved by the fact that while Bob was working it out on a primitive level on his own planes, engineers at aircraft factories were developing the same modification. Today the flentner is a standard adjustment on all modern planes, and is handled as a routine correction for the aircraft's altitude from the pilot's cockpit. "The modern pilot has the advantage," smiles Reeve. "He can adjust it while in flight. I couldn't. I had to come down to roost first."

One of the most intricate of Bob's modifications on his plane was his use of the basic principle of the turbojet engine, by the addition of a home-built supercharger that gave his engines close to sea-level performance at high altitudes. He recalled the specially built Pratt & Whitney Wasp engine that had been shipped down for the Andes mail route. It had a fourteen-to-one blower gear ratio installed, which had proved highly successful for the high-altitude flying. Even in the rarefied air this fourteen-to-one impeller had effectively provided rammed air, so that the engines maintained their rated power at sea level. "Why couldn't the lack of dense sea-level air, for which the altitude adjustment failed to compensate, be compensated for by feeding it to the carburetor under pressure?" If that fourteen-to-one impeller could suck the necessary increased air volume up through the carburetor jets, then the same required air volume could certainly be rammed through. Besides, it would relieve back pressure and suction on the impeller system, and enable the supercharger system to function more efficiently.

It took Bob months to perfect his supercharger. Using the cabin hot-air heat exchanger as a basic pattern, he tripled its capacity, designed a larger and more efficient heater air intake scoop, and incorporated an intricate system of baffles in the air passages. The baffles achieved the first purpose of preheating the cold air intake for a range from minus 65 degrees to over 150 degrees Fahrenheit. Its second purpose was to effectively trap the greatly expanded heated air so that it had only one outlet—pressure by expansion into the carburetor intake. All possible air inlets or leaks were sealed off. To get this pressurized air to 90 degrees—its most favorable combustive point when united with spray from the carburetor fuel jet—Reeve connected an auxiliary cold-air inlet to regulate the final mixture to the desired temperature. All functions were coordinated and regulated in conjunction with the readings of several thermometers by a series of push-pull controls located in the cockpit. The fuel mixture could be regulated to an exact degree. Another series of controls served the second purpose of modifying the ram air input when carburetor heat was necessary at low altitudes.

The supercharger worked. The higher Reeve flew, the smoother his engines operated. Although not attaining full rated sea-level power, they produced satisfactory power and a spectacular improvement over the former performance. "Maybe I had too much ram at the lower levels and not enough at extreme altitudes," says Reeve, "but oddly enough the valves and valve seats never showed any ill effects from what no doubt was seldom a perfect mixture ratio of fuel and air."

Although his device worked to Reeve's satisfaction, to this day he has a hard time convincing other mechanics or flyers that he actually used it. "There ain't no such thing!" is the consensus. Bob shrugs. "All I know is I used it—and it worked. At times, without it I couldn't have taken off."

No matter what he might overlook or disregard during busy flying activity, Reeve learned to be a stickler for proper propeller alignment. "You could have a bad plug, poor cylinder compression, a rough magneto, or valves set too tight or too loose, and all these faults would be effectively modified by a smooth-tracking prop. On the other hand, a rough prop exaggerated all other faults the engine might have."

Accurate blade settings served still another important purpose for Reeve. As he frequently landed in tight spots, it was often necessary for the Fairchild's engine to temporarily develop horsepower far in excess of its rated power in order to pull out. Since the horsepower output was measured in rpm and the rpm were governed by the amount of pitch in the blades, Reeve prepared for these emergencies by experimenting with various pitch positions of the prop to find the smoothest blade positions for emergency power as well as for normal operations. When he discovered the positions, Reeve made a single mated mark on the hub and the blade with the point of a knife. He was then able to make a manual adjustment, by loosening the hub clamps with a wrench, at any time he was on the ground. After he had made his own settings, Reeve ignored the factory marks, which had been worked out for ordinary flying. They were marked in half-degrees only, and Reeve found a fraction could make the difference between a smooth- and a rough-running prop. With his knife-blade marks to guide by, he could mate the loosened blade in the hub perfectly, at any time, without a protractor. "Another case where I was born twenty years too soon," sighs Reeve. "Nowadays you adjust it from the cockpit, with no exertion—even for the worst loafer in the league."

Reeve's endless experiments ("If Bob wasn't flying, you could always find him down at the field tinkering with his plane," says Noel Wien) carried him into realms far in advance of the aviation of the period. Concluding that the tapered tips of his props were inefficient, he squared them with a hack saw. Take-offs and cruising speeds improved appreciably. But scuttlebutt about this scandalous treatment of his propeller reached the ears of the inspector, and "he was on my neck in no time." "You can't do that, Bob! You are deviating from the blade profile specified in the manufacturer's Approved Type Certificate. Take it off or I will ground the airplane."

"Guess I'll have to compromise with you," grumbled Reeve. He took it off, privately thankful that the inspector hadn't removed the engine's motor cover and discovered some of his other "devices."

One of Reeve's experiments backfired. Tired with the drudgery of his mud-flat ski operations, he decided that the newly developed, oversized airwheels he'd read about might work on the shallow, hardened glacier snow as well as skis, in the summer months. He bought airwheels, and found "they worked fine when conditions were perfect." But the time he spent digging his plane out of crevasses over which skis would have slid proved he was better off where he started. Once, when he flew up to Columbia Glacier to land on a ten-foot-wide ice strip between the crevasses, where he had made a landing the previous day in a light snow, Reeve saw his own tracks, landed—and sank into four feet of fresh snow. Overnight the snow had actually fallen so gently that it had filled his tracks so that he could still see the indentation of his wheel tracks through four feet of snow. With the weather above freezing, Reeve had no chance of packing a frozen runway for a take-off. Straightening his prop, which had bent in the soft snow, he disgustedly mushed over to the Ruff & Tuff mine, three miles away, borrowed snowshoes, and tramped down a semblance of a runway, then waited for a freeze. A competitor, Jack Peck, who had recently moved into the Valdez area, flew over and circled when he spotted Reeve's plane. Bob laid out an "O K" in the snow with his emergency gear, so that the pilot could report to Tillie. On the eighth day it froze—and within seconds Reeve was airborne and "headed back for a new pair of socks." His constant tramping in the snow had worn the one pair he had on down to four ravels—one thread north, one south, one east, and one west. After that annoying session, Reeve put his new airwheels up in the attic and went back to skis.

In his efforts to support his young family, Reeve, by his own admission, "pushed too hard." Money was scarce in Alaska, and everybody was "scrapping for a living." Simple survival was a fierce ordeal. In an effort to get his hands on some of the elusive cash, Reeve took a few chances too many. In one particularly bad spell, he had five forced landings in that many days. The first one, out over Valdez Bay in the Fairchild 51, occurred when an intake valve broke. With no place to "sit down," Reeve forced the engine for all it was worth and made it into the edge of the Valdez field. But this was only the beginning of his troubles.

When the valve broke, Reeve later discovered, it had fractured into four secitons, each of which backfired into the blower section. Unable to locate anything but the stem during repairs, Bob surmised that they had blown out through the exhaust manifold.

Next day, with the cylinder replaced, Reeve resumed his flights. A few miles out it happened again. One of the sections of the broken valve, supposedly disgorged in the exhaust system, dislodged from the blower system, fell down an intake pipe into a lower cylinder, and blocked open another intake valve. The engine literally caught fire internally, with a series of explosions and a trail of flame from the exhaust. The oil temperature shot from 160 degrees to out of sight on the gauge within seconds. Bob got just enough power out of the engine in spite of the fire to maintain flight till he spotted a gravel bar.

Within the following three days, the three other valve fragments shook loose and caused three more forced landings. "The last one," reports Bob, "was nearly my last flight—my last clean shirt, as the undertakers say. I was taking off over high cottonwood trees with a fully loaded plane, and barely had flying speed when it happened. I just made it down to the mud flats straight ahead."

He had had enough. This time he dismantled the engine and searched for any remaining pieces of valve, but by now they had all jarred loose. Mute evidence of their presence were four sears in the blower section where they had lodged from backfiring.

The continual take-offs and steep climbs from sea-level Valdez up into the high peaks put stresses and forces on the engines for which they were never designed. An airplane engine is designed for 97 per cent of its use in cruising power in level flight, with only about 3 per cent of its use at full power. Bob, however, was using his engines almost 50 per cent of the time at full power, in order to reach the mining areas in the mountains.

Flying over the ragged peaks that were his daily routes, Bob kept his ears tuned for deviations in the engine. "I often heard things," he admits. "At one period I kept hearing a sort of screeching growl that made me think I needed a psychiatrist." One day, however, as he was crossing a high mountain, the engine let out a whining scream "like a wildcat," which Reeve knew was not his imagination. When he got back to his home base, he started looking for the cause of this strange noise in the Wright Whirlwind engine of his Fairchild 51, and soon located the propeller shaft ball-bearing race loose in the nose section. Its periodic turning had worn and elongated the nose section so that the bearing race and the bearing seat in the nose-section case were out of alignment. But with no spare nose sections or bearings and a "busy work season," Reeve performed repairs with "tin snips and brass shim stock." "It could not have passed an alignment test," he admits, "but it quit screeching."

Reeve had sixteen forced landings with that engine in nine

years. At about the tenth, he decided to treat the power case and accessory gear section to a first class "Stateside overhaul." He reinstalled the bright and shiny engine in the 51, confident that he had eliminated tumbling down for the life of the engine. Except for desultory firings, the engine failed to start. Next day, Reeve tried again and finally got the engine running. It was "off again, on again" for a month, then the engine finally quit for good on a flight in to the Big Four mine. Suspecting trouble in the cam gear, Reeve dismantled it. The came gear was floating in the gear race. The factory-specified hard steel dowel pins securing the gear to the race had been replaced by soft steel pins when it was overhauled. From then on, Reeve had his engines overhauled in Alaska and stood over the mechanics while they did the work.

There was no question—to anyone except stubborn Harold Gillam—that Reeve was the authority on the Valdez area and its peculiar hazards. On a wet, sticky day in the spring breakup season, Gillam came in scouting for passengers from the boat. Another plane, a strange Lockheed Vega, also circled the field and came in. In it was Jack Jefford,* the big, striking, black-haired flyer who had recently arrived from the States to work for the Hans Mirow Air Service at Nome. When they had their passengers and were ready to head out, Reeve cautioned the two flyers. "Snow's sticky, so don't try to take off downhill toward those high-tension wires. You won't make it. Take off uphill and into the canyon. The extra angle of attack on the wing will give you enough added lift to break loose, and you won't have any trouble."

Gillam, however, had to do things his way. When he had his passengers loaded, he took off downhill toward the wires, failed to attain the necessary lift in the short run on sticky snow, barely became air-borne, and ripped out the high-tension wires with his skis, one of which broke loose and hung like a broken arm at right angles to the fuselage. But the gods of luck were with Gillam. The power had been temporarily shut off for line repairs—or he would have tumbled down in flames. With his own brilliant knack for getting out of trouble, Gillam flew on, later managed to make a success-

* Jefford is now chief of Airways Flight Inspection Division for CAA in Alaska.

ful landing on an ice overflow on the Big Delta River, pancaking his plane in. But Jack Jefford was convinced. "It hadn't occurred to me until Bob explained it," said Jefford. "But after that I always used his technique of uphill take-off in a bad situation." Although a downhill take-off appears faster, Reeve explains, the plane, due to its decreased angle of attack, actually has much less lift by the time it reaches the bottom of the hill—and is apt to just "mush ahead" into rocks and trees. Flying uphill, the increased angle of attack of the wing gives the necessary lift to become air-borne in a short space in spite of the slower speed uphill of the aircraft.

Scrapping for business against severe competition showed its effects on Bob's personality. The floor of his planes was inch deep in butts from the cigarettes that he nervously chain-smoked. The owner of a roadhouse where he occasionally stayed confided to Tillie that when Bob stayed overnight she never went to sleep for fear he'd set the place on fire. Once, when he was making a landing at the Big Four mine, his lighted cigarette fell down his open shirt front. By the time he got to the ground, the front of his chest was a mass of angry blisters. "I spent more time flying sidewise to see if my plane was on fire than any pilot in the business," he jokes.

The gold boom that had briefly stirred Valdez was soon over. The fixed price which had at first been a shot in the arm to the mining industry soon became its main handicap. With costs of living constantly on the rise, there was not enough margin between cost and production to make further investment popular. With competitive flyers flooding into the Territory, undermining his rates and areas, and what meager cash existed being clawed for by a dozen hands, Reeve's quick temper reached its peak of irritability. "It was a bad time for us all," explained George Ashby. "Most of the mine promoters were running short of cash, and the mines were beginning to fold again. Nobody had any money. We were all broke. A man gets touchy. . . ."

Bob's "fights" during this period became legendary. Merle ("Mudhole") Smith who came to Alaska in 1937, worked for Gillam, and is now president of Cordova Airlines, tells with glee about seeing a plane land at Cordova. Bob climbed out "with a dish towel wound around his head and blood seeping through." When Smith asked Bob what happened, he shrugged, said tersely, "You should see the other guy!" Within a few minutes a second plane landed, a man crawled out with his wrist and hands bandaged up to his elbows! When he researched the fight, Smith discovered that Bob had revved up his plane and blown dust on the other man's shiny clean ship. When the fellow got mad and "crawled" Bob, it turned into a free-for-all.

Another famous fight, remembered by friend Mudhole, occurred when a trucker who had turned air-line operator borrowed one of Bob's props and failed to return it. Bob jumped him on the docks at Valdez, and the two men rolled over and over along the wooden dock, at the edge of the water. ("That fellow was so round and hard," explains Bob, "it was just like trying to get a good hold on a big rubber ball.") Baby Richard, toddling down to the dock, saw the fight, came running back to Tillie—who was by now, in her own words, "big as a house" with her next child. "Mama, Mama," screamed Richard, "come quick, Daddy's getting hell beat out of him."

Tillie rushed down to the dock. Bob looked up, saw her coming, and yelled, "It's all right now, Tillie. *I* got *him!*"

According to Mudhole, Bob made a Christian out of this particular gentleman, since he later became a preacher!

One local resident that Bob made no effort to mix with was "The Mad Trapper," prospector-flyer Hank Kroll. "The toughest man I ever saw!" Bob shakes his head in awed admiration. "The only man I wouldn't tangle with."

"Built like a bear," explains George Ashby. "Why, that man was so big he couldn't lace up his shoepacs!"

Contradictorily, the powerful man chose for his plane a tiny Curtiss Pusher, which he "completely filled up." The stocky, blond German would climb into the little plane, reach out with one long arm, and whirl the prop. Needless to say, he usually got an audience. But Kroll was not a competitor of Reeve's. He was not for hire. His interest in flying was simply to prospect in the mountains, and he made hundred-foot landings up among the snow caps that made veteran Reeve shudder. Once when Kroll landed in fresh snow, on wheels, he cut a cottonwood tree and made skis for his plane, tied the skis onto the wheels, and took off. In Valdez, Kroll liked to buzz over town, throttle the engine back, get out his accordion, and sing and play. Between tunes he shouted greetings (of questionable language) to his friends below. Once the young giant called on three teachers, entertained them for an hour by playing a guitar and singing, then suddenly threw down his guitar and demanded, "How about some food?" The ladies hastily retired to the kitchen, prepared dainty sandwiches, cookies, and coffee, and brought them in the tray. Kroll munched a sandwich, picked up his cup, then roared in horror, "Jesus Christ, you call this coffee! Why, you can see bottom in forty fathoms!"

When a zoo put in an order for a live wolverine, the big blond trapper disappeared into the woods, came back with one of the vicious beasts trussed to a pole slung over his shoulder, and a second one dragging behind him, collared by a heavy dog chain.

When he found a prospect that pleased him on Shoup Glacier, Kroll set up operations and built himself an airfield on a rock ridge at the end of the glacier. On one landing he hit the ridge short with the wheels of his plane and sheared off the landing gear. Reeve and other flyers looked for him, but found no trace. A week later Kroll showed up in town, afoot. "The most damage to his plane was not from hitting the ground," reports Reeve wryly, "but where Hank's body crashed into it!"

Eventually madman Kroll "softened up" his startling ways, married a nurse, and went into the cannery business. He is today a successful cannery owner who spends his vacations flying a Cessna to California or Florida.

Bob took every job he could get—flew anywhere, any time. "I always kept food ready," says Tillie, "so I could get a meal ten minutes after he showed up, no matter what time it was. I never counted on his being home for meals. I never knew when he'd appear, or how long he'd be delayed." When Reeve reached Valdez and headed home for a hot meal, he had a habit of picking up all the lone men he found along the way. "It was always me and six men around our table," smiles Tillie. "It's a good thing we could charge our groceries!"

The talk around the Reeve table was flying and mining.

Most familiar faces were old friends Noel Wien and Harold Gilliam, sometimes other pilots, often miners. In 1937 there was a new face: slender, lively-eyed young Bradford Washburn,† Harvard instructor and explorer, who had come to Alaska to map and climb the little-known mountains. It was with Washburn that Bob Reeve made his most historic flight.

† Bradford Washburn is now director of the Boston Museum of Science, still spends his vacation time on Alaskan expeditions. Petite Mrs. Washburn is the only woman who ever climbed Mount McKinley.

# 8. "Anywhere you'll fly, I'll ride"

Bob received a query in the form of a letter from Bradford Washburn in January, 1937. Two years earlier, the young explorer, on the National Geographic Yukon Expedition, had gone into the Saint Elias Range of the Canadian Yukon and surveyed the area preparatory to an attempt to climb the highest then-unclimbed peak in North America, Mount Lucania. One of the most difficult of all mountaineering problems, 17,150-foot Lucania lay in the isolated southwest corner of the Canadian Yukon, a few miles east of the Alaskan border. An approach by land from the nearest point of civilization, the Alaskan town of McCarthy to the west, involved not only terrible terrain but a prohibitive expense in pack-train equipment. In 1935 the Walter Wood expedition had tried the eastern approach, coming in from Burwash Landing in the Yukon, but had been forced to first climb 16,600-foot Mount Steele, which lies ten miles east, in the path of Lucania. The Wood expedition successfully scaled Steele but could not then proceed to conquer Lucania, due to the weeks of terrible back-packing required to reach its base, which both used up supplies and exhausted the climbers. The problem was to find an approach to Lucania that would allow the climbers' supplies and energies to go into the scaling of that single peak. Washburn had worked with other Alaskan flyers and felt the problem could be solved by the use of an airplane. But there were no ski planes available in the summer months when he was free from his position at Harvard to make the ascent. When he heard of Reeve's mudflat ski technique for summer flying, he felt this was his chance to be flown into the base of Lucania. Washburn wrote Reeve, outlining his plans for the expedition, and sent an aerial photograph (made by Russell Dow, a colleague of Washburn) that showed Mount Lucania and nearby Walsh Glacier, at the

116

base of the peak, which Washburn, himself a pilot, felt might constitute an adequate landing field. Walsh Glacier, however, lay at an altitude of 8500 feet. Could Reeve fly both equipment and men, on skis, in summer, to such an altitude?

Reeve studied the photograph. Although he had often flown into Whitehorse, in the Yukon, he had never flown over the top of the Saint Elias Range, or through it, near Lucania. Walsh Glacier appeared to be relatively free of crevasses for the last four or five miles at its extreme head. Both above and below that one comparatively smooth area, however, the glacier was a mass of treacherous slits and caverns. Bob had made numerous landings at six thousand feet around the Valdez area, and at eight thousand feet in Peru. Once at La Paz, Bolivia, he had made a twelve-thousand-foot landing with a specially equipped Fairchld. Since the Fairchild had originally been designed for high-altitude photography and had proved to be a capable performer at high altitudes, Reeve had an abiding faith in its abilities. But an 8500-foot landing with a load of freight was something else again. A few ski landings at higher altitudes had been made in the Alps, but they had been done as stunts, with empty planes. Washburn wanted Reeve to haul freight and passengers, which meant landings at an altitude approximately two thousand feet higher than had ever before been achieved by a loaded ski plane.

As usual, Bob wasted little time making a decision. In Cambridge, Massachusetts, only a few days after he'd written Reeve, Brad Washburn received a telegram date-lined Valdez, Alaska. On it was this terse answer, "Anywhere you'll ride I'll fly." Signed, "Bob Reeve." "You have no idea what a delightful shock that was," smiles Washburn. "No answer to my letter, no discussion, no details. Just that simple statement. I started making my plans for the expedition immediately."

Washburn was elated. Although the best climbing conditions occurred in April and May, when there was a combination of winter snow and spring sun, he was not able to leave his classes at Cambridge until the term ended in June. Reeve was the only flyer in Alaska who would be able to get Washburn into the glacier that late in the summer when the snow was off the airfields.

In March, Russell Dow, a member of the Washburn expedition, set out for Valdez with the party's equipment. The

plan was to relay the necessary equipment into Walsh, set up
a cache, and then when Washburn and his two other companions arrived in June, to have Reeve fly the men into the
site. As soon as the equipment arrived, Reeve relayed the
supplies to the town of McCarthy, near the Kennicott mine,
one hundred miles from Walsh Glacier. With snow still on
McCarthy field, Reeve was able to base his skiplane there,
and then he and Dow began trips in to Walsh. On their first
trip in, the wind was blowing so violently that Bob did not
risk a landing, but simply made a reconnaisance of the glacier and turned back to McCarthy. With seven hours' fuel
supply in the plane, the short run between McCarthy and
Warsh allowed a change of heart.

On his second attempt, with a light load, although a wind
was blowing, Bob was able to get the wind direction and
made a landing on the glacier, uphill into the wind, neatly
clearing the large crevasses. When the Fairchild settled to a
halt on the smooth snow, the altimeter registered 8750 feet.
Reeve and Dow unloaded the six hundred pounds of supplies,
covered them with a great tarp, marked the cache with orange flags, then set about the project of getting off the glacier. It was so narrow and steep that it was impossible to
turn the plane with power, so they did it manually, with
ropes, lifting and pulling the tail around until they got the
plane headed downhill.

Reeve and Dow made two more landings on Walsh without
difficulty, and wired Washburn that the supplies were all in.
These three landings were the highest freight landings ever
made with a ski-equipped plane.

Washburn and his companions, Robert Bates and Norman
Bright, arrived in Valdez on June 11, but were held up by
storms and low ceilings for another week before a flight
could be attempted. This time the problems would be very
different. With the snow gone from the McCarthy field, there
would be no landing place, except possibly for a forced landing on an occasional river bar, from the time they took off on
Bob's Valdez mud flats until they reached Walsh Glacier.
Once started, they would have to make up their minds to
turn back while they still had sufficient gas (Bob carried gas
for his return trip in the cabin, but there was no way to put
it in the tanks while in flight), make a forced landing and
mush out on foot—or fly the full 240 miles in to Walsh. Along

the way there were no communications, navigational aids, nor radios. There would be no way, except visual forecasting, of judging what lay in wait for them across the desolate ice field of the Chugach through to the Saint Elias.

For a full week after Washburn's arrival, the party waited out a storm in Valdez. Then, on the morning of June 18, the sun burned off the fog, and by noon the sky immediately overhead was cloudless. They decided to make a try. With the sun drying off his mud flats, Reeve decided there was no time for lunch. Settling for an ice cream soda apiece, the men hurried out to "Mudville," and Reeve began warming up the motor of the Fairchild 51. For the previous two days there had been no tide high enough to cover the flats, and the plane was so bogged down in the mud that it took the five of them half an hour, working in rubber boots, to get it free. But, once loosened from the mucky bed, the slick stainless-steel skis slid easily along the surface of the runway. Carrying nothing except their clothes and a minimum of emergency equipment so that Bob could haul his heavy gas load, Reeve, Bates, and Washburn climbed into the Fairchild, and Dow and Bright waved them off. The plan was that Reeve would land the two men, then return for the rest of the party and fly them in on the following day. Reeve revved up the Whirlwind engine, and they slithered over six hundred feet of mud and goose grass before finally shaking free and pulling safely up into the air. It was 1:15 P.M.

As they left the Valdez field behind them, a few streamers of clouds appeared in the east. A hundred and fifty miles out, storm clouds began rolling up, directly in front of them on their eastward course. The clear sky and bright sunlight in which they had taken off from Valdez began to darken relentlessly as they flew toward the new storm build-up. A strong southeasterly head wind made the plane crab to the left. To avoid the stiff winds higher up, Bob held his altitude at six thousand feet.

Sixty miles from their destination, Reeve motioned to Washburn to come up beside him. "That stuff ahead is too low," he warned. "We can go about ten minutes more before we'll have too little gas to get home."

Washburn studied the boiling clouds that lay ahead, his face serious. Then he smiled. "Anywhere you'll fly, I'll ride!"

"Okay," grinned Reeve.

Bob turned back to his stick and eased off a bit on the throttle as they started across what Washburn calls "the most godforsaken waste I have ever seen"—the snout of the Logan Glacier. Up until then there had been an occasional gravel bar on which they could have made a forced landing. Now, for the next twenty-five miles, there was nowhere they could have come down. "Till my dying day," Washburn recorded in his journal, "I shall never forget that nauseating desolation of dying masses of ice . . . veneered with a deep layer of reddish boulders and gravel. The valley walls on both sides were vertical rock and scree, bare, snowless and bleak. Potholes of horrid muddy water filled every depression. . . ."

"Hell's rear end, ain't it!" shouted Reeve.

It was like flying into the mouth of a whale. Below them lay masses of rotted, stagnant ice. Ahead and above, the clouds lowered ominously. By this time Bob was averaging about one cigarette a minute. "He had that inseparable rain hat pulled down over his ears," says Washburn, "and his cigarette holder clamped between his teeth. Every few seconds he'd hold the stick with his knees, while he took his pocket knife and flipped the butt out of the holder, then crammed in a fresh cigarette."

At 3:35 P.M. Reese turned. Ahead they could see the clouds lying menacingly in a black, unbroken ceiling. The air was "hellishly rough" over the pitted glacier. Reeve pointed to a likely-looking ore body on a hillside opposite the plane. "Anybody can have that gold mine that wants it!" he shouted.

Then, far ahead, they made out a series of ice cascades rising in the gray sky—the west wall of Lucania.

At 3:40 P.M. they reached the junction of the Logan and the Walsh Glaciers. Below them, the glacier face was a chaos of filthy, rotten ice and twisted moraine, gutted with huge crevasses. The valley had melted into a murky ceiling. Behind them, the storm was dropping down swiftly. By now the overcast was so low that they could make out only the tongues of the glaciers. Privately, Reeve crossed his fingers for the phenomenon that had helped him before: a low ceiling usually lifts just over the surface of the glacier and follows its contour.

Luck was with him. As they rounded the last elbow of their course and turned up onto the Walsh, the ceiling lifted for a few feet just off the face of the glacier. By now they were flying at about nine thousand feet, and the ice was barely two hundred feet below as they rounded the corner in violent air. The upper reaches of Walsh, where the landing area was, were gray and shapeless beneath the leaden sky that sped just above the plane. Snowflurries hid Mount Logan from view, and Hubbard Glacier was lost in the advancing darkness. A moment past four o'clock Bob yelled, "There it is!"

A tiny black dot seemed to float in the over-all gray of snow and sky, amid the wide fields of crevasses. It was the cache. At 4:05 P.M. Bob called out sharply, "We're going to land." The motor idled at last, the rigging hummed, and they lost altitude swiftly.

Using the black slits of the crevasses at the lower end of the runway to aim by and judge his altitude, Bob throttled back his engine, then dropped steeply toward the center of the black slits. As he came over them, Reeve gave the engine full throttle and pulled back on the stick. The glacier rose to meet them as Reeve flew up the face of the steep incline for about one thousand feet, with wide-open gun, at only ten feet off the face of the ice. Then, one thousand five hundred feet from the cache, he cut the gun, planning to taxi on toward the camp site at half-power when he hit the snow. The plane hit at about seventy miles per hour ground speed, but, once down, moved less than two hundred feet, then sank on her belly in a sea of slush.

Washburn jumped out—and went up to his armpits in watery snow.

It was the kind of paradox that only Nature could provide. In this, of all winters, only a few feet of snow had fallen over the Saint Elias. The weather was unseasonably warm: the temperature when they landed read forty degrees above zero. The snow was soft, sticky, and rotted by constant rain and fog. The six-thousand-foot landing strip had been cut in half by the melting snow, which had exposed the crevasses.

Washburn put on Reeve's Indian snowshoes and headed for the cache to get snowshoes for them all, poles with which to probe and test the snow, ropes and shovels, while Bates and Reeve started gassing the plane for its return trip. It took Washburn nearly half an hour to travel the three-fourths of a mile to the cache. "I approached it very gingerly by a series

of wide zigzags. I was terrified to walk over that riddle glacier without a rope."

When Reeve attempted to taxi the Fairchild up to a firmer
base, the plane ran a few yards, then plunged into slush up to
its wingtip. The three men dug for an hour, then tied a rope
to the tail, and Washburn and Bates pulled and jerked it
while Reeve roared the motor. They eventually got it out of
the deep slush, and Reeve taxied up a couple of thousand
feet. Another hour was spent putting blocks under the skis so
they wouldn't freeze fast. It was far too sloppy, foggy, and
dangerous to think of a take-off that day. But now, to add to
their misery, it had begun to rain. It was seven o'clock before
they hauled their supplies from the plane up to the cache and
started to make camp. While working with their shovels,
Bates and Washburn each fell into crevasses within ten feet
of their tent, but managed to catch themselves with the
shovels. The exhausted trio ate a little soup and cheese, then
climbed into their sleeping bags—to the tune of the relentless
splatter of rain, the roar of thunder overhead.

"Imagine!" says Washburn, "Rain and high temperatures
(it reached sixty degrees above zero that night) at an 8500-
foot elevation and sixty-one degree north latitude! It was like
running into a snowstorm on the Sahara desert."

The next day dawned foggy, rainy—and hot. It was actually so warm that Washburn and Bates had to throw out their
supply of fresh meat, which had been brought in frozen and
had begun to thaw. The problems presented by the strange
weather were, they realized, grave indeed. There was the immediate problem of getting Reeve and his plane out of the
sea of slush and into the air again. And secondly, the gloomy
realization that it would be next to impossible for Reeve to
haul in the other members of the party. Graver still, Reeve
would not be able to come back for the two men, which had
been their original plan. If they ever got the Fairchild off the
glacier, the two climbers were abandoned. They would have
to walk out over miles of unmapped country.

It rained all that day, and the temperature remained "hot
as pepper," according to Washburn. He and Bates made a
couple of desultory treks relaying some of their equipment on
to their next camp site. When they asked Reeve to join them
"and get some air," he snuggled down in his sleeping bag,
grunting disdainfully, "I'm a pilot, not a mountain climber!

You skin your skunks and I'll skin mine!" After his terrifying experience on the Valdez Glacier, Reeve was not about to set foot on the treacherous, rotten snow. "Thank the Lord those two boys were experienced climbers," Reeve says. "They found the crevasses and marked them off. Otherwise none of us would have got out of there alive."

On June 20, Reeve attempted to take off. The plane bumped and jounced along for half a mile, to the very edge of the big mass of open cracks at the limit of the runway—then stopped, sinking a yard deep into the sea of slush that lay under the thin crust of snow.

The three men tied a rope to the tail, turned the plane, and headed it back toward camp, planning to tie it down to wait for another, colder day. But Reeve had not taxied a hundred yards before the plane suddenly plunged halfway to her wing tips in a big crack. Again they set to work with shovels and ropes and dug the plane out. Reeve taxied it three hundred feet farther—and it almost disappeared as it sank into a tremendous hole. Washburn got the tent pole and tested to find the crack. But there was none. The plane was lying in a huge hollow between snowdrifts. This time the left wing tip was a full foot under the surface of the snow. The left ski had vanished from sight, its shockcord "disappearing into the snow like a fishline into water." Even the propeller was buried a foot and a half below the surface. For an hour the men worked to extricate the ski. Then they changed their tactics, and rather than dig the sunken ski out, they decided it was an easier task to dig the other ski "in" on a level with it. They dug down until the plane settled on hard ice below and the wings were once again level. Then they laboriously cleared a ramp ahead of the plane and "after about the tenth try" pulled it out onto a secure shelf. Then they again tied ropes to the tail, unloaded everything from the cabin, and she finally "roared out" and up to a safe hard spot, where they again jacked her up on blocks and left her, facing downhill, for another try, another day.

After this exhausting experience the three men agreed not to make another attempt until a real crust had formed. It would only eat further into Reeve's precious supply of gas. But so long as the fog remained, there would be no crust. What little layer might form in the day was rotted during the night by the wet under slush.

"Reeve is a stoic and a prince," Washburn wrote in his journal that night. "He took the two wrecks this morning calmly. . . . Bates and I have no alternative now but to walk out."

On the fourth night the murky rain finally gave way to cooler air and a moderate freeze. When the men awoke, at quarter to four in the morning of the fifth day, there was still fog, but it had snowed during the night, and a thin crust had formed over the slush. The temperature was twenty-nine degrees. While Reeve stood on the edge of the glacier, facing westward toward home, soberly figuring his chances of making it over the overcast which stretched up to twelve thousand feet, Washburn hustled around the cook tent fixing a "banquet" of scrambled eggs, bacon, and fruit compote. "My secret motive for such a large breakfast was to be well fortified to dig the plane out of another hole . . . although Bob Bates and I were certain that this time he would either take her off successfully or pile her into a hole out of which we should never possibly be able to extract her!"

After breakfast, Reeve warmed the engine, then they turned the plane to face the sun, so that it would burn the frost off the wings and tail surfaces, while they went back to camp to wait out the fog. At 8:10 A.M. the fog began to lift. They rushed down to the plane. Bob started throwing everything out: his tools, sleeping bags, emergency equipment—even the crank for the motor, after he had started it. "I had an impulse to remove the starter on the engine to reduce weight —but realized I'd lose all the oil in my engine."

With a wrench he flattened the prop to develop the utmost horsepower possible without causing the engine to fly apart. Washburn and Bates scraped the remainder of frost off the wings and tail surfaces, Bob jumped in and waved good-by and gave her full throttle. He figured if he could get started on the two hundred feet of firm snow and keep rolling, he would develop enough speed to climb out of crevasses if he broke through—and eventually become air-borne.

"I gave it the gun and off I went. But, by God, I hadn't gone a hundred feet when smack! down into a crevasse. But I wasn't stopping. The engine was developing tremendous power, far beyond its rated capability. I climbed right out of the crevasse and kept going. Then flop! down into another—and I lost the air speed I'd gained, getting out of it. Bumpety bump, it was just like driving over a plowed road. I realized I was getting nowhere. I'd already run a mile or more, and ahead of me I could see the big crevasses—wide enough to hold a boxcar. If I hit them, I was a goner. Then I happened to glance left and spotted an ice fall, sheering off the side—maybe 250 feet drop. It was my last chance. I made a sharp left turn and dove the plane right over that ice fall. It mushed straight for the bottom, and I thought maybe I was a goner, after all. But the plane had achieved just enough forward speed on the jump-over to become air-borne. I leveled out about ten feet from the bottom. That was the greatest feeling of my life—bar none!"

"I never hope to see wings hop and jerk and lunge back and forth the way that old 51 did!" says Washburn. "Halfway down the runway she still jerked. She had no speed, and her tail was still on the snow, bouncing up and down over each drift. I was just about to turn to Bates and say, 'She's all up, we'll have to tramp down a runway,' when Reeve suddenly turned the plane sharply to the left, down a steep sidehill leading toward an awful mass of cracks and a little greenish lake on the south side of the valley. There was a last roar and he disappeared out of sight. We could hear the 'rrrrr' of the motor. We waited for a crash. There was silence. Bates and I both thought we'd never in God's world get her out of that hole. Then suddenly we heard the rasping roar of the engine, and the plane came into sight going like fury in front of the lake. It suddenly began to climb, cleared the lake, and headed triumphantly for Logan, a black speck against the snow! Bates and I were simply spellbound. That steep hill had given Bob Reeve what he needed. It was a desperate maneuver which for almost any other pilot would have been suicidal. We shrieked for joy."

Within minutes Reeve had hit the solid wall of fog. He could either turn back and try to climb up over the fog bank, or fly blind. Reeve chose the latter, "the first time I'd flown instruments since I left Chile." He had no fuel to waste. Taking a sight down Logan Glacier, which led between nineteen-thousand-foot Mount Logan on one side and seventeen-thousand-foot Mount Lucania on the other, he set his compass course—and kept on flying. Clearing the mountains without mishap, he came out on top about twenty minutes later, at thirteen thousand feet, directly on course. Below him lay billowing clouds stretching as far as the eye could see westward toward home.

Reeve got out his maps and set a compass course direct for Valdez. About halfway home, he saw his first hole in the clouds. Looking through, he could see he was now exactly over the Bremner Mine, his old stomping ground. By the time he reached Valdez he was flying over broken clouds, and he let down into the Valdez pothole, skimmed over town, buzzed Tillie at the house, then flew on out to the mud-flat field. In minutes, Tillie appeared, pushing the old Model T at top speed out the dirt road to the flats, Richard on the seat beside her. Expecting Bob home the same day that he left, she had each morning gone out to the flats to wait, then home for the child's lunch, then back in the afternoon to sit and wait—and watch—till dark. The day before Bob finally appeared, Tillie had gone to Owen Meals suggesting a search be made, but the weather was too bad for any pilots to get off the field.

Of his return, Bob says with a slight smile, "Well, I took the rest of that day off!"

Next morning the Valdez *Miner* ran a banner headline:

MOST HAZARDOUS TRIP IN CAREER SAYS PILOT REEVE

Tuesday morning when Pilot Bob Reeve, flying his Fairchild 51 ski-equipped monoplane zoomed over town and set his plane down on the mud flats, little did his Valdez friends realize what a welcome sight this old town was. . . .

Reeve later told Washburn that when he flew into his Valdez field that day, "for five cents I would have dropped a lighted match in either gas tank!" There was not a drop of fuel left.

There was no thought of a second trip to carry in Russell Dow and Norman Bright—nor of a return trip for the two men abandoned on the rotten glacier. "The object of the expedition changed from that of scaling Lucania to that of getting out alive," said Washburn wryly. With the glacier and snow conditions so rotten below and to the west, the men decided that their safest chance for survival lay in going east to Burwash Landing. Although only 60 miles from Walsh to Burwash as the crow flies, it was 125 on foot, and included scaling Mount Steele and fording the treacherous, icy, nearly fatal Donjek River. As a sort of off-side project, Washburn and Bates also made a quick run over and scaled Lucania!

When Bob came back into Valdez, he brought a written message from Washburn for the climber's companions and the press, which was printed in the Valdez *Miner* and carried in Stateside papers:

Bates and I have been tremendously lucky to be able to reach this base cache under the existing conditions which are doubtless the most absurd in years, only six feet of snow have fallen here during the entire winter just passed. The rains have been heavy this year exposing many crevasses and although it is a tragic disappointment, both to us and the men in Valdez, Reeve, Bates and I feel that it would be running a tremendous risk to try even one more landing here. It is impossible to praise pilot Bob Reeve highly enough for his flying skill and resourcefulness which have got at least two of us safely into the highest glacier camp ever established by airplane. Any success which our expedition may have during the work we are about to do will be entirely due to his four magnificent flights which have landed us and our supplies at so great an altitude and so near our objective.

Later, Washburn, himself a pilot who had worked with French, Canadian, and Alaskan pilots, said in an interview that Reeve "is without doubt the finest ski pilot and rough-country flyer I have seen."

When the facts were in, Admiral Byrd issued a statement to the press that Reeve had broken the world's record for the highest landing on skis, which was over eighteen hundred feet higher than any point recorded in either Arctic or Antarctic expeditions.

There was no question in anyone's mind that without those

four landings Mount Lucania would have remained "virgin" for at least a while.

But the prestige of doing, as Ernie Pyle phrased it, "the most dangerous and exciting flying being done today" spelled neither money nor reassurance for pilot Reeve. The next year was to be the roughest he would ever know, the all-time low of his career.

# 9. "I ran out of planes—and luck"

Bob didn't fly any more on the day he got home from Mount Lucania, but next morning found him out on his daily milk run, servicing the mines. This time, it was a load of timber for a mine out on the Columbia Glacier. Reeve was just passing over the divide between the Shoup Glacier and the Columbia Glacier, where they flow into the open water of the Valdez arm west of the town, when the engine of the Fairchild 51 (the plane he had used for the Lucania trip) quit. "Here we go again!" Reeve muttered to himself, and headed back toward Valdez Bay. But there was no spot to come down. A high tide was in, which covered the flats where he had hoped to make a forced landing. The only possible spot Bob could find to come down was a boulder-strewn spit protruding into Valdez Arm. It looked as though he was going to have to swim out—if the load of timbers he was carrying didn't pin him in the cockpit.

Reeve decided his only hope for help lay in ditching the plane in the vicinity of the Cliff Mine, where one of the miners might see him crash-land and come out and help free him from the plane. He had just enough altitude left to circle over the mine, then he headed for the shallowest water he could find. His skis skimmed the surface of the water and then the plane came to rest, without tipping or sinking although water was seeping into the bottom of the fuselage. Fortunately for Reeve, the load of timbers held in place. He looked out of his window and decided he must have come down onto solid ground in about four feet of water. He opened the door, climbed out onto one of the skis, stepped off to wade ashore—and "went over my damn head." The plane had actually settled in a nest of boulders, in deep water. When Bob went under, the tide caught him and started to carry him out. But he managed to fight the current and head for shore. Exhausted and groggy as he dragged himself out of the water, Reeve felt arms pulling his shoulders, helping him out. Eighty-year-old Charlie Simenstad had been walking from one building to another at the Cliff Mine when he saw Bob circling overhead with a dead engine. Charlie started running, and had run over a mile in time to reach the scene of the ditching just as Bob made it into shore.

Enlisting the help of Owen Meals along with the miners, Bob managed to push the Fairchild off its bed of boulders with long timbers, and then roll it up to dry land. Once again the trouble proved to be in the timing gear. Uneasily, Bob thought back to the previous day when he had been flying in blind from Walsh Glacier. If the timing gear had failed during that run, he would have been a dead duck. There was no spot between Walsh and Valdez where he could have come down through the overcast. It was enough to make a man feel pretty spooky. With grim humor Bob recalled his stepmother's prophecy that he would meet a violent death before he was twenty. Maybe she'd been wrong by only a few years after all.

Owen and Bob repaired the plane sufficiently for Bob to fly it off the beach. Then they cleared the rocks off a stretch of beach and replaced the plane's skis with wheels, and Bob ferried the battered ship over to the Valdez field. With the soaking that the engine had received, he knew it was due for a complete overhaul. For the next eight months he spent all his spare time working on the plane, rebuilding the wings and fuselage and overhauling the engine. But all the time that he worked on the plane, a persistent thought haunted him. He had had sixteen forced landings with this plane—every one of them attributable to engine failure. Wasn't sixteen enough for one man? That last time he'd damned near drowned. If the engine had quit just the day before, he would certainly have been killed. There was still another sobering thing. While doing the overhaul, Reeve found that a spar was cracked from flopping into all those crevasses at Walsh Glacier. The wing surely would have torn off in flight in his next encounter with violent air.

During the long months that he worked on the plane, Bob's hunch grew increasingly strong. He was mighty lucky, he realized, to have survived those sixteen forced landings. But how long could a man count on that kind of luck? He had a haunting premonition that the seventeenth would be his last.*

When he finally had the engine overhauled, the fuselage repaired, and the plane ready to re-assemble, Bob stood there staring at it. "I kept thinking, 'Do I want to go swimming again?' I figured I'd run out of luck with that old Wright Whirlwind engine. So—I just let the darn thing sit there. I never did assemble the plane. I never flew it again." The remains of that Fairchild 51 are still lying around Valdez.

Reeve was now back to one plane, the Fairchild 71 with its Pratt & Whitney Wasp engine, a heavier-built and more serviceable engine than the Whirlwind. "My experience with that Whirlwind served its purpose in the development of aviation engines," Bob declares. "As a result of those weak points, among them the timing gear section, encountered by me and other pilots using it, Wright went on to develop the 1820 series which powered the [Boeing] B-17, and it and subsequent models proved to be one of the most successful engines in the world."

With so many near misses at death within the past couple of years, Bob was increasingly wary, high-strung, and spooky. It was time, he felt, to get off those glaciers. One day, as he attempted to take off from Columbia Glacier, the wind smacked him back to earth five times before he was able to become air-borne. Then there was the time he ran into the moraine and nearly broke his neck, and the time he got blown off the side of the mountain. . . . How many things like that had one man a right to survive? With a wife and growing family on his hands, what little daredevil urge he'd ever had forsook Bob. All he wanted of life now was the opportunity to make a living. He had survived thus far by doing the kind of flying no one else wanted. But he decided he had risked his neck long enough. Besides, with the first flush faded from the mining bloom, the Stateside investors were pulling out of Alaska, and there was no capital in the Territory to replace them. Servicing the mines would no longer provide an adequate income.

It seemed that each encounter with the mountains spelled more trouble for Reeve—almost as if they were deliberately

* Reeve actually survived five more forced landings (although not with a Wright Whirlwind engine), making a grand total of twenty-one.

showing him which was the stronger, after all. During breakup season that spring, a flyer named Don Emmons, who was a competitor of Reeve's, was lost over the Alaskan Range. Reeve spotted Emmons and his plane about three thousand feet altitude near Slate Creek. Emmons had tried to land on a runway near a mine, broken his skis, and wrecked his plane. Bob landed a mile away on Slate Creek—and the Fairchild promptly sank down through eight or ten feet of rotten snow to a bed of boulders below. The water melting off the glacier had run under the snow and rotted it, forming a cave under a thin surface shelf. Reeve looked at his plane with disgust. It was as bad as the mess he'd been in on Walsh Glacier! The snow was so rotten that Emmons could not walk through to Reeve, nor Reeve join him. Each flyer stayed with his own plane that night, and next morning, after the night's freeze, the crust was good enough for Reeve to be able to make his way over to Emmons. Emmons' plane was wrecked beyond any hope of flying it off, so the two men came back down to Reeve's plane on the following day and started digging out. They knocked down snow to fashion a ramp in front of the plane, then packed down their hand-made runway with shovels, so that the plane could climb up under power out of its rock bed. It took them two days to dig the plane out and make the runway—which they prepared for a take-off into the prevailing wind. By the time they were finished, the wind had shifted 180 degrees, and their runway was fashioned so that they would have to take off down a fifteen-mile wind. "By this time I didn't care if it had been blowing fifty miles per hour," snorts Reeve. "I'd have still tried it. Because I knew if I didn't get off soon I'd have to abandon my plane."

The two men climbed in, Reeve took off at a rush, "straight up," with a flattened prop. When they leveled out to cruise, the flattened prop could make no more than sixty-five miles per hour—but it had gotten them out of the hole.

A year later, Don Emmons repaid Reeve's courtesy by hauling him into the hospital at Cordova to get his hand set, after he had broken it in a fight with a miner.

In 1938 Reeve made his last glacier flight, when he flew Bradford Washburn to Mount Marcus Baker, in the Chugach Range, northwest of Valdez. "This," says Reeve flatly, "was

During his first six months in Alaska, Bob made a "stake" by servicing the Chisana mines, and was then able to buy this Fairchild 51.

Reeve working on his Fairchild 51. Note "official car" and "parts shop."

Bob ready to take off in the ski-equipped Fairchild from snowed-in Valdez.

Reeve arrives at the site of his Ruff and Tuff mine on the
Columbia Glacier.

Getting ready to warm engine of Fairchild 71 with firepot and engine cover, before a winter flight.

An 11,000-pound boiler being loaded into "The Yellow Peril" during building of Northway Airport. General Twining reported Reeve and his overloaded Boeing, with its cantilever added to fuselage to support extra weight, "looked like the Brooklyn Bridge."

The wrecked Boeing, as seen from the air at low tide. Coast Guard rescue plane stands by.

Biggest bear. Reeve's record-winning Alaskan brown bear taken at Cold Bay in 1948.

the last time I landed anyone on some damn unknown hunk of ice."

Reeve had learned in the past that it was safest to land as close as possible to the moraine of the glacier, where the crevasses were small. But this time he was fooled. "Those big crevasses stretched clear up to the moraine. I went through eight times. We spent all our time digging and mushing out. I figured if I kept this up much longer, I'd find myself stuck on one of those things for good. I decided there must be some better way to make a living!"

When they were at long past ready to take off, in his haste to get away, Bob gave it the gun, and "I was doing fine until I broke a cardinal rule of bush flying and tried to force the tail up with the stick, downwind to boot." The tail skid was dragging in the snow on the downhill take-off and acting as a brake, and with deep crevasses looming in front of the plane, Reeve tried to force the tail up. One ski hit a snow hummock, and the plane started to ground-loop. Bob rammed the rudder over and caught the plane just in time to straighten out. Once more, he had almost "had it."

On his way home from this last glacier fright, as he passed over the divide between the Klutina and the Valdez Glacier, Reeve noticed below him "the biggest grizzly I'd ever seen" wallowing in and out of the spring-rotted snow that covered the crevasses. "The stuff was so rotten he was surging up and down like a porpoise. I couldn't resist buzzing the rascal. I buzzed once, and that bear shot up twice as high as he'd been going, then sank down deeper. I didn't buzz him any more. That öld fellow had enough troubles already. I think he knew better than to stay in glacier country. I figured he was trying to get out while he was still alive!"

If Bob's dark hair had not already turned prematurely gray, 1938-1939 was the year that would have done it. He was at home with Millie when a wire came in from his father at Waunakee. Captain Richard Reeve, United States Air Corps, Commanding Officer of Lowry Field, Colorado, had hitched a ride on an Army B-18 from Chanute Field back to Lowry; a thunderstorm had hit and the plane had disintegrated, killing all aboard.

When he read the news, Bob said nothing. He put down the wire, got his coat, and started out of the house.

"Where are you going?" Tillie asked.

"I'm going to fly."

Blindly, Bob walked out to the field, climbed into his plane, and took off. A few minutes later he came back, landed, walked home. He seemed calm. "When I heard about Dick," he explained, "I knew I had to get in a plane—fast—or I never would again. It's like climbing back onto a horse after you've had a bad fall."

Richard Reeve, already a captain in the slow-moving peacetime Air Corps of 1938, had he lived, would, according to the men who worked with him, have been a high-ranking officer by the end of world War II, as were his closest associates.

In the spring of 1939 a violent windstorm hit Valdez. At 6:00 A.M. Bob went out to the field to check his plane and found it riding out the wind in fine shape. He had just gotten back to bed when a competitor yelled at his door, telling him he'd better go out and check his plane. Annoyed and irritable, Bob told the flyer where he could go—and to take care of his own plane.

Actually, the man had seen Bob's plane break loose from its moorings. Minutes after Bob left the field, an eighty-mile gust of wind had come hurtling down into town, off the Valdez Glacier, with such impact that it broke four one-inch ropes holding the Fairchild and tossed the plane, upside down, for about two hundred feet along the field. Bob bought a new set of wings from Pan Am, built a temporary hangar to house the plane while it was being worked on, and hired a mechanic who, with his wife, moved into the Reeve household while the two men worked on the plane. It took them the entire summer to repair the plane, and the night that they finally finished the two couples held a celebration supper and made plans for test flight the following morning. Later that night, as Bob and Tillie were preparing for bed, someone came running down their street yelling, "Fire! Bob, the hangar's on fire!"

Bob pulled on his trousers, rushed out of the house. The report was right. It was the hangar. And his plane. There was nothing he could do to save it.

But when he came home, to Tillie's surprise it was not with dragging steps and woebegone face. He seemed excited about something.

"You know, Tillie," he said, striding restlessly around the living room, "I'm really lucky!"

"Lucky?" Tillie echoed in a stupefied voice.

"Yes," said Bob, his voice gritty with excitement. "There's only one other Fairchild in the whole Territory like this one. Alex Holden's got it—and he isn't using it—and I can get it! Why, I've got enough spare parts for it to last a lifetime!"

Holden's Fairchild 71 had been in salt water and the fuselage had to be partly re-covered. Knowing Bob was out of planes, he made him a good price on it. Bob made the down payment and spent a month re-covering it, then brought it into Valdez and was once more in business.

However, during the five or six months that he was without a usable plane, other flyers had taken over much of his former business. To develop new business for himself, Reeve installed a camera aperture in the bottom of his plane, put in a pilot's sighting window, and went into charter work for aerial mapping.

It was at this inopportune (for Reeve) period that the Civil Aeronautics Board came into Alaska to regulate commercial flying, allot routes, and fix rates. Although the original Civil Aeronautics Act had been passed in 1938, the hearings on certifications were not begun until the following year in the States, and a year later in the Territory.†

A timely depression measure to regulate commercial aviation in the interests of a healthy over-all business, this government regulation of their highly individualized, free-for-all sort of operations came as a staggering blow to the Alaskan flyers. With no help from the government, they had built up a busy aviation business, and, like all pioneers, they were not ready to have outsiders come in and tell them how to run it. Already, with no help from the government, Alaskan citizens were flying twenty-two times more per capita than residents of the States. Alaskan carriers hauled one thousand times as much freight. Aviation in the Territory was individual, fero-

---

† Further hearings were held in 1941, and it was not until October, 1942, that temporary certificates were actually issued to Alaskan carriers. Subsidies, in the form of mail rates, were not established for Alaskan flyers for another five years. In all, it took nine years for the Territory's flyers to receive the benefits of the protective legislation that the States carriers enjoyed. And it was to be another nine years before they were granted permanent certificates.

ciously competitive, cutthroat. Rates were determined by competition, with staggering variances. There was no close supervision of operations or maintenance, on general safety rules. Pilots landed anywhere, however and wherever they chose, across runways, and sand bars and river beds, wherever they felt they could sit down—and survive. There was no close check on loading aircraft. "Our loads were determined by the length of the field and whether we could make it off the ground," reports Ray Petersen cheerfully. "We'd fill up all the seats, throw in all the freight our passengers' laps would hold, fill up the gas tanks, and take off. On a long trip we could take an extra load, because as the gas burned out we got the additional lift we needed to make it over the pass." (No matter where a pilot started from, there was always a pass to cross before he reached his destination, since Alaska is composed of a series of mountain ranges and valleys.) "When Brewster (the inspector) was around, we'd all wait till he went to lunch, then everybody would overload their planes and take off fast."

One of the biggest reasons for crack-ups, according to Ray, was "that last ten bucks' worth of freight." "However," fully. "Well, guess we might as well take off." He stuffed the those days!"

A CAB man described his first taste of bush style flying, on his initial inspection trip into the Territory. The "air line" with which he was supposed to make his first flight turned out to be a one-man, one-plane operation, with no fixed schedule or rates. "You my passenger?" the pilot asked cheerfully." Well, guess we might as well take off." He stuffed the man from Washington into the plane, then threw in freight "up to my neck," according to the inspector. After taking off in a questionable overcast ("I want to see my girl over at McGrath tonight, so I think I'll try to make it through"), the pilot flew along awhile, then plunked his plane down, without warning, "in the middle of nowhere," near an isolated cabin out in the Interior. A woman waved at the plane and shouted that since her wash wasn't quite dry, they'd have to wait a moment. "Might as well come inside," the pilot told the inspector affably, and the two men went up to the house, sat on the porch, and drank lemonade and ate cookies until the washing dried. Then the pilot helped the woman fold her clean clothes, she got her hat, locked the door—and the three took off.

"And we were supposed to turn that kind of operation into a scheduled, profitable business!" sighed the CAB man.

There was little doubt that the Alaskan scene was ripe for some sort of government control, both to stabilize the flyers' business and to insure safety measures and scheduled service for the passengers It was the inevitable and necessary control that eventually comes, as a civilizing influence, to frontier communities. But like the frontiersmen of our western plains, the flying frontiersmen of the Far North had a unanimous reaction: "What the hell!" After all these years, who was going to tell them how to run their business?

The laws and regulations written in Washington were based on conditions in the States, which were not always applicable to the unique physical and climatic conditions in the Territory. There was a several-year shakedown ahead for both the government agencies and the Alaskan flyers before an equable arrangement was reached, and only within the past few years has commercial aviation in the Far North become the healthy, profitable business for which the original legislation was designed.

Individual flyers met the inroads of legislation with attitudes ranging from disbelief to anger to downright terror.

"The first time I went before an aviation board," reports shy, quiet Noel Wien, "I thought it was just a friendly gathering. Then they started putting me on the carpet, firing questions at me—and I realized I better get a lawyer fast, or keep my mouth shut. I was scared to death. I went out of there wiping the sweat off my face."

It was a headache both ways. "They had no concept of government, they didn't know the difference between the functions of Civil Aeronautics Administration and the Civil Aeronautics Board," reports a CAB man. "First time I went up there, I was taking a reading on whether a pilot's business was furnishing adequate returns, and in an effort to impress me with how law-abiding he was, he insisted on weighing *me* as well as the freight! All I wanted to know was whether he was making money or not."

In order to give the Alaskan carriers the benefits of the CAA legislation, CAB inspectors had to have accurate accounts from the air lines, to determine whether or not the business was being efficiently run and whether it was entitled to government subsidy in the form of mail pay. But the bush pilots' systems of accounting proved a little less than adequate by government standards. "Most of the boys kept a record sheet of some kind," explained Owen Meals, with a twinkle. "One side was labeled Intake, the other Exhaust. They usually had more entries under Exhaust."

As late as 1944, when CAB member Robert J. Bartoo was in Alaska on an inspection tour, he found one flyer faced with what the pilot regarded as an insurmountable problem. A man had paid him in advance for a series of flying lessons. The pilot had mastered the art of entering a single cash payment correctly in his books, but, he asked Bartoo seriously, "What can you do with a thing like this?" Before the inspector's arrival the pilot temporarily solved his dilemma by leaving the full payment in a cigar box, by itself, in a drawer on one side of his desk. As each lesson was taken, he removed the amount for that one lesson, added it to his cash, and entered it as paid in his books.

Flyer Tony Schwamm—famous for having once made a landing on the back of a whale—greeted Bartoo's second trip with scarcely concealed delight. "I've got a whole new accounting system," he boasted proudly. The "new system" turned out to be a metal box with three compartments, a triplicate record sheet, and a part-time secretary. When, after looking over the entries, Bartoo explained to the girl that she must also charge tax and enter it, she burst into tears. "You're going to make me keep *two* books!"

The bush pilots had a hard time understanding the necessity of all this high-powered accounting. "If the government would just let me keep my records on a grocery pad in my hip pocket like I used to," sighed Ray Petersen wistfully, "we'd both have more money!"

When word came from the government that CAB was ready to descend on Alaska, Tony Dimond, Alaska's delegate to Congress, sent hasty notice to all the pilots in the Territory. With this terrifying prospect before them, the bush pilots decided that, for their own safety, they must band together. "We all rushed around and put on our white shirts and shined up our airplanes," recalls Merle Smith. "Then we decided to have a meeting."

For the first time in all their scrapping, competitive years, the Alaskan pilots turned to each other. They had a common enemy—government interference. There was more than just frontiersmen's hatred of regulation behind this. What few government people had turned up in the isolated, forgotten Territory to sporadically check the pilots were not particularly good representatives of national law and order. Like the British administrators who find themselves out in the remote colonies, the "remittance men" who for some perhaps personal reason were selected to be sent off to the "wilds of Alaska" were not always top-drawer personnel. Nor did they have any superiors on hand to check and see if they practiced a little shakedown, or "souvenir collecting" as it was called by the pilots. Most of the flyers had an active hatred for one official, whom we shall call Rooster, as perhaps they would have hated any outside interference. When someone asked Reeve why his friend Gillam kept three polar bears out at the Fairbanks field, Reeve snapped, "So he can name one Rooster and kick it in the tail every time he walks by!" Handsome, black-haired Ada Arthur Wien, accosted by Rooster on the main street of Fairbanks, pushed past, saying icily, "Some of the pilots may have to cater to you—but that doesn't apply to their wives!" There was no question that the feeling between the flyers and government men was far from good.

When the pilots convened at the Idlehour night club in Anchorage for their meeting, the night before they were all to appear before the CAB examiner, it was the first time in the history of Alaskan aviation that all the pilots in the Territory had assembled under one roof. "It was," reports Ray Petersen with a shake of his curly head, "just like a bunch of lions and panthers tossed in one cage!"

All the bitter competitors of years standing found themselves face to face in one room. The shock was too much. The "common foe" they had gathered to combat faded before ancient animosities, which rushed to the surface. "And," added Mudhole Smith with a twinkle, "a lot of new ones were made!"

"It was such a brawl," the report went round the Territory, "that *even Noel Wien took a drink!*"

Everyone got loaded. The next morning when Tillie took two-year-old Richard into the hotel coffee shop for breakfast, the waitress asked the child, "Honey, where's your daddy?"

and Richard answered, quite truthfully, "In bed with an *awful* hangover!"

Between drinks, at the meeting, various pilots aired their opinions. Reeve climbed on the table and spat out his hatred of CAB and said what he intended to do about it. There were roaring arguments, herculean consumption of refreshments, and eventually a rolling, howling swarm of fist fights. Of them all, only Harold Gillam remained serious, unruffled, thoughtful, concerned with the real purpose of the conclave. When Gillam got up on a table to make his speech, he was so eloquent that the other men actually stopped fighting long enough to listen.

Gillam had a cool, analytical mind, which held sway over his emotions. He, alone of all the pilots, had actually studied the imminent legislation and understood what it meant. It was, he realized, inevitable—just as he, unlike his laissez-faire associates, knew that in the future instrument flying was inevitable. It was the only way accurate schedules and efficient service could be maintained. He cautioned his colleagues that the modern air age was inexorably upon them and they must all prepare for it. Gillam didn't like government either—but he bowed to the future. The only thing to do, he urged them, was to make a clear statement of their facilities, their standing as pilots. Know what they wanted and ask for it. Show that they had a right to it. There was no point, he warned, in trying to fight anything as powerful as the law.

Although Gillam's "nerveless" nature withstood the emotional inslaught of the wild evening, the little man misjudged his physical capacities. Next morning, when all the battered, bruised, hung-over pilots poured in for the CAB hearings, Gillam was not among them. The pilots turned to each other, whispering curiously, "Where's Harold?" They had counted on his calming influence. They wanted to hear that wonderful statement he was going to make. But, alas, as time drew near, Harold was still among the missing. When the examiner finally reached his name, called out "Gillam Airways," there was silence. Not even Harold's lawyer was there!

As they neared the R's in the list, Reeve, exploding with all he wanted to say, bounced up and started talking.

"You're out of order," snapped the examiner.

"The hell I am," Reeve shouted. "Whenever I stand up in a crowd, I'm in order."

When the meeting was adjourned, some of the boys went to Gillam's room to see what had happened, found Harold sleeping off his "load" of the night before. They shook him awake, threw a little water in his face, and told him it was all over.

"The meeting's over!" Harold paled. "I've got to get a record of it." Pulling on his clothes, he raced downstairs, located a stenographer, and hired her to make a copy of the official record.

Twenty minutes after the girl was well at work, one of the pilots tapped Harold's shoulder. "Harold," he whispered, "did you know that thing'll cost you twenty-five bucks before she's through?"

Harold stopped the girl, who had completed four pages. He didn't have the cash to pay her for that much. And he never did get a copy of that hearing.

In order to allot territories in some sort of equable fashion, CAB granted charters to the Alaskan pilots under the famous "grandfather rights" clause, which determined a pilot's territory according to what he had been using for a period of four months prior to the passage of the Civil Aeronautics Act. Carriers operating during the period between May 14 and August 22, 1938, could file an application for a certificate for the route they were then using. Due to an odd quirk of fate, Bob Reeve was caught on this particular fishhook.‡ Although he had been servicing, most of the time solely, the Valdez area for the past six or seven years, the grandfather clause caught Reeve in the period when he was without planes. His most recent flying came out on the records as aerial mapping in the Fairbanks area, temporary work he had picked up when he found much of his old business taken over by other pilots. He put in a request to CAB that he be granted exclusive certificate for his old territory around Valdez, which he had pioneered. He knew, from the past years, that it would support no more than one full-time operator.

Reeve's request was denied. He was given certificate to one area only, the Copper River. His competitors were certifi-

‡ By another peculiar quirk, Ray Petersen was awarded the territory between Bethel and Anchorage, which showed up as his major area, since he was at that time based at Bethel and courting a girl who lived in Anchorage. "The only reason I have an air line today!"

cated to base at nearby Cordova and Gakona, with freedom to base and do business at Valdez.

The examiner's report set Reeve's quick temper to the raging point. In government terms, Reeve's operator didn't stack up very well. His equipment, the report found, was "one 5-place Fairchild monoplane, originally purchased in 1932. Plane damaged in windstorm and repairs not completed." His "only ground facilities consist of a small shed, which is used for the storage of gasoline supplies and tools." It mentioned that he had no steady employees and that his financial abilities were limited, and ended up, "It is apparent that public convenience and necessity do not require air transportation of persons and property beyond the Copper River area." In short, his hazardous ten-year record was being marked off as, Bob puts it, a "junk operation."

Reeve filed an exception, which has become part of the history of commercial aviation, and a favorite laughing point for the now amicable government agencies and commercial lines!

But Bob was far from laughter when he framed his reply. His fiery language was the enraged roar of a wounded bull:

> If we pilots who made Alaska what it is today had waited until the outlying bush and mountain "required" airplane transportation by virtue of public convenience and necessity, this Territory would be today just about nothing but a worthless wilderness. The oldtime Alaskan operator who made the country what it is was a man who made business where there had never been business before; he was a man who in most instances was forced to hustle and rustle or starve. It was the rustler who survived. I have deliberately gone prospecting with my airplane and discovered, staked and sold gold mining property at far below its actual value for the sole purpose of building up airplane transportation business to that district. On one property alone over $90,-000 has been spent for transportation, wages, machinery, etc. Gentlemen, suppose I had waited until that district or any of those other districts required service by virtue of public convenience and necessity? It would still be a wilderness. . . .

Furious at the tiny area allotted him, which he knew in advance could not support him and his family, Reeve turned down his certificate. "I regret to advise the Civil Aeronautics Board . . . that I find it impossible to subordinate my plans for the future to accord with Mr. Stough's (the examiner's) scheme for my regimentation. . . . Perceiving that under these rules . . . Reeve Airways of Valdez was a doomed organization . . . I moved my family and activities . . . to Fairbanks and am engaged in my old occupation of general charter operator. . . ."

In a rage at what he considered a totally unjust decision, Reeve packed up Tillie, the children,** his mother-in-law (who had come to Alaska on a visit—and stayed), and the cat in his Fairchild, and with sixty-five dollars which he borrowed to pay the first month's rent headed for Fairbanks.

"I was forty years old, with a growing family, one beat-up plane, and no future," says Bob. "I had to start out all over again and carve out a business somewhere."

When the family flew into Fairbanks that January day, the temperature registered sixty degrees below zero. "At least," says Bob wryly, "we had a warm house to move into. The landlady had to keep the fires going to keep the pipes from freezing."

When he left Valdez, broke, desperate, angry, Bob left behind a record of over two thousand glacier landings and over a million pounds of freight dropped into the surrounding mines; and, as Rex Beach had said years before, "the most thrilling story of adventure in the air I have ever heard."

He was also in debt. "Which was not unusual for anyone in those times," commented George Ashby. "What was unusual about Bob was, he came back later and paid off."

At the apparently bleakest period of Reeve's career, fortune, in a grim guise, lay just around the corner.

---

** The Reeves' second child, Roberta, was born the spring before they left Valdez.

# 10. "He who holds Alaska will hold the world"

When a friend once asked Seward what he considered the most important measure of his political career, he replied, "The purchase of Alaska—but it will take the people a generation to find it out." Just sixty-eight years later (February, 1935) in a speech before the House Military Affairs Committee, outspoken prophet of aviation General Billy Mitchell said, "Alaska is the most central place in the world for aircraft and that is true either of Europe, Asia or North America . . . I believe in the future he who holds Alaska will hold the world, and *I think it is the most strategic place in the world*." Mitchell recommended that Army planes and flyers be installed at strategic points over the Territory and out on the Aleutian chain.

But peacetime America was not yet ready to obey such a warning, nor change her traditional attitude of indifference to Uncle Sam's attic—that remote, desolate, cold country so far to the north. In 1937, when aviation inspector Hugh Brewster made a report to Washington, in line with the proposed regulation of Alaskan airways, he pondered the problem of establishing any sort of scheduled air service under the existing conditions. There were no big commercial planes in Alaska (let alone powerful, fast-landing military aircraft) for the simple reason that there were no adequate facilities for any. Although the bush pilots had, in 1937, kept their little planes in the air for a record 5,644,461 passenger miles, there was not a federal paved airstrip, a lighted field, or a radio beam in the Territory. Air route weather forecasting was nonexistent. Hourly reports often proved to be no more than booby traps. All flying was still contact, performed visually in daylight hours with single-engine planes which could be safely brought down on any likely looking sand bar or smooth patch of tundra. There was little effort at any sort of regulated schedules.

144

The only approach to a scheduled service, according to Mr. Brewster's report, was Pan Am's attempt at a weekly schedule between Juneau and Nome, using ships equipped with a two-way radio and ground stations set up along the route. In reviewing Pan Am's effort, Brewster said, "It remains for organizations of this type to determine whether scheduled operation is feasible in the Territory and if not, to lead the way in making the already common charter service safer and more reliable by the addition of emergency fields and weather reporting facilities." CAA mapped out a plan for an orderly development of Alaskan aviation, through the construction of a network of airfields and facilities across the Territory, such as had been set up in the States. But civilian pressure for funds was not enough to get the program under way. Although proposed in 1937, it was not until 1939-1940, when military leaders took over the project, that a beginning was actually made. The first appropriation went for the construction of a cold-weather station at Fairbanks (the Interior of Alaska is colder than the coastal area north of the Arctic Circle, which is tempered by the sea.)

Although it took Hitler's shadow across Europe to force a fresh appraisal of the potentially strategic position of Alaska in American defense, there was one Cassandra voice on the Alaskan scene who had already turned warnings into action. CAA official Chris Lample had become so impressed with the necessity for strategic fields in the Alaskan theater that he took it upon himself to order the construction of an airfield out at Cold Bay, at the end of the Alaskan peninsula, where it juts westward, by way of the Aleutian archipelago, toward Russia and Japan. When authorities in Washington found that Lample had gone ahead on his own, without authorization, to build an airfield out at the beginning of that bleak arc of fogbound, submerged mountains, Lample was called on the carpet, his job in jeopardy. When the Japenese bombed Pearl Harbor, however, the Aleutians suddenly took on vital and urgent importance, and Lample was praised for his farsightedness. That desolate string of volcanic islands about which Lample was so concerned provided our one real threat of enemy occupation of American soil.

Despite the handful of men like Lample, "Hap" Arnold, Twining, and Alaskan Delegate Dimond who were seriously considering the necessity of converting the barren North into an active wartime front, most Alaskans, long accustomed to being ignored in federal plans, were not giving much thought to the strategic position of the Territory. Certainly the foremost thought in Bob Reeve's mind, the winter he moved his family to Fairbanks, was the immediate problem of making a living. He could hardly know that the imminent threat of war would inadvertently bring to him, as it was to bring to all Alaska, the first real chance of economic security.

That the Territory would soon become the hub of wartime strategy and its deserted wastelands would soon buzz with fleets of military planes was scarcely evident to anyone living in Fairbanks in 1940. Like Valdez a town born of a gold strike (1901), Fairbanks had within the first year of its existence become the "biggest log-cabin town" in the world, boasting a population of eight thousand—and had dropped steadily ever since. Although still the only major-sized town in Alaska's vast Interior, its population, by 1940, was less than two thousand.* The log cabins that sprawled along the winding Chena River were now mixed with a sprinkling of frame cottages, but the streets were no more than wide dirt gashes, and as yet no one had figured how to install plumbing systems in the permafrost that lay a few feet below the city streets.† Fairbanks winters, Tillie found, meant a constant struggle to keep warm ("We had a furnace which periodically blew up!"); summers a constant struggle to "keep clean" as clouds of dust swirled in from the street outside, where trucks roared in from the Richardson Highway.

Yet Fairbanks had its pride. "The Golden Heart" of Alaska, it called itself. There was a tight clique of "old-timers" who dated back to the gold-strike days. And Fairbanks could boast that, of all Alaskan settlements, it had been foremost in the encouragement of aviation.

Out at Weeks Field, Bob Reeve found himself in the company of old-time friends Noel Wien and Harold Gillam, who had moved his base of operations from Cordova to Fairbanks in 1935. Gillam, Reeve discovered, was in a new phase of his career; his youthful daring had given way to scientific ex-

---

* Fairbanks, like Anchorage, became a war-built city, reaching its present population of 35,000 during the decade following World War II.

† This has now been solved by running "hot" electric wires along water pipes.

actness and a fascination with modern air navigational techniques. When Inspector Brewster had referred to Pan Am's project as "the only attempt at scheduled service" in the Territory, he had overlooked Gillam's private project. Although he personally reveled in the dart-and-swoop method of contact flying, at which he was an undisputed master, Gillam was aware that there would be no real aviation progress until flights could be put on exact schedules. And no exact schedules were possible without instruments. The first pilot in the Territory to install his own radio, Gillam was operating all his flights on tight schedules, with the aid of a directional gyro, a sensitive altimeter, and an artificial horizon which he installed in his twelve-place Pilgrim monoplanes (made by Fairchild). He had, however, no de-icing equipment, and no radio beam to follow. But he religiously practiced "blind flying" through the hazardous Alaskan weather. While Pan Am was still using a code and key, Gillam installed the first radio phone and an ADF direction finder. Since he needed a "home" installation to tune in on, and no stations were available in Fairbanks, he hooked up a battery charger in front of the transmitter at the field, which transmitted a signal on which he could tune in. "It knocked out all the radios in the area," reports Tom Appleton (Gillam's mechanic, who is now general manager of Reeve Alaska Airmotive in Anchorage), "and we had the Signal Corps on our necks all the time."

In 1936 Gillam had made a series of experimental high altitude flights for the Weather Bureau, to determine the condition of air masses (Jack Jefford did this same sort of weather testing in Oklahoma City in 1935, before he came to Alaska). The contract called for a twice-daily schedule, in which Gillam had to climb to six thousand feet (he could not dodge around, since he had to make exactly three hundred feet per minute), then come down in tight spirals. The weather instruments were attached externally on the wing struts, and installed and removed by weather bureau personnel at each flight. In winter the take-offs were performed before daylight in the morning; the last one after dark. During these "blind" operations, Tom Appleton stood below, on the field, and talked Gillam down by listening to the sound of his engine. If the flight was not made by exact specifications (regardless of weather), Gillam was penalized. In two years of year-round weather testing he was penalized only three times.

In 1937, when Sigismund Levanevsky, the Soviet Union's most popular Arctic flyer, was lost on a polar flight from Moscow to Fairbanks, an international search was begun, with flyers from Russia, Canada, and the United States, the latter led by Sir Hubert Wilkins. When the Russian consul asked Alaskan delegate Tony Dimond to find the Alaskan pilot best qualified for the search, he recommended Gillam. The Russians wanted the Alaskan flyer to take equipment up north of the Arctic Circle to Point Barrow, so they could set up a listening post in hopes of making contact with the lost plane. Gillam relayed the equipment to Barrow in a series of flights from Fairbanks north to the Arctic Ocean that made Alaskan aviation history. Flying without air navigational aids through recurrent fog and white-out across the flat, treeless tundra to the tiny speck of a village on the Arctic Ocean, Gillam "bored through" fog and weather on a regular schedule that left other pilots shaking their heads in amazement. Trader Charley Brower told of times when "Harold could not have seen anything till he hit the ice" at Barrow, yet somehow he always managed to get in. Those flights, in the opinion of Merle Smith, constitute "the greatest flying ever done."

Gillam's unique methods of conquering the elements were not answers that any other man could use. When he took over Pan Am's mail run from Fairbanks to Bethel in 1938, he established an unheard-of record of 100 per cent completed schedules. Pan Am had flown the route "sensibly," waiting out good, or as it got to be laughingly call, "Pan Am" weather. From a service standpoint, their project was pitiful. "We could set your watch by dog teams," complained the customers in the twenty-odd scattered villages along the five-hundred-mile route, "but no one knows when the airplanes are coming." But when Gillam took over, they could know—to the minute, regardless of what capricious horrors the elements were cooking up outside. Other pilots began referring to howling storms as "Gillam weather."

Ray Petersen described a day in 1939 when the platinum mines had just closed in Goodnews Bay and "all the miners wanted to get out at once." There were forty paid fares ready to move, and the old-timers were out to collect them: Chet Browne, who'd been flying out of Nome since 1930; Kenny Nese; Johnny Moore; Roy Holm; and Ray himself, who had by now put in a tough five years in Alaska that had "wised him up." "The weather was not flyable," Ray says flatly, "but one guy made the break out of Anchorage, and the stampede started. We all wound up at Bethel and spent the night. Next morning there was a blind snowstorm blowing—and we all just sat there, cooling our heels. A fellow there at the road-house was a ham radio operator and had a set. He got the word Gillam had just taken off from Fairbanks on his regular mail run. There was not a mile's visibility from Bethel to Fairbanks. Hearing that Harold was out flying, the boys were shamed—and took off. All but me, I wasn't that shamed! Chet Browne was back in ten minutes. "It just ain't possible to fly in that stuff." Kenny Neese lasted thirty minutes. Johnny Moore landed in the slough. Roy Holm, the youngest of the bunch, got a hundred miles upriver before he had to quit.

"When Harold reached Bethel, which was the end of the mail run, we were still sitting there. He walked casually into the roadhouse where we all were, calm as if he'd just come off a church picnic. 'Well, Harold,' Chet said, 'suppose you're turning around and flying back to McGrath?'

" 'Yes,' Harold calmly, 'I will.' He stayed long enough to warm his hands and get his plane gassed up—and then took off again into the blizzard. Three days later the rest of us were still sitting in Bethel—and Harold had made it back to Fair-banks, and completed his mail run on schedule."

It was a common occurrence, Noel Wien (who taught Gil-lam to fly) told Bob, for the Pan Am pilots to take off from Fairbanks and get weathered in at McGrath, be sitting there waiting out the weather, and have Gillam fly in, unload, take off. "Then darned if he wouldn't come through on his second trip—and those boys would still be there!"

All sorts of reasons are given for Gillam's phenomenal suc-cess at boring through blind weather, from facts to superstitions. There is dour talk of "cat eyes" that could see through fog and dark. Pilots point out that Gillam sat high above the engine of his high-winged Pilgrim monoplane, where he had exceptional visibility. Although he had no beam, he was al-ways "fiddling with instruments." When Ray Petersen asked him about his technique, Gillam said, "I keep my instruments in good shape. If you can't see, lock yourself on instruments at two hundred feet altitude. Eventually you will see a refer-ence point." To fly instruments, contact, at two hundred feet altitude, says Ray soberly, "took nerves of steel."

Another reason for Gillam's success, Reeve feels, can be attributed to mechanic Tom Appleton. Despite Gillam's early record of "running out of planes" in his Cordova days, from the time he came to Fairbanks and bought his own planes and Tom "nursemaided" them, Gillam never had engine trouble. Once Gillam told Reeve, "I pay Tom five hundred dollars a month [which was very high in those days]. I wish I could pay him double that!" Warm-hearted, competent Tom Appleton worshipped everything about his silent, handsome, ambitious boss. Except for one thing: the three polar bear cubs Gillam brought back from Point Barrow. Natives had shot the mother and dragged the hide in, and the cubs followed the hide. Taciturn Gillam, who had a soft spot for birds and animals (he couldn't stand to shoot a bird), brought the cubs home with him, raised them on bread and milk and cod liver oil, and kept them penned out at the Fairbanks field. But despite the lack of meat or fish in their diet, the cubs grew—into 650-pound bears! It was Tom's job to care for them. "I had to scrounge all the stale bread in town every day."

Reeve saw Tom out at the field at six o'clock one morning, found him still there at six in the evening, "Well, Tom," he said, "you're certainly putting in a long day!"

"Long day, hell," grunted Tom. "Two hours work—and all the rest of the time chasing those damn bears. I'm no chief mechanic, I'm a zoo-keeper!"

"It is due to the good heart of the people of Fairbanks," Tom reports gravely, "that Harold wasn't sued!" The bears periodically got loose, scratched people, raided gardens. They even managed to bite a few curious hands from their cages. But fortunately no one was seriously hurt.

One summer morning a carload of police roared up to Tom's cabin at the edge of Fairbanks. "Bears are loose!" Tom got a rifle and a car and drove into town. Since it was summer, the citizens of Fairbanks had their doors open, and the cubs were busily running up and down the narrow alleys, emptying garbage pails, then sticking their huge, sharp-nosed, curious faces into the open doors of houses. Tom started chasing them, trying to herd them out of town. But the bears were having much too exciting a time, poking around, making people scream. Tom gave up chasing them, got a whole fish, cut it up, bought nembutal tablets from the druggist, laced each piece of fish with the drug, then scattered them along the street. The bears obediently followed the pieces of fish to the outskirts of town. There the cubs saw some huge cabbage heads lying in a field and stopped for a game of ball. Then they got sleepy and started home, but the biggest one collapsed, asleep, before he made it to the cage. Tom had to get a cat tractor and haul him in.

Eventually Gillam sold the bears to the Bronx Zoo. Caged, on the truck, on the way to be shipped out, one of them managed to catch her head on a bar of her cage and hang herself before Tom could chop away the piece and set her free. She dropped dead to the floor of the cage, and the other two came over and felt of her. She was getting cold. They put their paws around her and lay against her, trying to warm her back to life. Even Tom felt sad about the poor old nuisances. The other two made it to the Zoo and, for all Tom knows, may still be there.

Although Gillam, with his heart set on a full-scale, scheduled airline, was working out instrument flying in his own fashion, Jack Jefford was the only pilot in the Territory who actually had an instrument rating. While flying weather tests in the States before he came to Alaska, he had applied for and gotten his rating, and when the federal airways came into Alaska in 1939 and decided to hire an Alaskan-trained pilot, Jefford was the only man qualified.

When the first federal airways were established over the four newly constructed CAA range stations at Fairbanks, Anchorage, Ruby, and Nome, Jefford began pioneering instrument flying in Alaska. A low-frequency simultaneous range, which gave four courses, was installed at the new fields, and Jefford made instrument approaches by orally following the beam, listening with headphones for a steady tone. The main problem with this type of equipment—which led to the eventual development of the modern omnidirectional range, which is followed visually—was that in the worst weather, when you most needed the beam, it was hard to hear it, due to snow static and electrical interference, especially severe in Alaskan skies. A brilliant bush-style flyer (Gillam was so impressed with Jefford's ability that he offered him a job the first time he watched him fly), big, easy tempered, black-haired Jefford, with his combined knowledge of contact and instrument techniques, was a perfect choice to test modern aviation aids in the Far North, and help prepare the way for safe flying for both commercial and military aircraft.

Reeve's first charter in Fairbanks came from an unexpected quarter. Noel Wien, whose territory Reeve had infringed upon when he came into Fairbanks, offered Bob a temporary freighting contract. "After I took a good look at that landing spot on Windy Creek," says Bob drily, "I couldn't decide whether Noel chartered me because of my hungry family—or because he didn't want to do anything that rough himself!"

Whatever the motivations, it was the cement of a lifetime friendship. This unexpected generosity where he anticipated a cold shoulder melted Reeve's suspicions, and he added Noel to his small list of "great friends." Actually, competitiveness and high pressure were foreign to Noel's quiet personality. Anything he'd won was simply the result of persistent work. "There would have been enough for all of us," he recalls in a gentle, wistful voice, "if everyone had played fair." The presence of the "bad boys" of Alaskan aviation, with their cutthroat practices, unethical flyers like wild, redheaded Dorbrandt and A. A. Bennett, who obeyed no rules and wished no good for their fellow flyers, had put all the men on their guard, caused them to distrust each other.

Reeve was fascinated watching Noel work. "He was a master flyer," Bob says admiringly. Known for his quiet deliberateness, his native caution, and refusal to be stampeded into anything smacking of danger, it is sometimes forgotten that Noel actually did some of the most important pioneer flying in Alaka. He made the first landing north of the Arctic Circle, the first nonstop flight from Fairbanks to Nome (which took seven hours in his clumsy Dutch Fokker). With his brothers, Sig, Ralph, and mechanic Fritz, Noel pioneered commercial flying north of the Arctic Circle.‡

The first flyer in the Territory after Ben Eielson, Noel arrived in 1924, and, when Eielson went to the States, he was for two years the only flyer, with the only plane, in the Territory. When he set out from Fairbanks, he knew ahead of time there would be no one to search for him if he were lost. He

‡ Ralph Wien was killed in a crash at Kotzebue in 1929; the three others run Wien Alaska Airlines, one of the most successful operations in the Territory. Sig is president, Fritz is in charge of operations, and Noel divides his time between office work as director of public relations and his real love, flying bush.

played it cagey, refusing to fly in anything but the best of weather, inching his way cautiously into the inevitable danger that lay around him. Each day he ran four miles around the Fairbanks field to keep up his leg muscles in case he came down on the Arctic tundra somewhere and had to mush out. And he did mush out—once over ninety miles through muskeg swamp in spring breakup.

Noel's friends loved to tease him about how he overloaded his airplanes. "Noel could handle a Fairchild with a 50 per cent overload with the same ease that I could with a normal load," says Bob. Both cautious in their own fashion, Bob would not risk the high overloads that Noel took on consistently. Once Hugh Brewster collared Bob on the streets of Fairbanks, peered into his face, and demanded, "Do you overload?"

"Of course I do," admitted Bob.

Disconcerted by this unexpected honesty, Brewster released his hold on Bob's collar. "Well," he said plaintively, "not 100 per cent like the other boys!"

"Any commitment, for Noel, was like a gold bond," says Bob. The Windy Creek assignment, for which he hired Bob, had been contracted for by a young pilot, flying for the Wien brothers, who then went on vacation and couldn't do the job. Windy Creek, Bob found, was a "unique experience." It was located in a narrow canyon in the Chandalar River country, and fierce winds and blowing snow spilled out of the canyon "like the milltails of hell." Trees were scattered around in the ice and snow, creating the unique, for Reeve, combined hazard of trees and williwaws. Landing conditions were next to impossible. Bob didn't like it a bit. But he got in enough of the mine supplies to satisfy Noel—and get himself back on his financial feet again. With the rent paid and groceries in the house, Bob was ready to take any and every charter he could pick up, flying trappers out to their camps, serving mines in the interior, carrying fur-buyers. He found that the district around the Upper Tanana River had been somewhat neglected by the other pilots based at Fairbanks—the Wien brothers, Gillam, Frank Pollack, and Bill Lavery—and Bob began picking up some business down there. One February afternoon when he flew into Tetlin, sourdough trader and trapper John Hajduckovich, known locally as John Hi-duke, met him with the news of an emergency at the Nabesna Indian village. He had had a call from Lucille Wright, the government nurse stationed there, that there was a baby ill with pneumonia that must be flown in to a hospital immediately. With John along for company, Reeve flew to Nabesna and landed on the river. Since it was already dark, they waited till the following morning, then loaded the nurse and baby and headed in for Fairbanks. Following the Tanana River bed, between tree-lined banks, Reeve ran into the beautiful and terrible winter phenomenon of Alaska's interior: ice fog. The moisture in the air freezes, blanketing trees, houses, and streets with an unearthly beauty. When he hit the patch of ice fog, as he followed the narrow river a few feet above the bed, Bob saw before him a complete white-out. His forward visibility had suddenly dropped to zero, and he was in it. He saw spires of trees rising up to meet him. There was no way to turn back, or even a choice of going on emergency instruments. He continued forward into the icy white blanket. In minutes the plane had iced up—the windshield, the wings, even the propeller. He had no alternative but to cut the throttle and land straight ahead— trusting that there were no bends in the river bed below. (Alaska's rivers are the crookedest in the world.) The Fairchild settled on a snowdrift in the river bed, missing a piled-up ice jam by inches with the left ski.

It was the Ole Hay trip all over over. Fifty below zero and a baby for a passenger. Bob quickly fashioned a tent from his wing covers, made up a pot of hot soup from his emergency rations; and he and John worked at keeping up the fire during the night. As soon as it was daylight, Reeve knocked the ice off the wings and propeller, warmed up the engine, and took off, in about a hundred-foot ceiling. But they had to get going. Another few hours' exposure, and the sick baby was doomed. As they left their camping site, John pointed down to the river below. "Good thing you landed where you did, Bob. There's a sharp bend right ahead."

Flying for about fifty miles under the hundred-foot ceiling, Bob finally came out in the clear, and delivered his passengers safely to Fairbanks. The child recovered. Old John had proved the perfect passenger for the let-down, helpful and handy. It was "routine" for the old trader, who had come down innumerable times with flyers Bennett, Art Hines, and Vic Ross.

Flying the Interior posed a set of problems different from the coastal, glacial, and mountain work in which Bob had specialized. He had to learn about tundra—the endless wasteland that looks flat and seems harmless as you let down, only to find that one of those "niggerheads," that little bunch of grass, turns out to be a hummock so tough that it can turn your plane onto its back. Past the Arctic Circle, north of Fairbanks, are the ever recurrent white-outs, when sky and land and sea become one color, with no horizon line, no reference points, not a single tree or mountain to guide by. Just the hundreds of snakelike, twisting rivers that all look alike, and the thousands of pothole ponds, one indistinguishable from the other. When Noel Wien and his friend, Anchorage flyer Russ Merrill (Noel's eldest son, flyer Merrill Wien, is named for him), made the first commercial flight to Point Barrow in 1928 for the Fox Film Company, they learned what a nightmare Arctic flying can be. Forced down by fog fifty miles short of their destination, the two planes made a landing on one of the myriad lakes that dot the tundra. Next morning Noel was able to get his plane off, and he flew on to Barrow with the promise to return for his friend. However, when Noel flew back for Merrill, to his growing horror he could not locate the particular lake where they had landed and pick it out from the hundreds and hundreds of similar ones. Days went by. Other flyers joined the search. It was a week before Merrill's two passengers were finally picked up, ill from exposure, by flyer Matt Nieminen, as they straggled on foot toward Barrow. It was another week before Merrill was found by trader John Hagnis, his face blackened, light-headed, and feverish from a diet of raw lemmings, from which he never fully recovered.

There was the yearly nightmare of the spring breakup when the Interior, according to one pilot, becomes "a land of icy rivers and lakes, surrounded by water." The first warm weather brings thaws that send the rivers into rushing torents, and make a bed of slush out of the topsoil of the tundra, which cannot drain, due to the permafrost beneath, but remains a trap of rotten snow and jutting hummock, a few yards of which exhausts a full-grown man, since each step sends him waist deep into icy water. After four precarious years of flying the Anchorage area and "smashing up a lot of planes," Ray Petersen had, in 1938, just managed to pay his debts and buy a plane, a Ryan B-1, which he was flying into Goodnews Bay ("I was flying along counting my money"—he estimated that with one good month he would be one thousand dollars in the clear), when a crankshaft broke, forcing him to land on a "smooth patch of tundra," whose hummocks rose to meet him, shearing off his landing gear. His freight load of eight hundred pounds of frozen meat smashed the instrument panel, another piece of freight smashed the spars. And Ray was smashed right back into a five-thousand-dollar debt!

Landing on rotten ice during spring break-up—and going through—was a common situation for the old-time Interior pilots. Reeve got his first dunking the spring he moved to Fairbanks. With a pair of muskrat trappers who wanted to go to the Nabesna area for passengers, Reeve made a wheel landing on the ice of Harding Lake, where he intended to change over to skis, preparatory to the Nabesna landing, which would be on snow. The "apparently solid ice" he chose was rotted through. The Fairchild sank to its belly. "But I wasn't going to lose that airplane—it was the only one I had!" Reeve gave it the gun with a wide-open throttle. The prop took hold and lifted the plane partly out of the broken ice and water. Slashing through the rotten ice, the prop carried the plane along for about five hundred feet, finally lifted it up onto solid ice. Reeve got out to look at the damage. The prop was bent, and the belly of the fabric fuselage was torn out.

He rummaged in his supplies, came up with a gallon of airplane dope. Using the engine cover for fabric, he cut off a piece big enough to patch the belly and stuck it on, securing the fabric along the ribs with lengths of fishing cord. Then, after straightening the prop blades with his inevitable sledge hammer, Reeve took off and successfully completed the trip.

The outer appearance of their planes, and the interior beauty, were not a consideration to most bush operators—except for Gillam, who liked "clean, shiny" interiors and neat paint job on the outside, just as he liked fastidious clothes that showed the trim lines of his body. (A deep-sea diver and wrestler in the Navy before coming to Alaska, Gillam had what a man friend described as "the most perfect body I have ever seen.") Reeve's particular brand of snobbishness went in the reverse direction. He liked things to show wear and tear, serviceability. He sneered at "spit and polish." The interior of his old Fairchild 51 in which he made his most spectacular glacier flights was so unique that Rex Beach described it in detail in the novel *Valley of Thunder:* the flooring made from old grocery crates with the labels still on; the gouged and scarred woodwork; the latch repaired with twisted bailing wire; the torn leather seat with the spring coils protruding. "A model T of a plane" some called it. "A sourdough." Beside the pilot's seat, in all of his planes, Bob kept a piece of sandpaper tacked to the side, to scratch matches on. A tide table hung from a peg. The question about a plane, for Reeve and most of the other bush flyers, was "will it fly?" As one pilot remarked wistfully, as he looked out at his wing, "I sure hope those termites keep holding hands." "Spare parts flying formation," said another. It was enough to give a Washington inspector something of a shock.

When he made it into Fairbanks with his patched plane that night, after going through the ice at Harding Lake, the news awaiting Bob at home was not good.

"Standard Oil man was here," Tillie reported, "and he refused to give me any oil for my stove until you pay them a forty-dollar bill they say you've owed for a year. If we're going to have any supper, you better get squared away."

Reeve went down to the Standard Oil Company to see Obie Reinseth, and demanded to know why he had refused to supply Tillie with fuel. They had had, argued Reeve, an Alaskan type of agreement, whereby he would pay when he got paid for a certain flying job. Reeve hadn't been paid—and in turn has not paid Reinseth. But since it was now a "humiliating issue," Reeve managed to cough up the cash—and increase some other, more sympathetic, debt.

Two years later Reeve had a modicum of revenge. With the war on, Reeve, who was flying for the Army, had a contract that stipulated that the Army provide him with fuel. When a lieutenant fresh from the States was reviewing the Army's accounts at Anchorage, he saw that Reeve had used up gas worth $32,000 in two years—and sent him a bill for it. The matter was promptly straightened out when Reeve produced his contract. But Bob kept the bill, and next time he was in Anchorage he cornered Reinseth. "Remember, Obie, how you worried about that forty-dollar gas bill I had on your books three years ago?" he asked.

"Yes, I haven't forgotten it," smiled Reinseth. "Particularly after that dressing down your wife gave me when I refused to give her any more oil."

"Well, Obie," Bob said, "I have a good gas company now that I do business with. I've got $32,000 worth of gas in the past two years and they only send me a bill once every two years. Take a look at this."

Reinseth looked at the bill, handed it back, and walked off without a word.

By April, 1940, a master plan for Alaskan defense, spearheaded by "Hap" Arnold, was at last under way. It called for the construction of a dozen airfields across the Territory, a northern air route reaching from the Canadian border on the east through to Nome on the west coast of Alaska—our shortest route from the United States to Asia and the Orient. An Army Air Corps base, Ladd Field, was being constructed at Fairbanks, and another, Elmendorf Air Base, at Anchorage. The network of fields was scheduled to be built from the southeastern entry into Alaska, at Ketchikan, across the continent to the west coast: Northway, Tanacross, Big Delta, Tanana, Galena, Moses Point, and Nome. Although no federal appropriations for this war-preparedness measure were scheduled until the time of emergency, the construction of the airfields was started, under CAA, without waiting for the necessary appropriation from Congress.

Reeve, one of the few flyers in the Territory who was freelancing without any certificated territory, was hired by the CAA to survey these new sites. This was the beginning of wartime service which led to Reeve's unique career as the only civilian operator under exclusive contract to the military, and eventually was to result in his pioneering the Aleutian run, which was to become his own individual air route.

# 11. The Northern air route

The problems of suddenly turning the Alaskan wilderness into an efficient defense front would, but for the necessity of war, have been virtually insurmountable. That it was accomplished in two short years is an amazing tribute to American ingenuity and patriotism. Stepchild of the States, with no voice of its own within the government, Alaska had been able to do little to divert any appropriations its way, and in 1940 was in about the same condition, so far as defense went, that it had been at the time of the Seward purchase. Although an evangelical Alaskan engineer named Donald MacDonald had been badgering the government with his plan for the construction of a highway from the States to Alaska since 1928, there was still, by 1940, no overland connection between the homeland and its frontier colony. When wartime emergency suddenly forced the hasty construction of Alaskan defenses, the only method available for transporting workers, troops, materials, and food was by slow boat from Seattle. There were no big planes for the job, since there were no adequate fields or navigational aids for them. In 1939 Jack Jefford had made headlines by flying from Seattle through to Nome in two days. (Pan Am was experimenting with Alaska-Seattle service and had built its own field at Juneau, large enough to accommodate multiengine equipment, but they had difficulty maintaining any sort of schedules due to the recurrent fogs and storms along the southeastern coast.)

Within the Territory, vital supplies had to depend on the vagaries of river boat in summer and cat tractor in winter to reach their destinations. Not only was there no overland route to Alaska, but, within this vast Territory, one-fifth the size of the entire United States, there was, in 1940, only one major road. It was only after the war had begun that a highway was built connecting the two major cities of Anchorage and Fairbanks. Construction of the international Alcan Highway finally achieved its long-awaited appropriation in 1942. A Negro worker from the States, looking out over the endless uninhabited tundra, forest, and mountain through which the highway was to be carved, shook his head and sighed his verdict: "Jes' miles and miles—of miles and miles!"

Much of the Interior was still unmapped. For CAA and military man alike, this was an untouched land with its own set of rules. The cold-weather experiment station, hastily erected at Fairbanks, was set up to determine what some of these new rules of operation were. Reeve and other Alaskan flyers assisted the military research program, by teaching Stateside Air Force personnel some of their own homemade devices for surviving Arctic flying. It was a completely new technique, which the military had to learn in double time.

By early 1940 the only armed forces in Alaska consisted of a couple of small infantry detachments in the southeast and a few scattered Navy and Coast Guard operations in the islands. But by mid-spring of that year, the first troops had begun to arrive. They poured into Anchorage to establish the Alaskan Defense Command, under the leadership of General Simon Bolivar Buckner.

While the Army and Navy concentrated on erecting bases at Anchorage, along the southern coast, and out on the Aleutians, CAA, under the direction of its Alaskan administrator Marshall Hoppin, set about the construction of the interior network of airways. For both CAA and the military alike, every item they needed for their accelerated work—from the workers themselves to their supplies, food, and clothing—had to be hauled up to Alaska by boat. There was no local source of supply—in the proportions the construction programs required—within the Territory. One CAA repair man, fresh from the States, arrived on his job with only the pliers and screwdriver in his back pocket for tools, and was forced to perform major radio repairs with this meager equipment. CAA mechanics soon learned to carry two hundred-pound tool kits wherever they went.

As soon as the survey of the network of airfields had been completed, the first and most important of them went into construction. Northway airfield was the "halfway port" between Whitehorse (in the Canadian Yukon) and Fairbanks, at a spot near the Nabesna Indian village in the Tanana River Valley, close to the Canadian border. Although there was no overland access to this spot, an airport was required, since the flight from Whitehorse to Fairbanks was too far for a plane to travel with no intermediate field. Already planes had been lost over this isolated, mountainous area.

Faced with the problem of how to get the tons of supplies they needed to construct a full-scale airport into the wilderness, the Morrison-Knudsen Company, which was to handle the construction for CAA, contracted Bob Reeve to fly in the supplies after they had been transported as far as was possible by overland means. Trucks could haul the equipment up the Richardson Highway, then over a "summer trail" as far as the Nabesna mine, about sixty miles from Northway.

On the first trip from Fairbanks into Northway, Reeve carried the Morrison-Knudsen foreman, the superintendent of construction, three shovels, three mattocks, twenty-four axes, and supplies for two men for two weeks, and landed them at Tetlin, about fifty miles northwest of the site. The two men then proceeded by river boat to the Northway site. There they hired a crew of twenty local Indians to tackle the job of carving a landing strip out of the forest, so that Reeve could begin bringing in men and supplies. The workmen literally hacked a little field out of forest, clearing off and leveling a hundred-foot by eight-hundred-foot strip in six days. For his base of operations, Reeve chose a smooth stretch of river bar on the Nabesna river bed, only about five miles from the Nabesna mine. The crated and barreled material was trucked from Valdez to the Nabesna mine, then loaded on athey wagons— flat-track wagons with continuous tractor treads—and hauled by cat tractors over the five miles of muskeg swamp to Bob's river-bar landing field. The muskeg was so soft that a trail could not be used repeatedly, and the atheys and cats were soon traveling all over the countryside, the muskeg "road" becoming miles wide. When the supplies reached Bob's field they were then cut into pieces by acetylene torch so that they could be loaded into the plane, and then rewelded at Northway. The entire airfield had to be hauled in this manner: from the navigational aid equipment to the tons of asphalt for paving runways, the workers, tools, and food.

All the necessary equipment could be carried by air with the exception of the big seventeen-ton "cats" and the twelve-ton scrapers. A Morrison-Knudsen crew, with Indian guides, set out to pick a path with the cats through the dense forests and icy streams, from Nabesna through to the Northway site. On one of Bob's flights in to the field, the foreman said uneasily, "You better take a look for those boys your next trip, Bob, they've been gone quite a while and they haven't shown up here yet."

Bob scouted for the men, discovered them a little over halfway, on a different route than the one originally selected. He flew back and made his report. "Looks like they've been having trouble. There are seven of them now, they must have picked up some extra natives along the way."

"They haven't got food for that many!" remarked the foreman. "You better drop them some."

Reeve made the group a food drop. Which, he learned later, when they finally got through, was greatly appreciated. It was the first food they had eaten in two days. When the cats got hopelessly stuck on a flooded river, Bob flew in some two-inch by ten-inch planks, eight feet long and the workers at Northway hurriedly built two barges. These they fastened together with logs to form a float, and then moved the cats across the river.

The cuts for the airstrip had to be made in both permafrost and sand. An entire two-inch layer of matted moss, which acted as an insulator, had to be removed. After that the soil thawed about six inches per day. Fill was spread in six-inch shallow lifts, then rolled flat by the cat-drawn scrapers.

With the work well under way and the weather turned warm and pleasant, Bob decided to move his family out from Fairbanks to his camp site near Nabesna. Compared to the dusty streets and house-found life with her two small children at Fairbanks, the prospect of a summer camping out appealed to Tillie as a perfect vacation. She had little hint of just how busy her vacation would prove to be. As soon as she had word from Bob, Tillie wrote her mother, who had been visiting at Valdez, to join the family. Mrs. Morisette was delighted with the idea and started making plans to hitch a ride up the Richardson Highway to Nabesna.

Traveling by truck up the 370-mile Richardson from Valdez, Mrs. Morisette followed the same path as the supplies destined for Northway. Having heretofore flown the route, she was fascinated and terrified with the breathtaking ride along the narrow roadbed, with its dangerous curves, steep

canyons, and hills, its drops of hundreds of feet to either side
with no guard rails. Reaching Nabesna mine, Grandma, just
like the airport supplies, was tossed high on an athey wagon
and hauled across the five miles of swamp. ("Those mosqui-
toes were as large as bluebottle flies!") There, at the camp,
she found Tillie and the children installed in a one-room cabin
that a hunting guide had loaned them.

The camp was a madhouse. Cats and athey wagons continuously chugged into camp and unloaded, and then the loads
were broken down and assembled for the plane. Bob was
flying six and eight trips per day, from early morning to late
at night, hauling loads as high as eleven hundred pounds in his
Fairchild. But supplies poured in faster than he could deliver
them; workmen arrived by the busload, to be carried across.
At first Bob was able to get the men over as fast as they came
in, but soon they were flooding into the camp, twenty at a
time, and stacking up there, awaiting passage. Tillie found, to
her horror, that there was no facility for their being fed—except her own cabin. The company cook had not yet arrived,
nor had a cook tent been set up. Bob magnanimously offered
that the Reeves would feed them all, if the food supplies
would be delivered to Tillie, until the camp cook house was st
up.

"My two babies had whooping cough," says Tillie, with a
smile that is still tired when she recalls those hectic weeks.
"Their clothes and blankets had to be washed every day, since
they were heaving all the time. And then I found myself with
twenty or thirty men to feed—three meals a day!"

For three weeks Tillie put out three hearty meals per day,
cooking the food on a sixteeen-by-thirty-six-inch Yukon stove.
An old Nabesna miner, Bill Weirs, who had been helping Bob
load the plane, forsook him and began helping Tillie, by
hauling water, peeling the bucketfuls of potatoes, and washing
dishes. Since there were dishes for only eight, each dish had to
be washed three times during each meal, and the men were
served at the small table in relays. "That little stove was going
night and day," reports Grandma, who arrived after Tillie had
already served two weeks as sole chef for the camp. "The real
trouble," explains Tillie, "is that I didn't know there was any
meal except meat, potatoes, vegetables, and dessert. I gave
those men roast, vegetables, hommade bread, and cake every
dinner and supper—although after a few days I did quit frost-

ing the cakes! Breakfast was mush, eggs, and a whole slab of
bacon, which had to be sliced by hand. But," she adds, "they
were a good bunch. They never complained about the service
even though I sometimes fed them off everything from pie
plates to breadboards when the dishes were going slow. And
when one of my babies whooped, someone would always pick
it up and give it a smack on the back!"

Three weeks of this hectic schedule was, however, at least
one week too much. Tillie collapsed with a violent sinus attack. And the company managed to come through with its
long-promised cook tent and professional cook. "That man!"
sniffs Tillie. "He had a full-sized kitchen range, all the supplies
he wanted, and I bet he never served more than ten people at
once!"

Once it got rolling, the equipment began arriving at an accelerated pace. Crews were working around the clock, on
eight-hour shifts, dragging in the equipment and preparing it
for Bob to haul across in the Fairchild. A thousand pounds, or
eleven hundred at the most, was all Bob could cram into the
Fairchild, and the piles of material soon stacked up, awaiting
shipment. At the beginning of the job, Morrison-Knudsen had
ordered a larger freight plane, a Boeing 80-A, and as soon as
Bob got word the plane was ready, he left for California to
get it. With the big trimotored plane on the job, Bob intended
to hire a copilot to help fly it, and another man to handle the
Fairchild, and then, with the two planes going constantly, he
hoped to get the majority of supplies in before cold weather
stopped the operations.

While Bob was gone, the workmen built a larger field for
the new plane. Within three days they had turned the whole
valley near the camp into a giant (for Alaska, at least) airfield, with one three thousand foot runway, another five thousand feet long and one hundred feet wide. It was one of the
biggest in Alaska, second only to the Elmendorf and Ladd
Army airfields. CAA christened it Reeve Field. Since it was
one of the few fields in the Territory large enough to accommodate bombers, the Army flyers began dropping in for a
chance to land, rest, and visit. The Reeves could be counted
on for a welcome, as well as some homemade cake or cookies
and plenty of steaming coffee.

"I came to Nabesna to be with Bob," says Tillie, "but he
was flying from early morning until late at night, and the only

time I saw him was at meals, with a row of people in between us. Then, as soon as things began to let up a little—he left for California!"

While Bob was gone, Tillie and Grandma moved from their temporary cabin to the tent quarters that had been set up for them. It was a fully floored, twelve-by-twenty-family-size tent, set on a log foundation and equipped with a Yukon stove, iron bunks, cupboard, table, and benches. Plumbing facilities were a "two seater" Chick Sale located about sixty feet away from the tent, in a clump of bushes, complete with burlap door.

The two women soon found that the firebox of the stove was so tiny that it would hold the pieces of wood only after they had been split three ways. There was only one thin sheet of tin for insulation between the firebox and the oven, and the first pie was a cinder. After a little experimenting, they found they could maintain moderate heat in the oven—if Grandma sat alongside the firebox, feeding in small pieces of bark, while Tillie baked the cookies and bread.

A platform was erected near the cook tent, two feet off the ground and covered with wire mosquito netting, to keep the meat fresh. With the air circulating freely around it, meat stayed fresh for two and three weeks at a time. Behind their own tent Tillie and Grandma made a sort of refrigerator by digging a hole in a shady spot and sinking a five-gallon tin can with a wooden lid. The cool, damp earth kept their butter and bacon firm.

When his whooping cough abated, three-year-old Richard helped keep the wood box full, but each time he heard an airplane motor overhead he rushed down to the new field yelling, "Daddy, maybe it's Daddy!"

After an absence of nearly five weeks, Daddy finally appeared, zooming in over the camp in a big yellow trimotor biplane. He had with him a copilot and "six boxes of fresh peaches, two crates of tomatoes, two crates of oranges, two of apples, and dozens and dozens of bananas!"

Bob had been delayed in California, waiting for the Boeing to be modified for the special cargo he would handle. A six-by-ten door opening was installed in the side, large enough to admit a thousand-gallon oil tank, since six of these tanks were destined to be hauled into Northway. Then, on his way back to Alaska, Reeve had a near wreck with his new plane when the throttle jammed wide open in one engine. The ground wire had shaken loose from a magneto to boot, and the engine couldn't be shut down. Making a forced landing near Sacramento, Bob repaired the plane and took off. Then a cylinder broke loose over Red Bluff, California, causing a second forced landing. "That was my first experience in several years flying a plane I hadn't personally maintained, and I never trusted to chance mechanical work again."

Although it was designed to haul four-thousand-pound loads, Reeve soon found that the "Yellow Peril," as the Boeing was known, could easily carry twice as much. "After a few days I never took off with less than seven thousand pounds. I've brought that plane in with engine failure with as high as a 100 per cent overload." This was the first time that Reeve deliberately overloaded—but the urgency of the wartime construction called for things "you wouldn't do otherwise." Since the work would have to cease after the big winter freeze-up, the entire airport had to be finished within the five short work months.

The big door that had been cut into the Boeing was fixed so that it could be removed, and Bob installed a truss on the door of the fuselage that would support several pieces weighing up to 7500 pounds. Eventually, pieces that reached 11,000 pounds were carried before the job was finished.

As soon as cold weather began to descend, Bob had constant trouble with the Boeing, which they had not taken time to winterize. The three engines seldom survived a take-off without one quitting. But Reeve found that in the dense air the Yellow Peril lumbered along about as well as two engines as three, and if he could get off the ground he kept on flying. Since his daily flights began at sunrise and seldom ended till after sunset, what maintenance was done had to be performed during the periods of loading and unloading. There was "always something" that needed to be done to the plane, which he couldn't take the time to do. When the starter broke on his center engine and he had no spares, Bob put in a call for help to Jack Jefford, the CAA pilot, then went ahead on two engines and kept them running all day long, never shutting them off when he was on the ground. Jefford found an old starter and flew it in to Bob, who was able to install it without missing a flight.

Once, however, he made a landing in a bad crosswind, and the motor mount broke on his right engine. With no welding equipment available, and no time for repairs anyhow, Bob simply took a log chain and secured the motor mount to the pedestal by weaving the heavy chain in and out. But with every take-off and landing the chain stretched a little, and the engine became shaky. "There were better ways than to unwind and rewind that chain all the time," says Bob with his sly Rube Goldberg smile. He put bolts in the chain links around the mount, and after every trip he tightened the bolts, making the chain taut again. To expedite this six-times-daily tightening, he left the cowling off the engine mount. The Yellow Peril, with her cowling off and a log chain around her neck, looked somewhat like a lady caught with her slip showing. As he was loading one day, Reeve heard a plane flying over, about to land. Thinking it an Army bomber on a practice run, he looked up casually, saw CAA in wide letters under the wing.

"Mindful of my past experiences with Hugh Brewster and Charley Burnett, who evidenced a lack of sympathy at some forms of 'Alaskan repair,' I yelled 'Quick, shut off that loading. We got to get out of here before they see this engine!' "

Reeve hastily flew over to Northway and was just about to unload there, when the CAA plane appeared, obviously trailing him. Reeve hurriedly fired up, took off ahead of them, keeping his log chair on their off-vision side. Back at Nebesna, Reeve jumped out of the cockpit, hustled to get the cowling, and replace it before his pursuers reappeared. When they landed, Reeve greeted the CAA men with a benign, innocent face—only to learn they were simply radio men from Washington who wanted nothing more than to see how operations were progressing at Northway! These days, when Reeve sees them, the men all get a good laugh over his big scare.

As the cold weather settled in, the baby buggy that Tillie had brought so Roberta could be wheeled down to the field each evening to meet Daddy was turned into a wheelbarrow to lug firewood, as more and more was needed to keep the tent warm, and they eventually moved into a cabin that the workers set up for them. Occasionally Bob was fogged in over at the Northway site, remaining overnight till the ceiling lifted. Each time this happened, his small son was puzzled. "How," he queried, "can you stay all night without your pajamas?" "That's when I sleep in my long underwear," Bob explained. One trip, Bob had Richard with him when they were socked in for the night. Next day, when they landed at the home field, the little boy jumped out of the cockpit and raced home exuberantly. "Oh, Mommie," he shouted proudly, "I slept in my underwear last night!"

A casualty of the newly arriving fall weather was twelve dozen eggs that Tillie had ordered; they arrived frozen. She promptly made one dozen sponge cakes and one dozen angel food cakes, then froze them for winter use. Some of the men shot some wild sheep, which they kept frozen, then sawed off meat as they needed it. At Halloween the four women in camp (Tillie and Grandma and the wives of the pilot and co-pilot employed by Bob) planned a surprise party for their men. Tillie made salads with pumpkin faces of peaches and cloves, Grandma sawed up the last quarter of sheep and roasted it, the other women made pies and biscuits and candy. They all worked at decorating the cook tent with flying bats, candles, and leaves. When their men came in that night and saw the festive spread, they all went back to their rooms to "recomb and rewash," then reappeared. After supper Bob let Richard set fire to the pile of stumps, brush, and trees that had been leveled off to form Reeve Field, and they all huddled around to watch the huge blaze, under a full October moon.

But by the middle of November the winds were blowing thirty and forty miles per hour, the temperature dropped to fifty below zero. It had become impossible to continue operating. Bob took his family back to Fairbanks. The only job left undone was the delivery of a shipment of oil drums. This job Bob turned over to Gillam, who had made a contract with Morrison-Knudsen to be their chief pilot, to fly in as soon as the weather permitted.

The last thing before they left Nabesna, the Reeve women made a flight over to Northway to see the "other end" of these mountains of supplies and hordes of men that had passed through their camp. There, to their amazement, they found "a city in the wilderness." Northway was a first-class modern airport, with nine buildings, radio towers, an office, electrical plant, and six-room houses for the families of the men who would come in to run the airport. Inside, the houses were completely furnished, varnished, painted, light fixtures installed. They had rugs on the floors, draperies hung, chairs and lamps placed—even radios. Modern baths had been installed with tub and shower, modern kitchens with cupboards, stoves, refrigerators, and silverware. The thousand-gallon fuel tanks for which the big door had been cut in the Boeing stood back of each of the houses, to furnish year-round heating.

As they headed back for Fairbanks, the Boeing 80-A was loaded with the Reeve family, their household supplies, and some last-minute passengers for Outside—fourteen people in all. "The extra men had to sit on top of the wash tubs, baby bed, and boxes in the tail of the plane," reports Grandma with a twinkle.

It had been memorable, in one way or another, for them all. Within the five months from June through October, Bob had flown in over eleven hundred tons of supplies to Northway, including the ranges, towers, everything needed for a full-scale airport—as well as three hundred construction workers. The heaviest load of all was the vertical boiler, which totaled nine thousand pounds, even with the firebox burned off. To handle it, the plane was stripped to a minimum and only enough gas to make the fifty miles to Northway was carried.

When CAA turned Northway Field over to the Army, the military moved in, multiplying the CAA facilities by ten. They added a church, a theater, barracks. During the European conflict the northern air route paid off in a spectacular fashion when thousands of fighters and bombers roared into Alaska above the Alcan Highway, into Northway, and on to Fairbanks and Nome. There, Russian pilots took over and ferried the planes across to Stalingrad and Moscow.

When the Alcan Highway was completed, Northway became the first stop on the Alaskan side. Now it is a permanent town.

The year following Bob's Northway contract, Mudhole Smith, who was working for Gillam, inherited the final job of freighting in the oil drums, as well as Bob's venerable Yellow Peril. "A bad job to fly," Smith says dourly. "One engine always quit in cold weather." Once, when Mudhole had just taken off from the Anchorage field, the right engine went out. He landed, ground-looped—and another engine went out. Unable to control the plane, he smashed through "a whole line of Art Woodley's planes." That old Yellow Peril just mowed 'em down!"

Next time he saw Reeve, Mudhole told him about the accident and complained that the Boeing had no brakes.

"Hell," snorted Bob. "You start yelling for brakes—and everybody will be asking for them!"

Bob finished the Northway job in November of 1941—just one month before Pearl Harbor. With the war on, all the pilots in Alaska had all the work they could do—and none of them more than Bob, whose total flying for the next four years was exclusively for the military.

# 12. Remember Dutch Harbor!

It took a war to put Alaska and the Aleutians on the map, so far as general American thinking was concerned. When the Japanese bombed Pearl Harbor on that December morning, in 1941, eyes turned anxiously to Alaska and the Aleutian chain, the American soil that lay closest to the Orient and was most vulnerable to the next attack. Alaska overnight became, in the words of Delegate Dimond, "a battlefield."

General Buckner, with a semblance of a military force already established at Anchorage, called for an instant alert. Soldiers hurried to their firing positions, Army trucks zoomed through Anchorage streets hauling vital material where it was most needed, picking up any stragglers not in camp. Civilian cars and trucks were cleared from the streets, home guards formed, Red Cross units set up. By night both Anchorage and Fairbanks had gone on a wartime basis, with fullscale blackouts, in which condition they would remain for four jittery years.

What few planes were already based in the Territory roared overhead constantly, on patrol; other planes and troops were rushed up from the States. Families of military and construction workers were evacuated; some Alaskans fled to the States. Most of them stayed. This was their home—despite the war of nerves, the persistent rumor of enemy bombers approaching, the imminent threat that Anchorage would be the second Pearl Harbor. They looked around, thankful for what preparation the past hurried year had achieved, and sighed at how little it was, after all.

So far as aircraft, Alaska's acknowledged medium of defense, were concerned, there was on Alaskan soil at the time of Pearl Harbor a total of six P-36 fighter planes and a handful of B-18 bombers. Within the first few weeks of war, all but one of the P-36's crashed during reconnaissance.

It was small wonder. Army flyers, trained in the States, had had little time to learn the special problems faced in Alaska flying. In the winter of 1941, Captain Dick Freeman, flying a B-17, worked on cold-weather techniques out of Ladd Field, Fairbanks. Reeve assisted Freeman, teaching him the methods worked out by bush pilots for winterizing planes: by lagging the oil tanks and adding additional cowlings to the engine to retain heat for continued cold-weather operations. When controls froze up in the dense cold, Reeve showed Freeman how to wash off the frozen grease and oil with kerosene, lubricate the parts with a mixture of kerosene and graphite. Airplanes designed to operate in warm climates would not work in Alaska—without extensive modification. Metal crystallized and snapped; hydraulic fluid leaked out of the fitting; electoral components, with different degrees of expansion in cold, froze and buckled; windshields frosted up. The pilots themselves were in danger of freezing to death unless adequate cabin heat was installed. All previous wars had been fought in temperate zones. The Alaskan theater offered a complexity and severity of climate never before experienced by our military aircraft. After months of intensive research on cold-weather flying, Captain Freeman, flying his B-17, carrying all the records of his experiments, crashed. The military were back at the beginning of their problems once more.

What aircraft could be spared in the States were rushed to Alaska. They were lucky if they arrived—since the long run from Seattle up to Fairbanks or Anchorage across endless forest and mountain and open sea faced a set of flying problems nearly identical to those in the Territory—for which few States pilots were trained. On one ferry flight six B-26's came down near Watson Lake, Canada. The place is still known as the Million Dollar Valley. The Army soon was calling upon commercial pilots who had knowledge of cold-weather flying. In the States, they found that the pilots of Northwest Airlines* had been flying along the northern boundary of our

---

* Northwest Airlines was the first commercial line to make a contract with the Air Transport Command. Having served as far north as Winnipeg since the early thirties, its pilots and technicians were trained in cold-weather operations, and they aided the military by setting up communications and ground service from Edmonton north, so that aircraft could be flown north; and then Northwest

country for years, in winters that approached, and often paralleled, Canadian and Alaskan conditions. Northwest turned
over some of its best-trained pilots "on loan" to the military to
ferry Army planes over the dangerous winter route.

There was a good case of wartime jitters in the Territory as
Alaskans crossed their fingers that the Japs would not realize
how pathetically defenseless the Great Land was to an all-out
attack, and prayed that our early defensive, holding tactics
would last out till production was in high gear and men and
equipment transported to strategic areas.

Japanese fishing boats had been spotted around the Aleutians and far western Alaskan peninsula for years. Now rumors
flew that the Japs would invade Kodiak—and march on Anchorage; that Japanese aircraft had been spotted over Naknek. Ray Petersen flew the first antiaircraft detail out to
Kodiak. A fine concrete runway had been installed, he found,
"fine for the Japs!" The only American planes there were
three goose-bellied, slow PBY's for Naval reconnaissance.
"The Japs could have taken the place," reports Ray, "revet-
ments and all—with spitballs!" Socked in by fog for three
days, waiting to get out for Anchorage, Ray got "nervous." "I
expected a bomb any moment." As soon as the ceiling lifted
he took off, fast, for Anchorage, with two passengers, Mrs.
Buckner, the wife of the Commander of Alaskan Defense,
and Mrs. Ladd, wife of the Army Commander who had gone
out to Kodiak on a social visit and been caught there at the
time of the Pearl Harbor attack. "There was fog all the way
in to Anchorage," reports Ray, "but there were no fields between, and I figured the Japs would come in as soon as the
fog lifted. I flew on top all the way." By the time he reached
Anchorage the mainland fields had begun to close in also. Anchorage's commercial Merrill Field was already closed. Half
of the runway at Elmendorf Army Air Base was closed off.
Ray called to the tower, requesting permission to land anyway. "Request denied" came the answer. "There I was up
there, with the wives of two generals on my hands—and
nowhere to land. I didn't have enough gasoline range to try
any other fields. That half a field at Elmendorf was the only

---

pilots ferried military craft over this route. Northwest later extended its wartime work out over the Aleutians for the Alaska
Defense Command.

place between Anchorage and Kodiak. I was getting desperate. So I got on my radio and said, 'Operator, you call General Buckner and ask him if I can't come in. I've got Mrs. Buckner and Mrs. Ladd aboard.' "

"Permission granted!" came the instant reply.

"I just got my wheels onto concrete when I ran into the fog banks," says Ray. "But we were down."

Bob Reeve heard the first reports of Pearl Harbor on his plane radio, between Anchorage and Fairbanks. Although a shock, it was hardly a surprise. The frenetic urgency of the building of the Northway Field had convinced him "it was just a matter of time." After his Northway "stake" Bob had contracted to buy three airplanes in the States: a Boeing 80-A for heavy freighting, a Hamilton, and another Fairchild, this an FC-2W2, similar to the Fairchild 71 and "an even better performer." There was to come a time when that Fairchild was the only plane Reeve had left—and he flew it alone for three years of dangerous wartime flying.

With his mind set on a heavy schedule of flying for the war effort, Bob went to the States where he had the Fairchild overhauled at Spokane, the Hamilton at Minneapolis. He ferried the Boeing to Yakima, Washington, where he rebuilt it at the Perry Institute with the help of mechanical students being trained there by the Air Force. He then hired a couple of pilots. While he was still working on the 80-A, however, Bob got a call from the engineering headquarters of the Army in Seattle. "We have an urgent mission to survey a route for a railroad from Prince George, British Columbia, to Nome, Alaska."†

When Reeve got the call he gassed up the Fairchild, which was in good flying order, and was air-borne within two hours. At Everett, Washington, he picked up Colonel James Truitt of the United States Engineer Corps, who was also an Alaskan, and Fred Hanson, who had worked on the building of the Copper Railroad from Cordova to Kennicott mines. They flew on, arriving at Prince George by nightfall,

---

† This was in line with the initial war strategy to press the attack on Japan from Nome, across to western Siberia, and then down through Kamchatka. The Yalta conference exploded this procedure, and the railroad was never constructed, although a roadway was cleared from Prince George to Nome before the project was abandoned.

and next day began the survey, traveling to Watson Lake, Selkirk, Dawson, Tanacross, Fairbanks, across to Nome, then retracing their tracks east toward Canada.

On the initial leg of the trip, when they made their first stop out of Prince George, at Watson Lake, Reeve needed gas. But when he asked the Watson Lake man how much gas cost, the answer was, "$2.75 a gallon." Bob had about fifty bucks in his pocket, and he needed enough gas to fill his special fuel tank, which had a two-hundred-gallon capacity. As he sat pondering his problem a Northwest Airlines plane flew in and Mel Swanson, the Northwest pilot, told the gas man to "fill up my plane." When the plane was full, Swanson, who was flying charter for the military, said, "Give me the book," and signed for the gas with his name and contract number. When Swanson had taken off, Reeve told the gas man to fill up his plane, too. Then he pulled his government contract out of his pocket and signed for the gas. Although he had no authorization to charge fuel, his contract did have a number, which he put down on the book. Then, smiles Bob, "I took off—fast!"

Two years later the bill for $550 finally caught up with him, and Reeve paid it.

All went fine with the survey until, on the homebound leg, they reached Burwash Landing, on the Canadian side of Mount Lucania. Burwash Landing was little more than a trading post, run by Reeve's old friend Jean Jacquot and his family. There was no landing field there, and Reeve brought the Fairchild down on a pasture adjacent to the trading post. The engineers had requested a landing at Burwash so that they could make arrangemnts for horses and pack trains, through Jacquot, for an additional overland survey to follow up the aerial work. Since the pasture where he had come down was a fairly long hike from the trading post, Reeve decided to be more obliging to his passengers, and flew on over in front of the post, where he landed on the ice on Kluane Lake.

Here he met with one of his oddest misadventures—a human hazard. Burwash, normally deserted, was at the moment housing over one hundred construction workers and soldiers who had been sent up to work on the Alcan Highway. When they heard the plane coming in, the men, glad for a little excitement, all ran out to greet it. The ice that Reeve had landed on was springy, just stable enough to hold the weight of the plane. When he saw the herd of men advancing on him, Bob waved and shouted at them, warning them to stay back or the ice would give under their weight.

The crowd waved and yelled back—and kept coming. When they surrounded the plane, the ice, as Reeve feared, gave way, and the Fairchild went through, until it was held up by the wings and struts only, the whole fuselage sunk in the watery slush.

Reeve looked at it and felt as close to a complete hopelessness as he had ever known. "I just didn't see any way of getting it out. For once, I gave a plane up for lost. I couldn't have felt worse."

Silently Reeve walked up to the roadhouse. Next day his passengers left him and hitched a ride into Whitehorse on another plane that had come through. But, just as unexpected human hazard had plunged Reeve into despair, an equally unexpected human help snatched him out of it.

Jimmie Joe, an Athabascan Indian guide and trapper whom Bob had known over the years he had flown in the Canadian Yukon, came to Bob the morning after the wreck, his wise face creased with serious thought. "Bob, I think I know how to get your plane out for you."

Jimmie Joe sketched out his plan for Bob, and they went to work. Shoving two long logs under each wing and fastening them together, the Indian then erected a tripod of wood in front of the timbers, to which he secured a chain hoist. Next he fastened the chain to the propeller hub and hoisted the plane up out of the water. Then they pushed the plane forward, along the timbers—and by afternoon the Fairchild had been maneuvered out of its slushy grave back onto firm ice. "Only a resourceful country man could have done it," says Bob admiringly.

When the plane was up on solid ice, Bob examined it. The belly had been torn out, and the engine and carburetor were full of water. He took the carburetor off and cleaned it out, drained the water out of the cylinders as best he could, and installed a fresh set of spark plugs. When he finally got the drowned engine started, he flew the Fairchild over to a dry cow pasture and tied it down. There was no time now to patch up the fuselage. He had to get back down to Washington and pick up his other planes and pilots and get back in business.

Hitching a ride, by local plane, over to Whitehorse, "who should I run into" there but old college pal and fellow aviation enthusiast, George Gardner. At this time president of Northwest Airlines,‡ Gardner was on his way back to Minneapolis following a Northwest survey of far western Alaska, preparatory to the line's program of contract flying there for the military. Hearing Reeve's present plight, Gardner offered to take him, in his Northwest DC-3, from Whitehorse through to Spokane. "Imagine," says Bob with a suspiciously misty eye, "he went a thousand miles out of his way to help me get back in business!"

Although the railroad survey had ended in a peck of trouble, Reeve's chore had been nearly completed. The divide which was surveyed on this trek, from Francis Lake (which drains into the Arctic Ocean) to the Salmon River (which drains into the Bering Sea) was officially recorded on the maps as Reeve Pass. "Everybody had taken credit for being the first man over that proposed railroad route," twinkles Reeve, "but I claim the credit—the pilot's seat was four feet ahead of the other claimants!"

At Spokane, Reeve ran into another old friend in need, this one, oddly enough, a fellow flyer he had never before seen. During the days he frequently prospected into the Yukon, Reeve occasionally made a landing in Dawson, to check with the Mounties and take on supplies. There he crossed tracks with another pilot who was also flying a Fairchild with a Wright engine, notorious for their habit of dripping oil. When Bob landed at Dawson and saw oil drippings on the snow, he'd say, "Well, I see Vern Bookwalter's been by." Bookwalter, flying into Dawson and seeing Reeve's telltale oil tracks, would similarly comment, "Well, I see old Reeve's been through." A veteran Yukon bush pilot and former airmail pilot, Bookwalter finally retired in the winter of 1941-1942, and Reeve met him face to face, for the first time, at the Spokane airfield. When he heard that Reeve was in a hurry to reach Yakima where his Boeing was being overhauled, Bookwalter offered to fly him over in his Bellanca. Reeve happily accepted—but was soon uneasy. A fine bush flyer, Bookwalter hadn't done any Stateside flying in ten years, and hadn't kept up on all the "newfangled rules." As he came in for an ap-

‡ Gardner is now president of Northwest Airlines.

proach to the bustling, wartime field at Yakima, he casually edged into the traffic pattern without waiting clearance. "Get out of the traffic pattern," roared Bob, terrified, as powerful B-25's and B-26's whizzed by the old Bellanca, making practice landings. Puzzled, Bookwalter looked around, realized they were about to be overrun, and withdrew. "Now," sighed Bob, "go around and take your turn in the traffic pattern and get in like you're supposed to!"

Confused and irritated by all these high-pressure operations, Bookwalter growled, "When did they start all this? The flying business is sure getting to be a hell of a note!"

The day after Bob got back to Yakima, on June 3, 1942, the Japanese bombed Dutch Harbor, on Unalaska Island, midway along the Aleutian Chain, only about five air hours from the city of Anchorage.

Alaskans' fear that Japan had an eye on its Aleutian Chain as a gateway to the States was terrifyingly verified. Out at Dutch Harbor, Reeve's friend, Seldovia cannery owner C. E. "Squeaky" Anderson, who had been hastily recalled on active duty with the Navy in September of 1940, to serve as commander of the Aleutian Patrol, described the havoc. "At Dutch we had oil tanks, float plane facilities, and a handful of PBY's." The first attack lasted two hours. The next day the Japanese planes reappeared, bombing the defenseless port for another two hours. The oil tanks were blown up, and about forty people were killed. A new Army group had just come in the previous night, and some of their men were killed as they marched to their barracks. "We had some antiaircraft," reports Squeaky, who was the port director at Dutch, "and we sunk some ships. They could have easily come in and taken us," he adds, "but for some reason they withdrew and made their landings on Attu and Kiska, instead."

Attu, the last of the Aleutian islands, lay 600 miles from Siberia, and only 650 miles from the farthest-north Japanese defense base, at Paramushiro in the Kurile Islands. When the Japanese took Attu, following the attack upon Dutch Harbor, they found a colony of forty-five Aleuts and a white schoolteacher and his wife the only inhabitants. The Aleuts and the white woman were taken prisoners by the Jap forces, the schoolteacher committed suicide. Since the tiny volcanic dot in the sea apparently had little strategic importance (none, before long range aircraft came into existence), the island had never been given a detailed survey by the United States, nor were there any military installations on it. Later, when the American forces came in (May, 1943) to recapture Attu, they had no information to go on, except for a map of the shore line. There was no map of the interior of the island, no information regarding its terrain, mountains, crags, and soggy tundra, over which the fighting men would be forced to "slog their way" in the face of concerted enemy fire.

On Kiska, the Japanese forces found a small detachment, composed of one Navy lieutenant and ten men, whom they took prisoner. Three months later they transferred their garrison on Attu to Kiska, and a new group landed on Attu. American forces hastily assembled to take over Amchitka and Adak and build airfields, which would be within easy bombing range of the Jap-held islands.

Realizing the conflict was "mighty close to home" and to his own family, Reeve hastened to get the Boeing ready, working around the clock. When he had time to look up from his own work Reeve was worried by the actions of one of the pilots he had hired. "He showed careless streaks that were bound to get him in trouble in Alaska." There was an old saying that Alaskan pilots were the best in the world because they had to be. They could certainly not afford to be careless. "Against my better judgment," says Bob soberly, "I didn't fire him. I should have followed my hunch."

When they were ready to head for Alaska, Reeve piloted the Boeing with another hand for copilot, the other flyer following in the Hamilton. At their first stop, at Spokane, two hundred miles away, Reeve landed—but the Hamilton did not show. Word came into the field that a plane had crashed one hundred miles south. "I had a feeling it was my Hamilton. I hired a car and drove to the scene of the crash. I was right. The plane was crashed and the pilot was dead." When he inquired of observers, Reeve found that the plane had been apparently functioning normally, but the pilot had been flying low. He saw a telephone line in his way, made a turn, but caught his wing—which plummeted him to his death. "What he was doing down there nobody knows."

It was a chilling, sobering lesson, which was to greatly influence Reeve in his later running of an air line. "Once, years later," he said, "I had the same kind of a hunch about a pilot—but since I had no real evidence to go on, I failed to follow it, much to my later regret. It resulted in a bad crash, but fortunately without loss of life. After that, I never took another chance on my air-line personnel."

With the loss of the Hamilton, Reeve's stake of $25,000 was starting to shrink. He took the pilot's body to his home, arranged the burial, gave the man's widow two months' salary—and ended up in a familiar recurrent position, broke. He didn't have enough money to pay his gas bill to fly the Boeing on north. "I had no banking connections in Seattle, but there was one fellow I knew, named Fowler Martin, who was vice president of the Pacific National Bank. I'd flown him all over Alaska in the early days, and I figured he might judge me a good risk!"

Martin told Reeve it was "most unusual" to loan money without security, besides which the bank had a set rule not to loan *anything* to bush pilots—but he couldn't quite turn down an old friend. Martin forked over the money (which Reeve was able to repay within a year) and then faced a dressing down from the bank's directors for his chancy loan. "For the next year," grins Bob, "old Fowler never picked up a daily paper without first scanning the headlines to see whether I had crashed." But Reeve, and others, soon proved to the skeptical bankers that "the airplane was here to stay." The bank eventually reversed its policy and became bankers for several air lines, including the highly successful Pacific Northern, owned and operated by Alaskan bush flyer Art Woodley.

When he forked over the loan, Martin told Reeve, "There are three Kodiak residents here who are anxious to get back to Alaska. Since there are submarines in the Gulf, they don't want to risk the boat. Would you fly them back?"

"I was more than happy to pick up some cash fares." Reeve loaded his Boeing with the three passengers, copilot, and three tons of spare engine parts. In addition he had four fifty-gallon barrels of gasoline, which he placed in the cabin, with a portable wobble pump and hose leading out of the window to the top of the wings so that he could transfer gas into the wing tanks during the long flight from Prince George to Juneau. With a four-hundred-mile range and a hundred-mile-per-hour cruising speed, the Boeing had to have one hundred gallons of gas to make the six hundred miles to Juneau, and one hundred gallons in reserve. Two hundred miles out of Prince

George, "we hit one hell of a storm. But I had a good map and I wasn't turning back."

Reeve's passengers, however, were "far from happy." In the extreme turbulence as they bucketed their way through the front of rain and wind, the gas from the open barrels permeated the cabin with fumes so that you "could slice the air with a knife." From the start of the trip, Reeve had issued a "no smoking" order. Now he ordered his three unhappy victims to stand up, since the gas fumes sank to the floor, leaving the fresher air on top. "There wasn't much ceiling, but I hit Telegraph Creek on the nose and was holding a good course—though I did just barely make it over the next hill to the headwaters of the Taku River, leading down to Juneau," reports Reeve. "I happened to look around once, and darned if one of those passengers wasn't writing out his will and a farewell note to his family!"

Reeve flew down the Taku River in about two hundred feet ceiling, then headed over the Juneau area on the downwind leg. But, as in Bookwalter's experience, times had changed while Reeve had been gone from Alaska. Juneau was now a major defense-control area. Principal port and capital city of the Territory, it was now fully protected by antiaircraft installations.

Reeve executed a landing, pulled up to the ramp, only to be immediately "surrounded" by a red-haired artillery captain and his armed squad of infantry.

"He was not a little angry with me," reports Bob modestly, "he was plenty angry."

The artillery men, assuming this unannounced plane was an enemy target, were ready to shoot, when at the last moment some keen-eyed individual noticed the United States registry of the aircraft and ordered them to withhold fire.

The captain dressed Reeve down thoroughly, ended up shouting, "Don't you ever come in here again without advising us and getting clearance!"

"I would have circled around so you could see me," Reeve said, "but this happens to be an airplane, not a balloon, and I'm out of gas and had to come down."

Between the storm, the gas fumes, and nearly being shot down, Reeve's passengers had had more than enough. "I think," grins Bob, "that at that stage a submarine attack would have seemed like peanuts compared to what they'd been through."

Only halfway home, they deserted their wild pilot and demanded half of their fare back. Since Reeve had a gas bill to pay, he couldn't also refund fares. "I'll have to send it to you later," he promised. A year later, he did.

The incident at Juneau earned Reeve front-page news stories, and the reputation for being a "tough case to handle." But his "What do you expect me to do, float around like a balloon?" was more truth than reckless independence. By the time he got near his home field at Fairbanks, he had learned his lesson and "wanted no part of control zones. Besides, this was my home base, and I didn't want to get in bad there." Reeve prudently landed eighty miles from Fairbanks, at Big Delta, and called Tillie to "come get me."

Back home once more, Reeve took his Dodge pickup truck to the Bank of Fairbanks and mortgaged it for five hundred dollars, for ready "gas money." Then, making proper clearance through defense-control area, he brought his Boeing into Fairbanks.

During his six months' absence, Reeve found, Alaskan airpower had come into its own, and with its modern airfields and navigational aids provided a network of airways that would have made Billy Mitchell proud. Reeve went to work on a charter contract to CAA at eighty dollars an hour, with fuel furnished. Flying vital supplies, construction materials, and workers into the new airfields at Big Delta, Tanacross, Galena, Moses Point, and Nome, Reeve soon found himself working on a fifteen-hour-per-day schedule, flying, loading, unloading, and doing maintenance on his Boeing. He did all the flying himself. On the run up from Spokane to Alaska, he had turned over the controls to his copilot while he filled in the log, then taken the wheel back in half an hour, asking, "Where are we?"

"I don't know," said the copilot. "Why?"

"Haven't you been following the map?" demanded Reeve.

"I've been used to following the east-west-north-south property lines in southern Washington," confessed the copilot, "and I have no landmarks here."

"Okay," sighed Reeve, "we'll settle this right now. From here on out, I'll handle all the flying from the neck up. You handle it from the neck down."

Reeve did the flying and navigating, the copilot did the gassing, and both of them the loading. "My job," said Reeve, "took five hours; his about fifteen minutes." Reeve realized he had taken too much for granted about his new pilot, "but he improved." The boy learned Alaskan flying so well that he later became a captain for Alaska Airlines—"a superb pilot," comments Reeve, "who graduated from the Reeve school for backward flyers!"

It was no disgrace to be "backward" in the complexities of Alaskan flying. Henry W. "Esky" Clark, Alaskan-born representative of Alaska Steamship Lines, who was sent by the military to survey towns and prepare them for the influx of troops, was flying over the Gulf of Alaska, listening to the plane radio, when he picked up the conversation of two Army flyers going over the Alaskan range. "My God," whistled one, "is that a mountain?"

"It ain't ice cream!" grunted the other.

Performing this "urgent" wartime work—loading and unloading four and five tons of lumber, oil, groceries, and machinery, placing it so that the airplane would be properly balanced, gassing, checking his plane before every take-off— Reeve found that the hours when he was actually in the air were the most relaxing of the hectic days. "After the tenseness of loading and take-off, it was nice to get air-borne and quiet down."

Despite his good intentions, Reeve finally managed to get tangled up in his home-town control zone. They were holding an air-raid warning at Fairbanks one night when he flew in from Nome, with just enough gas to make the field. The tower told him that due to the air-raid drill, no planes were to land. Reeve came ahead and landed anyhow. "The fellow started yelling at me, 'What are you doing here?'

" 'Heck,' I said, 'I had to come down. When I run out of gas, I got to come down. I can't change this plane into a kite and just hang up there till you finish your drill. I got to come tumbling down.' "

"Well," grunted the officer, "you're here. But don't let this ever happen again."

In November of 1942, Bob signed a contract with the Alaska Communications System, which was to earn him the title of "Air Force of the ACS."

With his heart set on a postwar air line, Reeve packed up

his family and household goods in the Boeing and moved them to Anchorage, which he felt would become the air center of the Northwest. Already little Merrill Field had more operations than New York's La Guardia. Big-time aviation was on the march in Alaska, at long last.

# 13. Ice, scud, and williwaw

When Bob moved his family to Anchorage, from which base he was, for the next three wartime years, to do the most remarkable flying of his career—out over the fog-bound Aleutians—he knew about as little about the Chain as the Navy and Army had when they first moved out to reconnoiter this suddenly vital area. Variously called "the birthplace of the winds," "the cradle of storms," "the birthplace of bad weather," the Chain had long been neglected, principally because it was generally conceded to have the worst weather, for planes or boats, of any place in the world. "Compared to the chain," Bob remarked grimly after a few months' experience flying it, "Cape Horn is a breeze!" And yet the Aleutians were to become Bob's special territory, the scene of his postwar business.

The islands—exposed peaks of a submerged mountain range whose volcanic eruptions finally pierced the surface of the sea—swing in a westward arc from the Alaskan peninsula toward Japan. Weather is literally manufactured at this juncture, where the warm Japanese current of the northern Pacific meets the cold air masses from the Bering and Arctic seas, resulting in violent winds and storms which form here and then sweep eastward over Alaska, Canada, and the United States. The Chain is known principally for its completely unpredictable weather, in which visibility may range from zero to twenty thousand feet within thirty minutes' time, and a moment's calm may give way to windstorms of sudden violence, williwaws that sweep down from the volcanic peaks, roar through the passes between the islands, and set up a surge of sea so powerful that no sandy beaches have ever formed. Countless ships have been raked to destruction against the unyielding rocky shores.

The second thing for which the Chain is famous is the blanket of fog that rolls ceaselessly over the islands. An oldtimer on Cold Bay, where the end of the Alaskan peninsula tapers into the chain, reported that during his lifetime, he remembered three consecutive days of sunshine. A photographic team sent out to Dutch Harbor by the Army in 1941 had to wait nine weeks to shoot fifteen minutes' worth of film.

It was a land most people were glad to leave to the elements. But with the Japanese holding Attu—only eighteen hundred miles from the city of Anchorage—something had to be done, and fast. The Chain had to be conquered by both ship and plane.

It was a grueling chore for all. (When the score was finally added up at the end of the war, it was estimated the heavy aircraft losses in this theater were due principally to the hazardous Aleutian weather rather than the enemy.) In 1940, when the Navy first set out to secure the Aleutians with the organizational brilliance that marked our military success in World War II, they looked for the man who knew most about the uncharted area and selected Bob's friend, trader and cannery man Squeaky Anderson, who had been running small boats around the Chain waters since 1910. Described by Samuel Eliot Morison in his history of United States naval operations as "a character of infinite resource, energy and cunning," the chunky, whimsical little Swede* was probably the only man in the military not afraid of the terrifying rip tides, uncharted reefs, and crumbly, precipitous cliffs that composed the shore line of the Aleutians. They were familiar landmarks of Squeaky's trading and trapping days.

Commanding an Aleutian Patrol that consisted of three seventy-five-foot fishing boats, Squeaky patrolled the Chain, selected landing sites for military detachments, then directed the shore parties when they moved in. The Navy had already begun air facilities for float planes at Sitka, at Kodiak on Kodiak Island, and at Unalaska Island. Squeaky supervised the construction of additional stations at Adak, Amchitka, and Dutch Harbor. As soon as the Navy had secured these spots, the Air Force moved in to establish air bases within bombing range of the Jap-held strongholds on Attu and Kiska.

---

* Squeaky shipped as a seaman on a three-masted schooner, from Hamburg, in 1908, arrived in America following a 242-day voyage, became a naturalized citizens, and during World War I attended Naval Officer's Training School at Providence, R. I.

In the summer of 1942, before navigational aids had been installed, most flights that started down the Chain from Anchorage were forced to turn back. The fog that summer was the worst it had been in years. In Washington, concerned with the slowness with which things were getting started out in the strategic Aleutians, Congress formed an investigating committee headed by Senator A. B. "Happy" Chandler, of Kentucky, who made a trip up to Anchorage to see what all the delay was about. The day that the Senator selected for his tour of the Chain was "the only clear day in months." He went out to Adak and back and saw hardly a cloud. The Senator reported, "I don't see anything wrong with this weather. You should have had the Japs out long before this." From then on, whenever one of those rare, once-a-season clear days with no fog or clouds occurred on the Chain, it was called "senatorial weather." Flyers who flew a mission in the Aleutians and got back to their home bases safely without crashing in the blinding scud and jutting mountains, or being hit by Japanese bullets, "sat around with wonderment and disbelief on their faces, doubting that they'd actually made it back alive." Colonel Everett Davis, who laid out the basic field systems in the Aleutians for the Air Corps, crashed into a fog-shrouded mountain near Iliamna and was killed, on his last trip on the Chain prior to his scheduled transfer to the States.

It was only, Reeve feels, when Major General Davenport Johnson (for whom Bob's brother Richard Reeve had once been an aide) took command of the Eleventh Air Force in 1943 that air navigational aids in the Aleutians were modernized and flying safety improved. A "hardened combat leader from World War I, "Johnson was "the first to really make the Aleutians flyable." Colonels under his command who refused to fly were busted; men who would fly were promoted and put in their places.†

---

† Northwest Airlines, working closely with the military, turned over two veteran instrument pilots, Captain Roman Justiss and Captain Lloyd Milner, to test safe flying procedures on the Chain. As soon as the modern aids were installed, Justiss and Milner pioneered the instrument letdown procedures and then took military crews out and instructed them in the proper and safe letdown techniques through the blinding scud. Milner and Justiss were later awarded the Air Medal for their invaluable aid in making the Chain safe for both military and commercial planes.

Reeve's move into Anchorage from Fairbanks was "somewhat different" than the previous move from Valdez to Fairbanks. "I had some money in my pocket," says Bob, "and I was moving my family into a new house"—which he had, on a previous trip, found under construction and rented from the owner, Zac Loussac. Not quite aware of the phenomenal wartime boom in population in Anchorage ("the fastest-growing city in the world," which expanded from 2000 to 12,000 in the period from 1940 to 1946 and from 12,000 to 60,000 in the period 1946 to 1954), Bob turned down a chance to buy the house a year later, since Loussac, who, Bob knew, had built it for five thousand dollars, offered it to Bob "as an old friend" for ten thousand. "I thought he was kidding," said Bob. But, after numerous warnings, Loussac finally collared Bob on the street and said, "I'm going to sell it if you don't take it."

"Your price still ten grand?" queried Bob, who was beginning to catch on.

Zac said, "Yes, and it's a bargain."

"Okay," agreed Reeve, "I'll match you to see whether I pay you eight thousand or twelve thousand."

A lucky gambler as usual, Reeve won and paid the eight thousand. Later, as his family enlarged,‡ he paid three times the purchase price to add two rooms!

In the previous year Tillie had not liked the Fairbanks winter, the midwinter daylight that lasted only from 11:00 A.M. to 2:00 P.M., the bleak cold. "Don't worry," said Bob, "next winter I'll take you south." The next winter, when Tillie reminded him of his promise, which she had imagined would mean a trip to California, Bob grinned wickedly. "You've had your trip south! From Fairbanks to Anchorage!"

Situated on Cook Inlet in the Gulf of Alaska, tempered by sea air, Anchorage does have a more equable climate than the Interior of Alaska. In midwinter, Tillie found, there was daylight from nine until four, about twice as much as at Fairbanks. When they moved there in 1942, the little railroad town, which had numbered about fifteen hundred persons when Bob first arrived there ten years earlier, was already on the boom, with a population of twelve thousand. Headquar-

‡ The three youngest Reeve children were born during the war years: Janice in 1943, David in 1945, Whitman in 1947.

ters of General Buckner's Alaskan-Defense Command, jumping-off point to the enemy-held Aleutians, Anchorage was America's most war-conscious city. Troops flooded in in preparation for the Aleutian campaign, scout planes zoomed overhead, Army bombers practiced landings. A complete black-out was observed. Street lights were shut off and curtains drawn each night. Air-raid wardens came by regularly to check. Out at bustling Merrill Field, where every kind of equipment with wings was being kept in the air as emergency supplies were rushed to the military zones, the landing and tower lights were put on only after aircraft had been identified, recognized, and were coming in. During radio alert no lights were turned on. Several times Bob was caught coming in "dead dark," when with no landing lights on his plane either, he had to "feel his way down" by searching for the dim outline of the runway, the line of trees.

The Anchorage bush flyers were all busy with wartime charter work in addition to their regular runs. Art Woodley's fleet of planes was operating on an accelerated schedule. Ray Petersen's Flying Service was now based at Merrill ("I heard a rumor Reeve was moving to Anchorage, so I moved there too." The Petersens and Reeves found themselves next-door neighbors). Haakon "Chris" Christenson, the Durable Dane, a favorite Alaskan flyer who loved flying so much that he stunted for fun, after following up some of Reeve's glacier work on the coast, was now busy flying military charters.** Lavery Airways also had a base at Merrill, as did Oscar Winchell. CAA had a hangar there. When military P-38's and B-24's could not get into Elmendorf Air Base, they made emergency landings at Merrill. With its constant taxiings, take-offs, and landings, little Merrill was the busiest airport under the American flag. For several months during the war it averaged over ten thousand landings and take-offs per month, more than New York's La Guardia.

The only bush operator under exclusive contract to the military, and the only civilian flyer assigned to the combat zone, Bob had the duty with the Alaska Communications System (a branch of the Signal Corps) of flying men and material to

---

** Christenson was killed in a private plane crash in 1956. "A hard-nosed guy," Reeve says, he had gone out on "a day when even the birds stayed on the ground." Jack Jefford found the wreck.

ACS bases all over Alaska, western Canada, and the Aleutians. By this time the hasty construction of Alaskan communications was being correlated with the Aleutian offensive and the planned attack on Japan by way of Nome and Siberia. Although ACS had a high transportation priority with the Army, they had to get their installations in "yesterday," and often the Army failed them. Deciding they must have a plane over which they had total control, they signed Bob as their own private air force. He began his contract using three planes: the Boeing and the two Fairchilds. When he went over to Burwash Landing to pick up the Fairchild he had left staked out in the pasture, he found that it had dried out with no internal damage, but cows had eaten the fabric off the tail surfaces. "This was no surprise," says Bob. "Once in Chile I went out to get in my plane, and a flock of goats had jumped onto the fuselage and wings, and their hoofs went through the fabric, making a hundred holes." It was one of the normal hazards of bush flying.

He patched up the fuselage with fabric and dope, then flew the plane back to Anchorage, where he worked at recovering it between flights in his other planes.

The month of December, 1942, just one year after the Pearl Harbor attack, found Reeve "in the air every day" to some part of Alaska, carrying personnel or hurry-up repair parts for the ACS. At the end of the month Reeve made his first flight out to Cold Bay. While flying for CAA, Reeve had been out the Alaskan Peninsula as far as Bristol Bay and Port Heiden ("nothing surrounded by nothing," one civilian pilot called this piece of rock), but he had never before been out as far as Cold Bay. "To us in the old days, both the peninsula and the Aleutians were 'nowhere.' No one went out there, except on rare occasions."

By now the Air Force had established bomber runways and defense installations at Port Heiden, Cold Bay, Dutch Harbor, Umnak, and Atka. The Adak field was still under construction. While Cold Bay was being constructed, at Lample's insistence, for CAA, by the Morrison-Knudsen Company, back in 1941, General Buckner, like Lample anticipating the Japanese attack through the Aleutians, had at the same time secretly begun the construction of Umnak airfield. Sending the materials out stenciled for a cannery, he built the field without the knowledge of the enemy. After the attack, this lone outpost spelled the difference between our tenuous hold and complete loss of the Aleutians to the Japanese, who were operating float-fitted Zeros out of their well-entrenched strongholds on Kiska, Attu, and tiny Agatu.

Because of the heavy military traffic along the Aleutians, Reeve wouldn't risk making the normal instrument approaches in the blinding fog. He was sure that if he moved his small, slower plane into the traffic pattern of the swift Air Force planes, he would certainly be overrun in the limited visibility. As he flew out over the Peninsula that December day, the Aleutian weather was up to its normal tricks, providing blinding snowstorm and ice fog. The only map Reeve had was prepared by the Coast & Geodetic Survey and showed nothing but depths, soundings in fathoms at mean, high, and low water. He had marked out the air navigational range legs of the military fields on the map—but he did not dare fly them. His purpose in knowing them was to stay off. While the big fast planes zoomed by on instrument, Reeve flew his smaller plane on contact, depending on a bush type of ingenuity to work his way in and out of the fogbound fields. When he got within fifteen miles of Cold Bay, his Fairchild loaded with Signal Corps technicians, "I started circling around [in ice fog] about ten miles out there, drawing into narrower and narrower circles till I hit Cold Bay. I was staying at about fifty feet altitude in order to be under the heavy air traffic above." Reeve reported to the tower that he was coming in VFR (Visual Flying Rules), then described to the tower what the particular spot he was in looked like. They recognized his position, and when he asked permission to enter the immediate control zone, it was granted.

Staying overnight, Reeve got his first taste of the freak Aleutian winds. When he went out to the field next morning he couldn't find his airplane—although he had tied it down with four fifty-gallon drums lashed to the wings. He finally found it—about two thousand feet down the runway from where he had left it, the drums still attached to the wings and the propeller windmilling in the fierce gale. "Fortunately I had parked in a remote section of the runway—and it hadn't banged into other aircraft." This, Bob found, was to be standard procedure. He learned to alert the ramp crews to come fetch him from his bed, or a poker game, whenever "Leaping Lena" broke loose from her moorings. Frank Judd (vice president in charge of operations for Northwest Airlines) described a wind at the Shemya field that was so strong that they had to tie down a Northwest passenger liner DC-4 with two trucks on each wing tip to keep it from blowing off the field. The first time Reeve landed at Shemya he saw a log chain hanging from a pole, and "bit." "What's that for?" he asked curiously. "Why," said the ground-crew men, "that's our wind sock!"

Few jokes can exaggerate Aleutian winds. Base personnel walked with a slant. "When the wind stops blowing, everybody falls down." Aloft, they reach terrific velocity (they have actually been clocked at two hundred miles per hour). Caught in one of these "blows" at ten thousand feet altitude over Dutch Harbor, Reeve once hung there for over an hour "just flapping my wings," unable to get down. He finally had a call from the tower at Dutch: "Better come down to three thousand, feather merchant. It's only blowing fifty miles per hour down there and you might make it in this week." One blast of hundred-mile-per-hour wind picked up an entire tent at Adak, including its floor, stove, and eight occupants, and rolled it one hundred yards. The same blast seized the steel matting on a nearby emergency landing strip and rolled it up into a ball one hundred feet in diameter. That matting still lies there as a monument to the "birthplace of wind." Reeve also claims that they were painting their tower at Umnak one day, and four hours later the same coat of paint was discovered neatly plastered over the Catholic church at Cordova, on Alaska's southeast coast!

The morning following his arrival at Cold Bay, Reeve had a call to report to the commanding officer. The C.O. queried Reeve about his operations in the combat zone, and asked particularly about his odd method of approach to the Cold Bay field. "I would rather have you come straight in," he told Reeve, "than in that unorthodox manner. From now on we will permit you to enter as routine traffic—on proper identification, of course."

The winter of 1942-1943 provided the hard-pressed Air Force with one of the worst winters in the history of the violent Aleutians. It was literally impossible to forecast the shifting weather. In all the time Reeve flew into Cold Bay, he doesn't remember seeing a correct weather forecast made. His favorite greeting to the boys at the weather bureau was, "Good morning, how's Cold Bay's Liars Club?" In the States, where the forecasters had had their previous experience and training, a front would move through, leaving clear weather behind. In the Aleutians, one front followed on the heels of another, with no respite between. "You never knew it was coming until it hit you!"

When Bob made a landing on a Chain field, he was always surrounded by an eager group of bomber pilots who had been sitting around waiting out the weather for a chance to "dive through." "How's the route?" they'd ask Reeve. "How's the weather where you've been?" Bob would tell them what he had just been through "upstairs," and the flyers would hastily take off—and at least get as far as the place Bob had just come in from. A pilot's report was more valuable than the weather forecast, particularly on the Chain, where the ground conditions and those "on top" were greatly dissimilar.

Reeve enjoyed flying the Chain, in his own perverse fashion. "The weather was actually no worse than it had been around Valdez—just more consistent—and here I didn't have all those mountains to plow through. I could go back to my old tricks and fly the beach line ten feet above the water. The only time I quit flying was when the ground wind exceeded fifty miles per hour, since my airplane would blow away before I could get it tied down."

The landing and take-off speed of the Fairchild was approximately fifty-five or sixty miles per hour. More than once, swept by a sudden gust of wind that exceeded fifty miles, the plane would become air-borne again after Reeve had already touched down, and he would have to fly it down to the ground a second time.

Making constant trips to Cold Bay, Dutch, Umnak, with loads of Signal Corps personnel, tools, and emergency materiel, Reeve flew so continuously that he never got around to re-covering the other Fairchild till after the war was ended. By then, he had converted to DC-3's to meet new business requirements, for which the Fairchild was too small. It is still sitting around Anchorage's Merrill Field. Reeve and a copilot kept the Boeing and the other Fairchild in the air "every day." In addition to the Signal Corps men and equipment, Reeve carried "everything from a private to a colonel" along the Chain on his regular runs. Anyone connected with the war effort who wanted to get out there, and didn't have a high enough priority to find an immediate place on an Army plane, "rode with Reeve." "My seating arrangements," he says modestly, "were strictly informal." When both a freight load and passengers were carried, seating was on a rank basis: the highest rank got the seat, the others sat on top of freight.

On a trip from Cold Bay to Anchorage, Reeve stopped at Naknek to refuel, and a civilian fisherman, who had been waiting a week for transportation, asked him if he could go along.

"Sure," said Reeve, and tossed the man's suitcase into the cabin of the Fairchild. "Climb in."

The fisherman looked into the loaded plane. "Where is my seat?"

Reeve took the suitcase, tossed it back out. "That *was* your seat!" The finicky fisherman waited another week for transportation out of the Peninsula.

Once when Bob flew into Umnak a GI ran out to meet him. "I've been here a year," the boy pleaded, "and they promised me a pass to the mainland, but they always tell me the planes are full. Will you take me?" Reeve checked, and found that the boy's superiors didn't intend to let him go, but had just told him that "to keep him happy." (Men stationed too long in the Aleutians developed the "Aleutian stare," the bleak, glazed, half-mad look that came from the unrelieved driving winds and rain, combined with the threat of enemy attack.) Reeve told the boy to come along. The kid climbed into the plane in his coveralls, and Bob hauled him in to Anchorage. "Later," reports Bob, "I really got hell for that."

Although not a member of the military, Reeve was soon accepted as one by the men along the chain. He made a practice, as he had done for the miners, of bringing out personal items they needed or simply wished for: film for their cameras, cigarettes, magazines, liquor. Frequently fogged in at the Chain bases, Reeve spent many a night helping the boys pass time over bull sessions, poker tables.

With the endless hours of waiting that made up military life on the Aleutians, poker was the one respite. "Aleutian dollars," frayed, dirty, dog-eared bills that had been in every game on the Chain, became favorite souvenirs—along with the short-snorters that were back in vogue during the war. (Reeve had one from this period signed by Eisenhower, Eddie Rickenbacker, and Bernt Balchen.) Individual games became famous. Frank Judd told of one at Cold Bay that was hastily broken up when a Kodiak bear crawled through the window. At Umnak, the busiest of all the Chain bases, "The Little Red Schoolhouse" was in constant session. It was there that Reeve nearly lost his airplane.

Stuck at Umnak in a dense fog, Reeve got into a game with a bunch of dive-bomber pilots en route to the Kiska invasion. Within an hour Reeve, usually lucky, was cleaned of all his ready cash. Reluctant to lose a customer, the pilots voted to let him stay in on jawbone credit.

"I'll pledge my airplane for five thousand dollars' credit in the game," offered Reeve. He was given that amount in chips, went on playing, and within one more hour the five thousand had disappeared. Reeve was voted a second mortgage on his airplane for five hundred dollars' worth of chips. His luck took an upward swing, and within the first day he won back the propeller and wings. Progressively he also won back the fuselage, then the landing gear, the ailerons, and the stabilizer. But, play as well as he might, the rudder and the elevators refused to materialize.

In the meanwhile the weather had cleared. "But I had no plane yet," says Reeve. "I was just as remote as Robinson Crusoe!"

At three o'clock in the morning of the tenth day, in a lucky bluff, Reeve won back his elevators—finally the rudder. He jumped up from the table. "Gimme that I.O.U. back! I got to get going!"

Outside, he looked at his Fairchild with affectionate eyes. "You'll never conceive the fond feeling with which I regarded my old Fairchild—nor the haste with which I fired up and headed home!"

Without waiting for the tower to give him a green light, Reeve headed for the runway and was air-borne at ten thousand feet in half an hour. Flying over Dutch Harbor, he saw a battle cruiser that showed evidence of severe battle damage being warped into the dock. As Reeve flew over the battered ship, he said softly, "I know just how you feel—getting out of the bite and back to port!" Later he found that this was the cruiser *Salt Lake City*, limping back from the terrific three-and-a-half-hour battle of the Komandorskis.

Reeve hated his first flight into any field. The wartime flying in the combat area was complicated by a secret code device. When Reeve approached a new field, he was forced, first, to fly his plane around over it, so that the men at the antiaircraft guns could get a look at him and identify him. "They were trigger-happy with the Japs so close, and my plane was 'a strange plane'—it didn't look like a U. S. military plane. I always expected someone with itchy fingers to shoot me down before I was properly identified."

Of all the fields he went into, Umnak was the busiest. The Amchitka base, which was eventually used to blast the Japanese off Kiska, was not yet completed, and all the forces and planes stacked up at Umnak. Japanese Zero fighter planes, on floats, were occasionally spotted cruising around and observing the Air Force installations. Reeve made no contact with a Zero—that he knows of. "Anytime I saw a plane faintly resembling a Zero I got up in the clouds and stayed there." At Umnak, the P-40 and B-24 pilots glared suspiciously at Reeve's red Fairchild, his black Boeing. Once, when an Umnak fighter group had been flying fighter cover, they took a closer look at one of the planes in their formation—and found it was a Zero, flying in with them!

One of the biggest breaks of the war was when one Zero, out of gas, made a forced landing on the soft muskeg of Unalga Island, which killed the pilot but left the plane intact. American forces salvaged it and took it back to the States, where valuable information was derived about its performance.

Reeve won a reputation for bush bravado for his contact flying of the Aleutians without instruments or navigational aids. Actually it was his shrewd Yankee sense of survival that dictated his unique performance. He stayed consistently off the military airways, flew high from Anchorage west; then as he neared the busy control centers he flew a safe distance out over the ocean, then ranged in low beneath the other traffic. When he couldn't find a hole in the solid cloud bank that clung so tenaciously over the islands, he let down 40 or 50 miles out, then skimmed in low, just over the water, where there was a slight ceiling such as he had found along the coast of Chile. "I never told them about my technique," says Reeve, "because I didn't want to upset them by these unorthodox methods which might have canceled my landing privileges!"

It has been said that crusty, old-hand pilot Reeve was contemptuous of radio, refused to install or use it in his planes or yield to such newfangled devices. This is far from the truth.

When radios were first required in commercial aircraft, in 1942, Reeve put in a token installation to satisfy the authorities, then seldom used it since the commercially available radios of that period were relatively unreliable. When he reached the Aleutians, however, Reeve realized that modern navigational aids might well save his life some day—and he became a serious student of radio, applying his characteristic concentration to the exact length of antenna for best reception on various frequencies. Although the old Wasp engines in his Boeing and Fairchild had no modern radio shielding to eliminate the static generated by the spark plugs and magnetos, Reeve developed his own method of eliminating this by wrapping the magnetos with wire fly screen. "It was rather complex to unwind all that and check the megnetos—but worth it!"

Reeve talked to old-time radio men over the Territory, learned to mark the length of the trailing antenna to the inch for best transmission and reception on the several frequencies allotted him. Before each flight he checked the radio power generator to make sure it was giving proper power. His radio installation functioned so well that operators in Nome, Umnak, and Juneau remarked, "We've been listening to you all over Alaska. Your transmissions nearly blasted us out. How do you do it?"

Although he did not usually fly the radio beam for fear of being overrun, Reeve used his radio to make position reports. When he had skimmed in low to a position ten or twenty miles from the field, the tower would clear him to make a visual approach when other planes were out of the way.

Practically all of Reeve's Aleutian flying was visual except when he "couldn't find a hole in the cloud" and used the beam briefly to orient himself for a letdown. "But I always stayed to one side, at least ten or fifteen miles off the beam." A few times when he was caught in "real zero-zero" blizzards, Reeve notified the tower that he was going to come in on the beam, then relied on them to keep all the other traffic stacked aloft until he could get down.

En route to the Chain with his Boeing in the spring of 1943, one propeller "froze" when an outboard engine failed. Although he carried a 100 per cent overload, the plane flew well even though deprived of the benefit of a windmilling prop until, coming in at three hundred feet altitude, he hit a patch of violent air that caused him to lose altitude until he was down level with a ridge on the outside of town. "I had to decide quick—whether to continue over the housetops toward Merrill Field or turn around and try to gain altitude." He decided to risk coming over town. Halfway across Anchorage Reeve hit another downdraft which carried the Boeing down almost in the middle of Eleventh Street, his own block! He saw his own back yard rising to meet him, nearly hooked the wing on a transformer sticking on a pole. "Here I've flown in almost every country in South, Central, and North America," he thought, "and damned if I'm not going to crash in my own back yard!"

He managed to lift the wing enough to clear the transformer, then he got on the radio and "started yelling to Merrill Tower." He told them he was in trouble, coming in low, and to clear the field. Fortunately they were able to, and Reeve skimmed the treetops, brought the Boeing to a safe stop on the runway. He borrowed a new engine from CAA and was on his way again the next day.

But the Boeing was destined to give Reeve repeated troubles. In June, on a trip to McGrath with three two-ton spools of cable and three passengers, Reeve heard a commotion in the right-hand engine, saw that the number one cylinder had snapped off—and taken part of the wing with it. Already a hundred miles out of Anchorage, he turned around and started back. But the fractured wing kept him from maintaining altitude. At one hundred feet, however, he found enough lift in the air and was able to hold at that. But he had to get up to at least two hundred feet to clear the town of Anchorage. He managed to climb up to two hundred, was halfway across Cook Inlet when strong downdrafts caught him. He turned back for the tide flats and looked for a place to come down, finally spotted a berth that looked safe "amongst the stumps and creeks" about three hundred feet long. He flew over, started making the wide turn for final approach—and lost sight of his tiny field. He flew around another twenty minutes trying to get the limping, cumbersome plane lined up with the little spot of smooth beach. When he finally did get lined up, Bob ordered his passengers to run to the back of the plane, so that if he hit the bank, and the cables broke loose and rolled forward, they wouldn't be killed. With the passenger weight in the back, the plane was tail-heavy, which eliminated any chance of going around again. Reeve cut the gun and brought the plane to a stop in 150 feet of soft mud, the tail wheel just grazing the bank as they came in.

Calling Art Woodley on his radio, Reeve asked him for help, and Art flew over in his Travelaire and hauled everyone back to Merrill Field. When Bob examined his motor he found that, when the cylinder had blown off, the connecting rod had whipped around, destroying the engine. He remembered an old emergency engine he'd bought two years before, while flying the Northway contract. Looking for it, he found Morrison-Knudsen had "purloined" it and had it overhauled in their Anchorage shop. "There was a little hassle," admits Bob, but the bill of sale with the engine number on it, which he had remembered to keep, turned the trick. He had to remove the cylinders before he could load the engine into the Fairchild, but finally managed to get it in, and flew to "mudville" where the Boeing lay incarcerated. He also hauled over a load of twelve-foot timbers, then built a scaffold so that he could pull the old engine out and install the new one. "I did the work alone—except for the assistance of Richard, who was then seven," smiles Bob. "That emergency landing on mud flats had a bad effect on my copilot's nerves. He promptly went on a good drunk to recover from it."

The work went well until, in his hurry, Bob failed to install the master rod cylinder till the last thing. He had the master rod blocked with a wooden pin, and when he pulled out the wood to install the cylinder it dropped, pulling the pistons out of most of the remaining cylinders—and he had the job to do "all over again." But he had it finished by the morning of July 4, and ferried the Boeing to Merrill, where an emergency call from ACS was awaiting him. "A load of radar equipment and four technicians vitally needed on Amchitka." "I'd suspected some big stuff was going on out there," says Bob. "They had the North Pacific Fleet anchored at Cold Bay, and there were some twenty thousand combat troops assembled for an unnamed destination."

Late the next afternoon Bob was headed for Amchitka in his Boeing with the radar men and equipment aboard. It was ten at night, and still fifty miles from Cold Bay, when the fog started rolling in to meet him. By the time he reached the field it was closed. After several unsuccessful attempts to land, he finally headed for an emergency field ten miles south, which was reported still open. As he made the final approach, it socked in. He tried again, but could not get lined up in the dark, pea soup fog. "I found myself one thousand feet on top of the fog, had one half-hour of gas, it was midnight, no moon, blacker than hell, and I had no place to go. I was in just about the worst fix of my life."

Hovering on top of the fog in his "balloon" that would have to come tumbling down somewhere, Reeve did some split-second thinking, raking the crevices of his memory for an "out" to this apparently hopeless situation. He recalled that on other night flights between Port Moller and Cold Bay he had observed that, in similar dense fog, a rift always appeared along the streams flowing from Cathedral Valley near Mount Pavlov as they poured into the Bering Sea. The difference in the temperatures of the fresh stream water and the cold Bering Sea created enough difference in the dew point to clear the air. Reeve headed the Boeing for the coast, on the watch for one of those rifts. He finally spotted one, just as one engine quit, warning him that the gas was almost gone from the tanks. "I probably had five minutes left in the air."

He dove down, following the rift from the fresh water down to where it met the salt spray—which Bob recognized by the light of the phosphorous in the surf. Then, radioing his position into Cold Bay, he ditched the plane into the sea. "We hit like a ton of bricks, wheels down in the surf."

Everyone but the copilot was hurt. Reeve had injured his back; his passengers suffered concussion, shock, bruises. The Boeing was up on its nose in about five feet of water; six-foot rollers washed over it. Bob got a long rope and tied it to the tail of the plane, then led the rope to shore, riding in on the rollers. Then the others climbed down the rope and used it to make their way to shore. As soon as the high tide subsided, Reeve went back out to the plane and got matches and emergency rations. When the tide was completely out, he got out his radio and carried it ashore. Unlike most pilots, Reeve never carried his radio fixed or bolted into the wall of the aircraft, but had it in a portable box where he could easily salvage it in an emergency. He salvaged a battery out of the plane to work the radio, hung the antenna on the tail of the ship, then made regular reports to Cold Bay, giving the position of the crash. The men got a campfire going, then they all lay down in the sand to keep warm and rest from their shock and injuries. When one of the passengers remarked that he had a quart of whisky among his belongings, Reeve made another trip out to the ditched plane and fetched it. "We all took a shot—then fell asleep."

At daylight Reeve woke up "with a queer sensation"—and looked up into the curious face of a huge brown bear, who was standing over him sniffing his legs. While Reeve "froze" the bear moved on down the line of men, sniffing everybody. The last man was sleeping with his head turned the other way, the empty whisky bottle next to him. The bear took a big sniff, let out a startled "woof," and galloped off into the fog.

"It was Tom Burns Whisky," reminisces Bob, "reputed to cure everything from flat feet to dandruff. It sure lived up to its reputation. That ole bear got a snootful of that—and immediately thought there were half a dozen panthers lying around."

Wondering if the whole silent scene hadn't been a hallucination, induced by shock and liquor, Reeve got up and looked around, found huge bear tracks in the sand where the animal had been circling the group of sleeping men. Bob built up the campfire to smoke signal their position through the fog to rescuers, and in a little while heard, above the fog, the sound of an airplane engine. Within a few more minutes the plane was circling the area at a lower level, and "thermos jugs and sandwiches started raining down on us from out of the fog. We all ran up on a bluff to keep from getting hit." Reeve's pals from the Forty-second and Fifty-fourth troop-carrier squadrons had not forgotten him. They dropped enough food and refreshments to last a week! At noon, when the fog finally burned off, a Coast Guard PBY landed to pick up the injured men and took them in to the hospital at Dutch Harbor.

Bob elected to stick with his plane and deliver the radar cargo to the Army. A crash boat was already on its way through False Pass, piloted by Warrant Officer Mike Uttecht, who had been born and raised in the Aleutians. Uttecht arrived at the scene, Reeve saw the cargo safely loaded, and then he went back to Anchorage.

It was not until he got back to his own house, pulled off his shirt to the accompaniment of a startled cry from Tillie, that he realized he was injured. His back was solid black and blue from waist to neck. It had been wrenched in the crash, and added internal injuries still give him trouble.

But a "bad back" was minor compared to Bob's other worries. He had had no insurance on the Boeing—and it was a total loss. "I was back where I'd started the day I left Valdez: broke and down to one plane. The only difference was I had another kid and I was a few years older!"

In an effort to salvage something from the disaster, Reeve sold the engines to Morrison-Knudsen Company for $4500— F.O.B. Anchorage.

His Army buddies sent a boat from Cold Bay, then sawed the motor mounts off the plane and loaded the engines aboard. Although corroded by the salt water, they still could be repaired. Reeve kept check and received daily reports from the Army Transport Service of the voyage of the engines from Cold Bay into Anchorage. But the day they arrived he was out on a flight, and the engines were delivered to Fort Richardson. When Bob got home and went out to the base to claim them, he found the boxes with his name on them—but no engines inside. Nearby he saw a bunch of pulverized metal scrap—which he had a sickening feeling were the remains of his $4500 worth of engines! But when he demanded to know if they were, he met a "blank wall." Finally, at his angry, frustrated queries, one young GI gave in, whispered, "Those are your engines all right. We had orders to smash them up."

Reeve went to the sergeant in charge. "I know that's my engines," he said. "Now you tell me why you smashed them."

The sergeant told Reeve the story. "A general from the States came through here on a whirlwind tour—he whipped through this camp like a hurricane. When he saw your boxes, he said, 'What are those old Jap engines doing here? Smash them for salvage.' The soldiers tried to tell him they belonged to you, but he kept saying, 'I know a Jap engine when I see one. Smash them up!' He stood over us till we had the job completed."

The general was "Concrete" McMullen, a nickname won from the fact that he had survived numerous bad crashes without a scratch. Reeve had known him in South America. Bob wrote McMullen, suggesting the least he could do was give Reeve three engines of the same type. McMullen answered that mistakes were mistakes, and the law prohibited him from giving away engines. "I suggest," he said, "you sue the government."

"But I had learned early in life to keep out of court," said

Bob. "I was just plain out of my $4500. I told McMullen that from now on, he wasn't 'Concrete' to me any more—he was 'Sledgehammer.' "

Reeve's only souvenir from his Boeing wreck was a copy of *Time* magazine which he picked up in the cabin when he was transferring the radar equipment to the crash boat. Scribbled on the margins are the comments of his passengers, who couldn't make themselves heard above the roar of the engines. There are a few general remarks: then, "I think something's wrong." "Do you think we'll ditch?" And finally, the tersely humorous comment, "Walking ain't crowded."

Bob feels, however, that his wreck may have inadvertently saved American lives. The delay in the delivery of the radar equipment allowed the Japanese to secretly evacuate Kiska without detection. The bloody battle of Attu cost three thousand American casualties; but when our forces made a landing on Kiska six weeks later, not a shot was fired from the empty island.

## 14. I lay in bed and marveled
## I was still alive

In January of 1943, while he was flying the Aleutians on a tight wartime schedule that brooked no delays, Bob got some news which, though not a surprise, was a profound shock. Harold Gillam had crashed. Chief pilot for Morrison-Knudsen Gillam had taken off in an MK-owned Lockheed Electra from Seattle on a stormy January day, with five passengers, four men and a young girl, and headed north for Anchorage. Near Ketchikan he ran into dense fog and storm, the plane iced up, he had to come down. But Gillam's maps did not show the latest wartime installation of air navigational aids, and the direction on the Ketchikan range leg had been changed. Flying in on the wrong side of the range, he couldn't orient himself, one engine quit, and the Electra crashed into a mountain. Oddly, no one of the six occupants was immediately killed. Fatally injured, the girl died within hours. Gillam, dazed and with a gash on his head, went about the motions of making camp, then left the group to work his way down the mountain to the coast line, looking for help. His body was found a month later, wrapped in a parachute, his flyer's boots and red underwear strung on a pole beside him, signaling for help. An autopsy disclosed that the flyer had died of cerebral hemorrhage, the result of concussion suffered in the crash, and subsequent exposure.

In one of the shameful blots on aviation history, the search was called off before any trace of the crash had been found. It was a month before the four survivors, in critical condition, were picked up by the Coast Guard.

"Gillam's death," says Bob soberly, "was no big news to any of the pilots who knew him. The kind of flying he'd done, he'd already run out of luck ten thousand years in advance!" But it was nonetheless hard to believe. A fine instrument flyer, Gillam, Reeve feels, could have eventually found his way, if his

204

engine hadn't quit on him and the plane iced over, forcing him down. "His luck ran out, that's all. In a critical time like that, when he most needed luck—it went sour."

Noel Wien attributes Gillam's crash to the plane he was flying. "The Lockheed Electra was underpowered. It was not a good instrument ship. It got so heavily iced he couldn't stay airborne."

Questioned about Gillam's crash, all the flyers come up with some reasonable explanation. No one says "pilot error." For, of all the Alaskan flyers, Gillam was the flyer's flyer, "the greatest Alaska ever had, or ever will have."

"He got himself in a trap," comments Reeve. "He was a brilliant flyer. But he got a reputation built up that he couldn't live up to without killing himself. Harold was a little guy, you know, and he loved to show up his contemporaries. He got so he couldn't turn down any job, or any risk. He had to live up to his reputation."

Gillam's superhuman exploits are as vivid today, in the minds of his fellow flyers, as they were when he was alive. "There was no one like Gillam," they will tell you, shaking their heads in amazement. "Gillam bored through—where no other man could go." There is no argument about his standing. They agree that of all the brave and exciting flying done in the Far North, Gillam did the most amazing of it all.

And yet, Gillam was often a "rough flyer." While Reeve, according to contemporaries, was never seen to make any other than smooth, technically expert landings and take-offs, Harold's plane might "flop all over the field." Iron-nerved and daring, he was a curiously Alaskan product, his virtue that of the young frontier: supreme guts! Coming up to Alaska as a wiry kid, Gillam had quickly identified himself with the robust new land: he had taken a job as a "cat" driver when he'd never been on one before; survived the first fatal crash in Alaskan aviation when his instructor was killed. With only a few hours' flying time, the youngster had stampeded north in the Eielson search, showed the older pilots a surprising thing or two when he barreled through weather they wouldn't touch. Although Gillam's contributions in blind flying, bad weather techniques, and early instrument work, were so individual as to be of little value to the men who followed him, his Fairbanks-to-Bethel mail run, his participation in the Levanevsky search, his brilliant rescue work, were dramatic, well-loved chapters in the history of Alaskan aviation. For all the men who watched him fly in his own morose, perverse, nerveless fashion, Gillam lives as truly today as within his lifetime. "There was only one Gillam!"

Unlike Gillam, Bob had learned early in his career that the "greatest hazard to a flyer is overconfidence." "All pilots glory in their ability, their good luck," explains Bob, "and I was no exception. But time after time as I sat in that cockpit I'd say to myself, Fellow, if you think you are good, you are riding for a fall!'" As in his days flying the violent Andes, Bob forced himself to fly the violent Aleutians "always a little bit scared." He knew that the day he began to take his press notices seriously, would be the beginning of the end.

When the Army bases were completed at Amchitka and Adak, within bombing range of the Jap-held islands, the time had come to "clean up the Aleutians." The first on the list was Attu. But the Chain, as usual, had no intentions of cooperating with the military. Despite the airpower now concentrated on Amchitka, the ceaseless fog make it next to impossible to get out the planes. A few took off—and crashed into the mountains. The rough, muskeg-covered terrain also prevented the use of mechanized equipment. Attu, like so many other physically hazardous battlegrounds of World War II, thus became an infantryman's battle. A job for the man who could come in on foot, using for weapons what he could carry in his own hands.

Getting the foot soldier and his supplies onto the Attu beach was a job for Beachmaster Squeaky Anderson. As the flagship Pennsylvania inched its way into fog-shrouded Massacre Bay toward enemy-garrisoned Attu, one of the Navy officers, peering tensely into the dank, danger-packed gloom around them, heard an odd sound. "What?" he asked incredulously, turning to Lieutenant Commander Anderson, who stood beside him peering dreamily over the ship's rail.

"I said," repeated Squeaky clearly, "that democracy is a wonderful thing." Thoughtfully he caressed the new gold braid on his sleeve, then pointed into the murky water below. "See there—just one year ago I was being chased by the Coast Guard for poaching fish, right over there. And now——" again he patted the gold stripes with loving fingers, "now I'm wearing these!" (When Squeaky was first appointed commander of the Aleutian Patrol, a Coast Guard officer paled.

"My God, don't send that man out there—he'll kill all the sea otters!")

After the long, nerve-wracking wait, the boys who went in to Attu were overeager. The cry to "get a Jap" went down the lines, sent them splashing helter-skelter to their deaths in the face of the well-entrenched enemy fire. Squeaky screamed for order, lashed out at one young ensign who had let his landing-barge crew go AWOL and run up with the front lines of the infantry, "Young man," he screeched, "I vould court-martial you for this! Yes, I vould." Squeaky shook his fist in the boy's face, "I vould—if I yust knew how!"

It was not just eager boys who threw order to the winds and rushed forward to take front-line part in the battle. Colonel William "Bill" Eareckson, "the fightinest airman of them all," whose bombers had stopped the Japs at Dutch Harbor, frustrated by the fog that kept his planes on the ground, borrowed a rifle and joined the infantry to help knock out the enemy on Attu. Wounded in hand-to-hand fighting, Eareckson was later awarded the Purple Heart by General Buckner in an elaborate presentation ceremony. With the staff all smartly lined up, wise, white-thatched Buckner said, somewhat acidly, "Now, Eric, there are two parts to this ceremony. This is the formal part." He pinned the medal on Eareckson's breast. "Next is the informal part. Turn around." Eareckson complied, and General Buckner gave him a swift kick in the pants. "That," said Buckner, "is for being so damn careless!" (It was, however, the gallant general, not his precipitous colonel, who was later killed in combat, when struck by shellfire while on reconnaissance on Okinawa. Buckner died, goes the legend, with a smile on his lips—"the way he'd have liked to.")

The bloody battle of Attu lasted from the initial landing on May 11 (1943) until May 30, when the last Jap was dead. In a suicidal last stand, the entrenched Japanese could not be ferreted out and taken prisoner, but remained at their posts until all of their forces (with the exception of three men whom the Army managed to capture before they could commit suicide) were killed. The Japanese were determined to take as many American lives with them to their deaths as possible. Even after the last Japanese soldier lay dead, several hundred more American lives were lost when the soldiers fell for "booby traps" that had been cunningly planted by the Japanese, with bomb attachments. "They had beautiful fur coats, jewelry, all sorts of things lying around," reports Squeaky sadly, "all the kinds of things that boys would be tempted to pick up."

Squeaky served as beachmaster at the Kiska landing, on August 15, expecting that they would all be "shot like rats." But no one was there. In the interim the Japanese forces had quietly sneaked off—savings thousands of lives.

When the Navy had secured the Aleutians, they moved their ships and men on to the Central Pacific theater. Squeaky, who had served as beachmaster for the infantry and Marine landings on Amchitka, Adak, Attu, and Kiska, went on to the Pacific to become "king of the beachmasters," his foghorn screech "the most familiar sound in the Pacific theater." Serving as beachmaster for sixteen amphibious landings, the bloodiest fighting of the war, on Tarawa, Peleliu, Saipan, Iwo Jima, Okinawa, Squeaky was eventually made an admiral for his spectacular work, the only beachmaster (and the only Alaskan) ever so honored. Asked his definition of his job, Squeaky explained earnestly, "To get the Marines their bullets and beans when they needs 'em!" His recipe for his fantastic ability to get men and supplies ashore amidst chaos and gunfire: "I'm the orneriest sonofabitch around." His special knack for getting work out of the most unwilling and terrified worker he ascribes to this recipe: "The admiral gives me hell all the time, and I parcel it out."

Most of the Air Force fighter and bomber squadrons also moved to the Pacific theater, with the exception of several bomber groups stationed at Shemya and Attu, to bomb northern Japanese islands six hundred miles over water, "about the most rugged bombing missions of the whole war," according to Bob. Once, when Reeve was on a busman's holiday with a bomber group at Shemya, a bomber took off in a crosswind, drifted into a hut on the side of the runway; all the bombs exploded, killing several men. Among the seriously injured survivors was the son of the Reeves' next door neighbor when they lived at Fairbanks.

Although locally based enemy bombers and fighters were frequently active in the vicinity during this period, only once was American soil struck by bombs from the Japanese mainland. A mission came over to bomb the Attu field—in return for the havoc the American bombers had wreaked on Paramushiro. In those forays some of the Yankee bombers, hit by antiaircraft fire and unable to return to their home base, were forced down on the Amchatka peninsula, where they were interned by the Russians and their planes confiscated. Fascinated by the work of the B-24's and B-25's off Shemya, under the direction of Brigadier General Harry "Swede" Johnson, Reeve requested to go on a mission—but was refused. He had been given a taken commission as a captain in the United States Army so that he would be given the was refused. He had been given a token commission as a captured by the Japanese, and not shot as a spy—but that "token," the Air Force informed him, didn't buy him a ride on a bomber!

Once, before the Aleutians were secured, when she was pregnant with her fourth child, David, Tillie heard the phone ring late at night, and Bob, who was due to go out on an early flight, answer. The one side of the conversation that she heard was hardly reassuring. "Yes, I have my card [stating he was rated as an Army captain]. Yes, I have my gun." It occurred to his listening wife with chilling clarity that Bob needed a gun—to shoot himself if captured. "Damn those Japs," she whispered to herself as she fell asleep.

Although the Japanese forces had been driven off the Chain, "the big push" was on—toward the west. Japan still had control of the seas surrounding her home islands, and the accent in fighting was on the air, demanding that the airfields and navigational aids be constantly expanded as the main task force pushed through. Eventually, when the Japanese Navy had lost some of its power, the strategy was switched to the amphibious island-hopping technique that eventually won the war. But from 1943 through 1945 the pressures of Bob's work were as great as when the enemy had actually occupied the Chain.

"I got so that I paid no attention to storms, wind, violent air—just pushed on through." To get from Cook Inlet to the Bering Sea, Bob had a choice of two passes: Iliamna or Lake Clark, neither of which he usually could get through "without a fight" at any time of year. "I'd try Lake Clark a few times and take a beating. Deciding Iliamna was never like this, I'd switch to it—and find it worse."

So long as the wind was head on, he bucketed through. Once, hitting a terrific crosswind in Lake Clark Pass, he found it impossible to remain airborne. He held out till he reached Iliamna airfield, but was so busy fighting the wind he did not have a chance to use his radio and call in for field instructions. Coming in for a landing, he was startled to find rows of iron stakes planted over the surface of the entire field. He came in anyway, plunking down between two of the stakes. He found that the field was closed and that the stakes had been placed to mark low spots in the runway which needed surfacing. "Couldn't you have at least put up wooden ones?" demanded Reeve. "We tried them," the field officials explained, "but they blew away!"

The turbulent air through which he flew daily was such a normal condition that it became routine. On one flight in from the Chain, after being socked in for a full week and living on Army rations, Reeve hit the usual patch of violent air in Lake Clark Pass, fought his way through, and landed at Anchorage. When they were safely down, one of his passengers said to Reeve, "In civilian life I am a psychologist. And I couldn't help but be curious as to just what was going through your mind when we were being tossed around in that violent air. Would you tell me?"

Reeve scratched his head, thought back. "Oh, I remember. I was wondering what my wife was going to give me for lunch."

The man turned his back and walked away without another word.

Although he was unruffled by it, the sheer physical effort of controlling the plane during the severe turbulence became a problem for Bob. "When I hit violent air, I could have gone back where I started and waited for it to calm down. But I decided if I started doing it, I'd be doing it all the time. And then I'd be through as a flyer." The thing he could not control was his limit of muscular endurance. Once in Chile, caught in a violent storm in a deep canyon while flying the Lockheed Vega—which had a very short control stick—Bob's arm muscles actually gave out, so that he could no longer hang on. When he let go, the plane plunged from six thousand feet altitude down toward the bottom of the canyon, hit calmer air near the earth, and proceeded forward on its own, at two hundred feet, in level flight. His arm had not yet "given out" on his Aleutian run, but Bob feared it was only a matter of time. To offset that risk, he added a full foot to the length of his control stick and installed a pistol-grip extension, which gave him both greater leverage and a comfortable hold over long periods of time. "After that it was duck soup." But during those wartime years Bob's right arm grew until it actually doubled the circumference of his left and felt "just like a stick of wood."

Bob added some other modifications for the special problems of Aleutian flying. He built up a tail wheel instead of the skid, since it was easier to maneuver and park on the ground. He took off the airwheels and replaced them with old-style hard tires, which added five more miles per hour to his air speed because they had less drag. He carried two radio sets installed in the plane, and stretched his antenna in multiple angles from the wings to the tail surfaces, so that directionally he would have equally good reception no matter which way the plane was turned. He added a trailing antenna for long-range reception and transmission.

He learned, although flying contact, that he could keep on going through both moderate and dense fog—if he could follow a coast line with combers to watch. Once, on a trip from Port Heiden to Cold Bay, a GI asked to go along for the ride. A little way out they hit zero visibility. Bob made a beach landing to wait out the fog, was so tired he fell asleep sitting in the cockpit. Three hours later, when he woke, the combers were already awash up to the fuselage of the ship. "Why in hell didn't you wake me up?" he roared. "I went to sleep too," said the soldier, "then when I did wake up, I didn't bother to waken you because I didn't think there was anything we could do about it now!"

They sat there for three hours more waiting for the tide to recede. When it had gone down a few inches and the fog had risen a little, they fired up and went on to Port Heiden.

As in his mud-flat days, tide became as important to Bob as his maps. One day the weather officer at Cold Bay warned him of an approaching storm, but Bob felt he could get through before it would hit. He got about fifty miles out when it moved in fast, blacking out "the whole damn coast line," not leaving even misty combers to guide by. Bob turned back to Port Heiden, got near the field, but the fog was so thick he could not find his way down. A tantalizing glimpse of land—then it socked in, so that he was unable to get lined up with the runway. He decided to get out of there and try Naknek. "There were lots of radio towers sticking up around the field, and I didn't want to make their acquaintance in the fog." He whipped down the beach with a thirty-mile tailwind—then remembered that there was a place where the coast made a sharp right-angle turn. If he overshot the turn he would miss the coast line, and thus lose all visual reference to land. He'd have to pull up to go on instruments, and the air was saturated with water, which meant he'd run into heavy icing conditions a few hundred feet up, since it was already near freezing on the ground. He decided he'd better come down—somewhere.

A few days before, flying along this coast, Bob had noticed a dead walrus on the beach and, watching it, had also seen—and recorded for future reference if he decided to get the tusks—a strip of beach long enough to land on, just beyond the trophy. Now he glued his eyes on the dim beach ahead, looking for the walrus!

Finally he caught a glimmer of the white tusks through the fog, promptly cut his gun, and landed straight ahead. At the rate he was traveling he had overshot half the sandy spot, but, coming down onto the soft sand, he managed to stop the airplane before hitting the bank at the edge. Bob unloaded the four passengers he had with him and ordered them up above the tide line. The tide was only a few feet from the plane, rolling in with big, six-foot combers. Bob studied the setup uneasily. Since the beach ended abruptly in a high bank, there was no hope of pulling the plane up past the tide line. But he sure didn't want to lose his one last airplane! He got on his radio, called Port Heiden.

"This is Fairchild 7039. I have landed on the beach. What is the tide today?"

"You're not a boat. You're an airplane!" came the reply. "What do you want with the tide?"

"A few more of these goddam rollers and I'll be a boat. Now, you give me that tide!" The operators went for the tidebook, and came back with the report: "Today is the highest tide of the year."

"Well," reported Reeve, "it's zero-zero here, but I'm getting off the first second it lifts."

He turned the plane to head it into the wind, flattened the prop, got the motor running, tossed out all the emergency rations—and abandoned the passengers. "I've got to get this plane out of here," he explained, "or I won't have one. But I'll send a weasel back for you as soon as I get in." Five minutes passed, and the combers were still climbing. Bob knew he had to get off in minutes or he would be literally sunk. Noticing he had a broken tail wheel, he took his ax and chopped it off so it wouldn't whip around—then waited, poised to go. The ceiling lifted about one hundred feet. He gunned off the sand in less than one hundred feet, made it into the Port Heiden field, thirty miles away. As his wheels touched the runway, the weather socked in around him, zero-zero again—a violent storm that lasted five days. The field sent a weasel out for the passengers. Reeve thanked his luck and thought back to Captain Cooper's words that morning when he took off. "I'm warning you, Bob, you'll never make it this time!" "From then on," says Bob, "I quit cloud-watching, gave up personal forecasting, and made Cooper my Aleutian sector weather officer."

Reeve's Aleutian flying was uncharacteristically reckless—and he knew it. "A man will do a lot of things," he says soberly, "with a war to win and a wife and bunch of kids to support." Reeve's hair, which had begun graying during his glacier flying, turned completely white. He gained weight, eating nervously between flights. He smoked incessantly. His speech was abrupt, his manner jittery. Sometimes when he was just going to sleep his heart felt as if it were stuffing his throat. At an age when most men begin to taper off their most vigorous activities, Reeve was performing the most consistently dangerous and exhausting flying of his career. Down to that one lone little red Fairchild as his total means of saying in business, he became increasingly spooky about losing his plane.

Out at Merrill Field one day, as he lay under the plane working on it in his greasy coveralls, a fastidious young Air Corps major approached, watched curiously for a few minutes. "What," he finally asked, "is that aircraft?"

"Fairchild DGA," growled Reeve.

"DGA, old man?" asked the youngster.

"Damn Good Airplane," roared Reeve, getting to his feet, towering threateningly over the young officer. "And if you call me 'old man' again, I'll turn you over my knee!"

Only a novice sniffed at Reeve and his dilapidated little antique plane. For the knowledgeable airmen, Reeve's flying was some of the most extraordinary performed in World War II. "Even the boldest Army pilots . . . cross their fingers and utter profanely respectful comments when they see Bob Reeve's airplane on an Aleutian landing strip," reported a UP release from the headquarters of Alaska's Defense Command. "A veteran combat pilot shuddered recently when Reeve's battered old Fairchild slipped in through the fog to a three-point landing on Umnak field. 'I'd as soon kite around them volcanoes on an ironing board,' confessed the vet."

Both friends and officials often felt Bob was pushing too hard.

Knowing that Reeve was flying vital wartime supplies, CAA Inspector Burleigh Putnam left him pretty much alone, except for three occasions when he felt Bob's flying procedures deserved a dressing down and warning not to repeat. He called Reeve on the carpet about losing his Boeing, and once for getting lost in a storm. There was one other time. Flying in from Cold Bay on a black winter night with five passengers aboard, Bob ran into ice fog as he approached Cook Inlet, which sheathed the propeller, fuselage, and wings within minutes, causing the Fairchild to "lumber along like a hay barn." With no deicing equipment, Bob had to "sit down" fast. But he did not dare try to land in the Inlet, since the tide was out and he would have hit the huge ditches on shore, wrecking the plane. Besides, it was pitch dark, and he couldn't see to make a forced landing. He opened his window, peered out, and kept his plane lined up with the line of the beach. Since he could not fly across to Anchorage without any visual reference, he followed the beach around the Inlet, wondering if he could keep his heavily iced plane in the air till he reached the field. By the time he reached the city, at an altitude of 200 feet, the iced-up prop was barely rotating with enough thrust to keep the plane air-borne. Since he couldn't bank or turn his "iced barn," Reeve called ahead to clear Merrill Field for a straight-in approach—and made it down. Burleigh Putnam took a look at the ice-sheathed plane and shook his head: "I didn't think it was possible." When Putnam gave Reeve a lecture for flying in an ice storm, Reeve agreed with him. "I get your point. But I didn't pick up that ice on purpose."

Sometimes it seemed that Bob had as many lives as a cat. Most Army pilots, and many Alaskans, shunned Rainy Pass in the Alaskan Range between Anchorage and McGrath, if possible. But one afternoon Bob flew the treacherous, winding route three times within one half hour. There was good reason for Rainy's reputation: You never know, when you started through, whether the clouds were high enough for the full run. You never knew whether, once in, you would have a chance to run around. "I lost more copilots there than anywhere else", reports Bob cheerfully of the days before he lost his Boeing. "They suffered a silent death every trip." Coming in from Flat with a load of twenty flasks of high war priority quicksilver, Reeve was only fifteen miles into the Pass when he switched on to his last remaining fuel tank—only to have the fuel pressure gauge drop to zero. Condensed water had settled in the bottom of the sump of the full tank and frozen enroute, blocking the fuel line. "A lifetime practice saved my neck," explains Bob. "I never let a gas tank go completely dry, but always left five or ten minutes' reserve in it—for emergency." He switched back to the "good" tank with its ten minutes of gas. But there was no place to sit down. He was in the mountains, over Bud Branham's lodge and weather station on the lake. Reeve looked down and considered. The lake had four or five feet of snow—he was sure to nose over, the flasks would break loose and "give me a good massaging when that sixteen hundred pounds of quicksilver came to rest on my back." As usual in emergency—there had been so many now!—Bob's mind worked lightning swift, sorting out possible solutions. He thought of an old bush field that had been constructed on the Rhone River at the west entrance of Rainy in the old days, and abandoned. When he had entered the pass he had noticed that the wind had blown the snow off this old field. He turned back—hoping his gas would hold till he came within gliding distance of the strip. The pass was about fifteen miles long, it was another five to the field. He had not less than ten minutes left in the good tank, nor more than fifteen. He climbed to lengthen his glide, and the gas held out till he was five miles short of the field. He went into a glide, but the heavy load of freight made the plane descend rapidly. He realized he could not make the field—but a strange new possibility occurred to him. The sun was shining directly onto the front of his airplane. Could it have melted the ice obstruction in the fuel tank? He switched back onto the fresh tank with apprehensive fingers. As the plane descended, the temperature rose till it was above thirty-two. By the time he had slipped down to five hundred feet, the engine suddenly caught, the fuel pressure bounded up. The line thawed. At two hundred feet altitude—his lucky number—he found himself on full power once more.

Now he didn't need to land. He turned around and went back through—his third flight through the pass in one half hour! "I flew home wondering what kind of a rabbit's foot I'd got hold of."

After flying the Aleutians steadily for a year, the old Fairchild's power plant began to "buck" for no apparent reason, and developed serious engine trouble. The first warning was the blowing of the exhaust valves. Reeve discovered that the lip of the valves had become leaded and burned, which caused improper seating of the valves and resulted in blow-bys. Once blow-bys started, the valves were on the road to ruin. Next trouble showed up in the intake valves, which caused a substantial loss of engine power. The twin spark plugs in each cylinder became so leaded that they functioned little better than a single plug. When one plug became leaded the firing of the remaining plug caused a torching effect of the compressed fuel mixture that seared the top of the piston and both valves. Reeve had no time to stop and remove the cylinders and grind the valves and reseat them every trip—so he lapsed into an unorthodox bush-pilot answer for his troubles. Each day, after landing, he placed each cylinder at top dead center and whacked the valve rocker arm above the valves with a rubber mallet. The spring back of the valves knocked off the lead and reseated them—to some degree, at least enough for that next trip.

Bob talked to all the mechanics he knew about the leading that troubled him, but no one seemed to understand the cause. But Bob was enough of a mechanic to realize that he could not go on as he was. In addition to the danger of flying violent weather over water with constant engine trouble, the daily hammering of the valves distorted the valve seats. When Bob reseated them, then pulled the prop through to listen for a blow-by, there finally came the check when every cylinder blew by! He realized now that progressive deterioration had caught up with him. He took the engine into the Wiens' shop at Fairbanks to get an overhaul. When Elbert Quam, Wien's chief mechanic, took a look at it, he shook his head. "I've seen everything! I don't see how you ever got this engine started— let alone flying it all these hours!" Three of the intake valves were "down to stems."

With the engine torn down, Reeve could understand the internal explosions he had frequently experienced during flight. The raw gas had blown back from each cylinder through the leaking valve into the exhaust system—with resultant torchings and explosions. The obvious hazard was, of course, eventual failure of the engine. "I had become reconciled to flying over land with an exploding engine, but out over water, flying only fifty feet above the waves and having the damn thing explode was hardly conducive to my peace of mind!"

The answer to Reeve's puzzling problem lay in the famous experiment of his friend and fellow Alaskan Jimmy Doolittle with highly leaded hundred-octane fuel for military planes. A success for modern Air Corps planes, the heavily leaded high octane gas, which was all Reeve could get at the Aleutian bases, played havoc with his old Wasp engine, which was a low-compression engine designed for the use of eighty-octane fuel. With its low compression ratio, the result was improper combustion—and the impurities in the gas impregnated the valves, pistons, and spark plugs.

Reeve was not the only one who suffered from the leaded gas. When a big flood carried the caches of Air Force gas away from the banks of the Kuskokwim, all the Indians, trappers, and fishermen along the river soon had their private gas cache "for years in advance." But within a week the Northern Commercial Company trading post was swamped with demands for new outboard motors and Coleman gas lamps. The highly leaded aircraft gas had destroyed both the boat engines and household lamps!

Reeve's perilous flying drew a lot of attention from the military and the press—and some jealousy on the home front. Then at last his fellows "had one on him." An Air Force DC-3 became lost and crash landed on a ridge at Dillingham near Naknek. In order to retrieve the plane the Air Force dug out a four-hundred-foot field along the ridge, so that they could fly the plane out—quite a feat on the extremely short and hazardous run, but they made it. The emergency field was generally regarded as one to stay away from, but the Signal Corps had supplies labeled for Dillingham, and Reeve flew in, landed on the four-hundred-foot strip in a strong wind with no difficulty. Other pilots, who were reluctant to land there, decided Bob was a "traitor to the profession." Reeve made three more successful landings at Dillingham, but on the fourth he overshot the tiny field in a crosswind and ended up fifty feet off the strip "out in the niggerheads." The word sped around by "mukluk telegraph," and next week the story was going the rounds, as pilots gleefully reported that Reeve had overshot "a thousand feet." A month later it was by fifteen hundred feet. "They were getting such a kick out of telling it there was no use spoiling their fun," laughed Reeve. "I told 'em any time I can land and only overshoot fifteen hundred feet, that's fine with me!"

Bob's initial survey route, from Edmonton to Nome, had brought him into contact with Russian flyers. There were substantial Russian colonies in both Fairbanks and Nome, where they picked up lend-lease planes, flew them on to Russia. The flyers were principally fighter pilots, and they "gunned around," according to Bob's frugal eye, "with great attrition to both aircraft and human life."

They also furnished Bob with one of the most surprising aviation sights of his life. In Nome one day he looked up at the sky, saw a lend-lease C-47 come in from Siberia with a piece of stovepipe sticking out of its fuselage and a trail of black smoke behind it. When the plane had landed, Bob couldn't resist going inside the cabin for a look. There, he found a potbellied coal stove installed in the middle of the cabin floor, a hole cut out of the top of the fuselage for its pipe.

"How does it work?" Bob asked curiously.

"Fine now," said the Russian flyer through an interpreter. "At first, though, we had trouble getting enough dampers in the stovepipe to keep the coal from flying out while in flight."

The early planes of the war had water-jacket heaters only, which were not designed for Arctic conditions, and froze up. The Russians had, at least, managed a way to keep warm. "When I saw that stove installed in that C-47," said Bob, "I decided I'd seen everything!"

Although the native Aleuts of Attu and Kiska had been taken prisoner by the Japanese, and those on the American bases evacuated to southeastern Alaska "for the duration," Bob got to know a number of the islanders. They had, through their first-hand knowledge of the Aleutians, become an important part of the war effort, serving on surface craft along the Chain, and being active in ground, sea, and air rescue parties. He liked the Aleuts, their ingenuity, helpfulness, honesty. During the years he flew the chain, whenever he found an old-time resident (the Aleuts were not evacuated from the Alaskan peninsula) who did not have a priority needing medical care, he hauled him in to Anchorage for free.

As he became increasingly familiar with the islands, an idea began to take hold in Bob's brain. He had no certificated territory; the war would eventually be over, and his contract as well. He needed a postwar territory. Why not the Chain? With its great natural resources, coupled with its new strategic position in American defense, the Aleutians would always have some sort of population.

In peacetime the Chain, as well as the nearby Shumagin and Pribilof Islands, would always be populated by those whose livelihoods stemmed from the natural resources of land and sea. It was one of the richest fishing areas in the world; the only place in the U.S. possessions where fur-sealing was carried on. At that time, there was no scheduled air transportation available. Islanders were forced to rely, for their mail and supplies, one a once-a-month summer boat, two to four boats during the stormy winters. There was no emergency medical aid beyond an on-call Health Service boat in summer. When the war was over and the people came back to their villages, there would be a year-round, stable population of both Aleuts and whites. During the summer season, fishermen flocked in to the Shumagin Islands and the Alaskan Peninsula from Seattle and the Alaska Mainland. There would be seasonal cannery trade, for which flying would certainly be a valuable saving in time—and probably money.

Harold Gillam had talked of perhaps adding Aleutian service to his fast-growing Gillam Airways. Northwest Airlines had applied for a Seattle-Alaska route in 1942, and now, with military fields available along the Chain, they made plans to apply for the "great circle route" to the Orient, which would bring their planes out over the Chain on the shortest route to Asia.

Bob thought in terms of a local Alaskan line, based out of Anchorage, to serve the Chain dwellers and the seasonal cannery interests. It would take, he realized, bigger planes than his single-engine Fairchild. He would need dual engine transports, such as the military used. Something like the Army C-47's, big enough to haul freight, mail, and passengers, and equipped with air navigational instruments so that they could fly the Chain in all weather on a regular schedule.

By early 1945 the European war had come to an end, and, due to the final strategy of Central Pacific island-hopping, the Alaskan theater also tapered off. There was no longer any plan to move into Asia, by air, from Nome. When the "big push" was finally over, Reeve "lay in bed and marveled that I was still alive."

As soon as his wartime work slackened, Bob resumed bush flying, with his Fairchild, until the time came when he could buy a larger plane. On a trip to Kotzebue, in March, 1945, carrying two old-time Alaskan traveling salesmen, Clark Andreson and Bailey Covey, Reeve was met by old-time Arctic bush flyer and trader Archie Ferguson. Before Reeve could climb out of the cockpit, Archie stuck his head inside the plane. "Larry Shelton is down with my Cessna some place between here and Fairbanks. He's got a woman and two children with him, and we gotta find them fast before they freeze."

Bob promptly refueled and, with Archie for guide, started back over Shelton's route. They flew east for 250 miles, the limit of Bob's return gas supply, without finding a trace of the plane, and then headed back for Kotzebue. Thirty miles west of Kobuk, just as the sun was setting, Reeve spotted a T-shaped shadow on a small lake. Bob circled the lake. It was the downed plane, all right, but the prospects were not good. Shelton had come to roost among ice hummocks from a foot to three feet high. However, the temperature was thirty below zero and old hands Reeve and Ferguson knew they had to get the passengers out or they would surely freeze. Bob made a landing—which broke his tail ski but did not other damage to the plane. They found the woman and two children in the plane, cold but unhurt. Shelton, they said, had started walking out to find help. Bob loaded the passengers and flew them in to Kobuk, where the local trader put them up for the night. Next morning Bob started out again, looking for Shelton. After a fruitless search, landing at Shungnak to take on gas, Reeve found that Shelton had reached there the night before. The flyer was "suffering from bad frostbite as a result of wearing a short parka": Reeve carried him, along with the passengers, into Kotzebue. Poor Shelton had to be hospital-ed to thaw out, and merciless Archie christened him "the Kobuk Capon" on account of his frosty injury.

With his "stake" from his Aleutian flying, Bob began looking around for some business opportunity, in which to invest his savings until modern airplanes were available for purchase.

Anchorage was obviously, as he had predicted, the hub of aviation, the transportation center of Alaska. It would grow rather than lessen in population after the war. Reeve looked around for a solid investment, finally found a small hardware store for sale on Fourth Avenue, the main street of Anchorage. But when he approached the owner, who had said he wanted to sell, the man was hot one day, cool the next.

Impatient as usual, Reeve decided to speed up the man's decision. He told his poker friends out at Fort Richardson to go to this hardware shop whenever they were in town, nose around a bit, then drop a little advice to the owner. "With our war strategy moving to the South Pacific, in a few months from now you'll be able to shoot a gun down the main street of Anchorage—and not hit a dog!"

A month went by, and Reeve was no nearer a deal with the owner. When he complained to his buddies that they weren't doing their job, they hotly denied the charge. "We've been in nearly every day—giving the old man the works."

About this time the largest hardware store in town went up for sale—cater-cornered across from the one Reeve had tried to buy. Although the price was several times higher than that of the smaller store, Reeve interested some partners in the investment, and the men decided to make the purchase. When they delivered their down payment and had signed the sales agreement, the owner of the store said, "Fellows, I hate to tell you this. But the strategy has moved to the South Pacific, and in a few months you'll be able to shoot a gun down Main Street here—and not hit a dog!"

Reeve's buddies had been in the wrong store, talking to the wrong man!

A few months later, the owner of the building in which the hardware store was located suffered a heart attack and offered the building for sale, giving Reeve & Company first chance. "Had to raise a lot of money to buy the building—but we had to buy it to save the store." Today the property is still rising in value.

Despite his rigorous flying schedules, Bob had not forsaken

his interest in mining. Wherever he landed and found die-hard miners still operating during the war, he bought up their raw gold, then hauled it into Anchorage and sold it to the jewelry stores—which netted him a little profit (he paid the standard thirty-five dollars per ounce, sold it at fifty dollars) and also saved jewelers the price of a chartered flight. In 1942, when his mining friend Carl Whitham had wanted to get in on the war effort, Bob had found him a job as construction superintendent on Dutch Harbor. When that job was finished Carl came into Anchorage, and he and Bob formed a partnership to develop some of Whitman's old prospects that dated back to the early 1900's. Few of them had any merit, but it gave Carl and Bob some happy hours reminiscing and planning, and occasionally a brief horseback prospecting trip—a welcome letdown after Bob's hazardous flying.

On a flight Bob made into Canada, Jean Jacquot at Burwash Landing showed him some coarse gold from claims he had on Burwash Creek. Reeve recognized tellurium in the gold, and a qualitative analysis showed it to be petzite. In the fall of 1946, Reeve and Whitham made arrangements to take over Jacquot's claims. Jean had more samples that the Indians had brought in from an extensive outcropping fifteen miles west of Burwash. Whitham recognized nickel and other minerals, and set out with a pack train to stake the claim. A sudden snow storm, however, prevented him from locating the outcroppings. The following spring Whitham died of cancer, and Reeve, without a partner, gave up his longtime search for gold. Eight years later the nickel claims were staked by the Hudson's Bay Company, and drillings revealed one of the biggest discoveries in the northwest.

But Bob's gold days were over, for good—their only legacy in the Reeves' youngest son, born one month after Carl's death, and christened Whitham Reeve.

As soon as planes were available, Bob was to embark in the air-line business, which left no time for daydreams or prospecting trips. His greatest hope for a successful line, Bob decided, was that he had picked a territory "nobody else wanted." All of his life, his successes, his very economic security had been based on flying where no one else wished to fly, doing things no one else wanted to do.

# 15. Wanta ticket to Alaska?

No country inherited more from a war than Alaska. As a result of its important role in World War II, Alaska got fifty airports and 8300 miles of navigational airways. Although CAA did not come into Alaska until 1939, once there, it worked with fantastic speed. By the time of the Pearl Harbor attack in 1941, it had already in those two short years put in 4000 miles of operating airways. Three years later there were over 7000, and by 1946, 8300. Alaska, which had developed aviation on its own, with no federal aid, and had existed without communications or paved runways until the war, found itself, by 1945, equipped with a network of airways as good as, and often better than, those anywhere else in the United States. "The Territory," said General Twining, at the time he was commanding general of Alaska, in a statement before CAB, "is itself a natural air theater. ... As we picture it, the cities here are islands in the sea, just as divorced from each other as if out in the ocean."

To see to it that the islands were properly linked, CAA had installed half a hundred modern airports, of which forty-two had runways five thousand feet and more in length, forty maintained RON (Remain Over Night) facilities for pilots and travelers, twenty-six had control towers, twenty-five had hangars. Weather information was gathered from 150 different stations, and broadcast to flyers from 49 stations. Fifty-four radio ranges had been installed in the Territory. There was a major airport at approximately every 150 miles, one airport to every 1700 people in the Territory. With the fighting over, the Army began rapidly turning these wartime facilities back to CAA, as fast as CAA was able to take over their maintenance with its limited personnel. When the wartime furor died and the military pulled out, citizens of the Territory looked around—to find that their legacy was a setup of aviation facilities as fine as any commercial line in the States was accustomed to, Alaska, with its imposed dependence on air-power for all of its facets of life, had exactly what it most needed. It was ready to meet its destiny as "crossroads of the world." It had the necessary facilities to be hospitable to world-wide aviation.

CAA spread the word of the facilities now available in the Far North, and encouraged both commercial and private flyers to try them. But they gave States-trained pilots this note of warning: "Some of the older bush flyers frequently fly contact through the mountain passes. However, this procedure is not recommended, not only on account of downdrafts, but also on account of the possibility of taking the wrong valley which may end in a blind alley." They recommended that all flyers venturing North carry full bush-style equipment: maps, guns, emergency rations, first-aid kits, matches, flares, and pocket compass. Despite its modern fields, Alaska still required bush-type know-how to survive.

Northwest Airlines made plans for a seven-hour tourist run from Seattle to Anchorage, using DC-4's (later expanded to a five-hour run, with comfortable Boeing Stratocruisers and DC 6-B's); and eventually meant to fly the Orient route, via the Aleutians to Tokyo, Hong Kong, and Manila. Canadian Pacific Airlines ("the strangest schedule in the world, from South America, Asia and Australia to Vancouver, and thence to Amsterdam"), added Hong Kong to its certificated route, and made plans to fly out over the Chain, using Cold Bay as a refueling station. Pan American and Alaska Airlines established mainliner service from the States to Fairbanks. Art Woodley made plans for a States-to-Anchorage schedule to be based in Seattle, for his Pacific Northern line. The Wien brothers mapped out a regular schedule north of the Arctic Circle to serve the Eskimo towns of Point Barrow and Kotzebue, as well as Nome. Ray Petersen merged with Gillam Airways, Bert Ruoff's Bristol Bay Service, Jim Dodson and John Walatka to form Northern Consolidated Airlines to serve Fairbanks and Anchorage and connect these major cities with the Bristol Bay and Kurkokwim areas.* Merle Smith bought out the Christenson Air Service and took over Cordova Airlines to serve the Copper River Valley, the Gulf coast, and Prince William Sound. Alex Holden and Shell Simmons went

---

* Petersen is now president of Northern Consolidated.

together to form Alaska Coastal; Bob Ellis became Ellis Air-lines of Ketchikan.

Alaskan aviation was booming—or would be as soon as they could all get their hands on bigger planes. The bush pilots furrowed their brows over books on instruments, talked gleefully of the future when, according to one, "I'm going to get me one of them big, double-breasted tin airplanes with two motors and holes punched for two more!" By 1945, twenty Alaskan air lines had been certificated by CAB, and thirteen others were seeking certificates.

The bush pilots looked around happily at all the fine new equipment, sometimes found there were "things to learn" about using it. Flying into the handsome new 7500-foot run-way at Nome, Jim Dodson hit a thirty-mile crosswind and, electing to land with the wind rather than against it, calmly set his plane down across the 500-foot width of the runway, di-rectly in front of the tower. Army personnel in the tower scat-tered, sure the "wild man" would crash into the building. But the CAA control man laughed. "He knows what he's doing. He's been landing on 500-foot fields all his life!"

Madman Archie Ferguson decided there never had been anything as much fun as a plane radio to fool with, and kept up a running monologue during all his flights, describing his every motion in a high-pitched screech that drowned out all other transmissions. When he also developed the endearing trick of carrying on family feuds with his wife, who had a transmitter at their trading post, CAA personnel ordered him off the air "unless there is an emergency." "Hell," screeched Archie, "any time I'm flyin' it's an emergency!"

As the military pulled out, the burden of maintenance of the network of fields fell on CAA. Over at their Anchorage airport, CAA's own Alaskan supply service, the Happy Action Traction Faction, as Pilot Jack Jefford and copilot Fuzz Rog-ers called their outfit, kept the CAA's DC-3, King Chris (named after CAA prophet of preparedness, Chris Lample), in the air around the clock, hauling federal airways person-nel, food, and airport equipment over the Territory. A second plane, a Boeing 247, served as the "grocery and light delivery truck for CAA personnel," while the work horse, King Chris, was given a five-and-a-half-foot-square big door in its left side to haul oversized loads—such as Diesel engines, generators, iron platforms. The King Chris then became, according to its whimsical pilots, a DC-3½-BD—Big Door. Jefford installed a hand-operated winch at the head of the cabin for loading and unloading heavy equipment, also carried a demounted A-frame to set up where local manpower was short and the pilots had no help in the unloading. The oddest load the King Chris ever swallowed was a Taylorcraft airplane that needed to be hauled from Juneau to Anchorage. (It was not flyable at the time.) The resourceful pilots knocked the pins out of the wings and put the plane through the BD nose first. There was just room enough to make the turn into the cabin, and finally the tail was slipped inside, then wings added last (as well as ten passengers!) It looked, said observers, just like "a snake swallowing a frog."

In February, 1946, Reeve got a call from an old barnstorming friend of his, Colonel (now Brigadier General) Leslie Mulzer, who was then commanding Elmendorf Airfield. "We're about to declare some of our C-47's surplus," he tipped off Bob. "My private plane is going to be first. The price is twenty thousand dollars each, three thousand dollars down and the rest in three years. It will be handled through RFC."

Reeve hurried to the RFC headquarters in Fairbanks and put his name in the hat for the first airplane. He was the first applicant, and within ten days he had the first DC-3 turned loose for surplus in the Northwest. (When Archie Ferguson heard that Bob had bid for a twin-engine plane, he screamed with horror. "Jeezus, Bob, what d'ya want that for? You'll just have twice as much trouble!")

Although the initial price was remarkably low, the operators desiring the planes were slowed up because of the reputed cost of converting them from military to commercial use. The quoted cost of conversion of one military C-47 into a commercial DC-3 with license for commercial use was about fifty thousand dollars. When Bob read the specifications for conversion, he estimated he could accomplish the preliminary licensing himself and get the plane for about $5,000. The requirements were far less critical than he had feared. He heard rumors of a boat strike in the offing, which would paralyze service between Seattle and Alaska—just as thousands of wartime workers were leaving, and others who had left Alaska during the war were swarming back to their homes. Despite all the postwar aviation plans, the only States-Alaska air service actually in operation was Pan Am's Fairbanks-to-Seattle route. Realizing there would soon be a tremendous demand for air service, Bob decided to take advantage of this fluke and cash in when the opportunity offered itself. He ferried his new plane to Spokane and began working on its conversion round the clock. He had it equipped for commercial operation and got it licensed the very day the steamship strike went into effect.

He flew the plane over to the Seattle airport—and was promptly besieged with more passengers than he could haul from Seattle to Anchorage. He had gotten his plane in shape to meet the deadline, but although Bob had a multi-engine pilot's rating, he had never taken out an instrument ticket. He hired bush pilot and friend Merritt Boyle, who was a good instrument and multiengine man, and for copilot, young Bill Borland, son of Alaska's Alex Borland, who had been killed with Carl Ben Eielson in Siberia. Big, blond, twenty-two-year-old Bill had learned to fly in Alaska before the war, made a spectacular record for himself as a Marine fighter pilot in the South Pacific. (Borland is still with Reeve, now his chief pilot.)

Boyle, an old-time flyer from Skagway and the Yukon, was an expert mechanic as well as a talented pilot. The three-man crew—Boyle, Borland, and Reeve—began a series of daily round-trip flights between Seattle and Fairbanks or Anchorage, with a stopover at either Juneau, Yakatat, or Annette field for refueling. They could carry twenty-one passengers in the DC-3, and always had a full load northbound and "all we wanted to carry" southbound. Although no airplane seats were yet available for sale, Bob had made his own for the plane, seven iron seats that would hold three people each and were bolted to the floor.

In the next fifty-three days they made twenty-six round trips, keeping that one DC-3 in the air on an average of ten hours per day. On the first trip out of Seattle, they got their shakedown by a CAA inspector, but, says Bob proudly, "I was legal as hell." Seattle to Anchorage averaged nine and one-half hours flying time, eleven hours en route; Seattle to Fairbanks was eleven hours flying time, fourteen hours en route. Reeve carried boxed lunches, coffee, and fruit juice. He bought them at Boeing Field in Seattle for the northbound trip, and Tillie made them for the southbound trip (as well as answering phone calls for reservations and looking after her four children). "Nobody wined or dined on those trips," says Bob, "but no one starved." Between refuelings and loading, a trip averaged about six hours on the ground between daily flights.

When the weather was bad along the coastal route "it was no reason for stopping." Reeve shifted over to the Interior route, an old bush route he'd often flown, which led into Anchorage via the Skolai Pass, going through passes "with ten feet to spare." Or he navigated "over the top" of the wild Saint Elias and Chugach Ranges at fifteen-thousand-foot altitude. (The modern commercial route is coastal only.) "Our engines never cooled off."

Reeve's furious activity was getting the jump on the other Alaskan carriers —and they decided to stop him. Other planes had been released, other operators got them, and within weeks after Reeve initiated the route, "Many nonscheds were competing for that golden harvest." One of the best-run of his competitors, Reeve felt, was the Mount McKinley Airways, founded by bush pilot Jack Scavenias, who was fresh out of service as an Air Force captain. There were also Arnold Air Service and General Airways.

On one of Reeve's many landings at Anchorage, he was met by a CAA inspector. "Bob," the man said, "you certainly must have been operating this airplane without maintenance and inspection. Let's see your logbooks and maintenance records."

"I was prepared for that," says Reeve gleefully. "That plane had had periodic fifty- and one-hundred-hour inspections— and I could prove it." On each trip into Seattle Reeve had taken the plane over to Spokane, and with the help of friends at the Wallace Air Service had worked all night on inspections, then at daybreak flown over to Seattle in time for the scheduled take- off. "All it took," says Bob, "was no sleep!"

By the end of those twenty-six round trips in fifty-three days, Bob had taken in $93,000—enough to pay for his plane and buy three more DC-3's. He had, in one month's time, put in 266 hours flying as a crew member.

When he had his stake for the fleet of planes, Bob abandoned the hectic Seattle-to-Alaska run to his competitors. Although the record verifies Reeve's claim to have been the first carrier between Seattle and Anchorage, the route later taken over by Northwest and Art Woodley's Pacific Northern, Bob had no desire to compete with the big carriers. He wanted to be a small operator in his own private territory. When CAB wrote, claiming that he was operating without authority between the States and Alaska, since he had not been certificated or obtained an exemption order for that route, Reeve answered that he was only interested in that run during the emergency caused by lack of surface transportation. He requested that they take a fresh look at the application he had filed, that winter, with CAB, for scheduled service on the 1783-mile run between Anchorage and Attu.

During those fifty-three days of States-Alaska operation, Reeve had spent the odd day making a trial run down the Chain, to Cold Bay and Dutch Harbor, with eleven passengers. Although they could not get a report on field conditions at Dutch, Reeve and his crew elected to go on and "take a look" anyway. They found the field at Dutch (voted by our military flyers as "the field we'd most like to stay away from") covered with two feet of fresh snow. There was a two-thousand-foot stretch, about fifty feet wide, along the side of the runway that had been sluiced off by a recent tidal wave. "I think we can make it," said Boyle.

Standing behind his pilots, Reeve watched the approach. They landed, rolled along, and "were just about to run out of runway" when they saw before them the whole end of the runway strewn with huge boulders that had been flipped out of the sea by the tidal wave. "Here we go again!" shuddered Reeve. But the plane's brakes held just short of the boulders—and Reeve Aleutian Airways' first eleven passengers debarked on schedule.

That summer, Reeve made once-a-week flights down the Chain, as well as maintaining charter service to Seattle and over the Territory. Operating nonsched, Reeve had no agents at the fields he went into, no facilities of his own along the routes he was using. When his pilots took off from Merrill Field for an Aleutian flight, they simply loaded up their plane with passengers, freight, and mail, put a "couple thousand bucks in their pockets" to pay for fuel and landing fees to the Air Force, CAA, and Navy personnel who were maintaining the Chain fields, and took off. They were out of contact with their home base until they flew into Merrill on the return trip.

It was a bush operation all over again—with slightly larger planes.

Reeve's only overhead for running his air line, at this point, was pilots' salaries, gas, oil, insurance, and maintenance of aircraft. "My only personal expense was the desk I bought, which I installed at my house to do the paper work."

By the end of his first season, he had four fully equipped DC-3's paid for. "All I had to worry about then was the tax at the end of the year."

But such simplicity of business operations was not to last long, for Reeve or for any of the other bush operators who were slated to make the painful and complicated transition into full-scale scheduled commercial operators.

# 16. Air line headaches

There were a whole new set of problems for the bush-flyers-turned-air-line-owners to learn about the "big business" of running a full-scale air line; concepts that were completely new to the old-style informal, one-man, one-plane operation. There were accounting, personnel problems, passenger comfort—and biggest of all, SCHEDULE. "The days were gone," sighed Ray Petersen, "when we could take off today—or next week." He described buying a new trimotor Stinson that delighted the passengers he served from Anchorage to Bethel. It had comfortable seats, a good warm cabin. "Why, it even had a toilet!"

No longer were Reeve's problems those split-second decisions that lay between himself and fate. He wasn't "the pilot" any more. He was merely one man in a group—which he had to regulate. From the beginning his Aleutian run did good business, and he had soon hired six more pilots, paying them one thousand dollars per month flat pay, at that time, he says, "the highest DC-3 pilot scale in North America." Before the first year was over, he was running two scheduled round trips per week down the Chain, keeping his four DC-3's busy all the time. At first he hired civilian mechanics from the Air Force to work for him in their off time, at nights. Later, when Pacific Airmotive was set up out at Merrill Field, he farmed out his maintenance work to them on a contract basis.

A great deal of postwar construction work was being carried on over the Territory, and many of Bob's charter hauls were planeloads of workers, which Reeve Airways carried to their work sites on a planeload basis. They were a rough lot. Particularly the pile-bucks—the men whose job was to knock in piling—and the steelworkers. "The carpenters and cannery workers were a pretty decent bunch, but the others spelled real trouble. They could climb on a plane carrying a quart of

whisky, then proceed to get drunk in flight." On one trip to
Seattle a gun fight started between Anchorage and Juneau.
Reeve's Captain Anse Tibbs wrestled the gun away from the
man, made a landing at Juneau, and called the marshal. The
marshal told Tibbs he'd have to go into town, place formal
charges, and reappear later as a witness. Tibbs didn't want to
lose all that flying time, so he carried the disarmed trouble-
maker on to Seattle.

From then on Bob "frisked" his passengers and took away
all their guns, knives, and booze. (Cot Hayes, Northwest's Anchorage manager, says the modern custom of serving liquor
on planes "is a lifesaver," since, if they know they can buy a
drink on the plane, the passengers don't take a bottle aboard
and drink it dry. Also, the air line can always "close the bar"
if anyone is getting too much.)

When some of the men objected to being frisked, Bob got a
five-celled flashlight and filled it with shot, then carried it under his arm, ready to conk any uncooperative passengers.
"Fortunately, I didn't have to use it," he says grimly, "since
word soon got around what was in my flashlight."

To fool Reeve, the workers began stringing pints of liquor
inside their pants, from their belts. Reeve missed this for a
while—till he heard one of the men bragging; then he began
frisking for that bottle too. "I didn't much like bending over
to inspect their legs—and leaving my head and back defenseless," says Reeve, "so I asked Bill Borland (six foot three
inches, 220 pounds) to stand behind me. I always had a feeling they'd all jump me like a bunch of wolves when I bent
over—but they never did with Bill standing there looking like
a ton of granite."

The Reeve pilots and copilots carried guns as part of their
regular flight equipment, and locked the door that led to their
cabin. "It wasn't so bad," grinned affable Bill Borland. "When
we heard 'em fighting back there, we just shoved back the
stick and smacked 'em back into their seats. You know," he
added, with his rippling, jolly laugh, "a pilot can put his passengers on the floor—or the ceiling—whichever he wants!"

If the pilots became aware that there was drinking going
on, despite the precautions, they had orders to "put on your
oxygen masks and go up to twelve thousand feet." The thin
air caused the drunks to pass out. "If they don't quiet down at

twelve thousand," ordered Reeve, "keep going up till they do!"

Reeve learned how to handle the "rough ones." But he had a lot to learn about the comfort of orderly passengers. When they boarded one of his planes at Anchorage, to go out to the Chain, passengers who made the trip cautioned the new ones, "Don't eat that box lunch all up the first round. It's got to last you clear to Attu!"

The DC-3's had no lining inside the cabins, only a bare metal interior. Without proper insulation, a thirty-five-below-zero ground temperature which dropped to sixty below in the air meant freezing conditions in the cabins. "If we ever ran into a temperature inversion enroute, the roof would drip like a tropical rainstorm!"

"You should of seen those planes," Reeve confesses with a guilty giggle. "When they landed, there'd be two inches of frost on the inside walls of the cabin!"

"We're just paying for freezing to death," screamed the passengers. Some threatened to sue Reeve. The pilots "robbed" what little heat there was by diverting it all into the cockpit. "There was always a steady stream of passengers up front to get warm." Reeve decided those fool Russians hadn't been so crazy after all, installing the potbellied stove!

"Public opinion got so bad," admits Reeve, "that I finally lined one plane for women and children."

Alaska Airlines added to Reeve's problems by beginning to fly to some of the Chain bases—with lined aircraft. Sparked by this competition, Reeve hastily lined all his planes. Although Bob had his application in, he was actually at this point running a scheduled airline without certificate. But those reviewing his case at CAB ordered Alaska Airlines off his projected route until his case was decided.

So far, Reeve was using the wartime Chain bases, which were being maintained by the military. After a few months he began to get urgent letters from the Navy, whose fields he was using at Kodiak, Dutch Harbor, Adak, and Attu, stating that he was using their facilities without authorization and that he must get a formal landing permit or get out. Reeve made a trip to Washington, to the Bureau of Yards and Docks, and found that, as an air-line operator, he was eligible to a lease on the Dutch Harbor field, which he took, thus getting control of the field. He also negotiated landing permits to use Kodiak,

Adak and Attu. Then he wrote the Navy, suggesting they get a landing permit from him! He had no trouble with the Army Air Force at Shemya. "They were always delighted to see me," smiles Bob. "I was their only source of mail!"

A "grandnanny" about safety, and frighteningly cognizant of the hazards his pilots faced in the Aleutians, Bob fretted constantly about his "boys." (Actually, although Aleutian flying is still rated as some of the most hazardous in the world, and takes skilled pilots, the instruments and navigational aids that were installed on all of Reeve's DC-3 fleet made the flying far less precarious than his own visual, contact flying of the Chain had been.) The men Reeve hired were principally former Air Force fighter pilots, fresh from combat, a wild, unruly bunch. "Hiring and firing became an onerous part of my job of running the line," says Reeve. With his old-time hatred of spit-and-polish and "show," he rather liked their independence and their somewhat sloppy appearance. "Always use Reeve Airways," he advertised in the Anchorage newspapers at the time Alaskan Airlines (with its elegantly uniformed pilots) was competing with him. "No zoot suit pilots or characters in our employ. Old reliable Aleutian pilots only." He referred contemptuously to his competitors' "captains." "All it takes to make a pilot today is two hundred hours (fifteen in a cub, fifty padded, and the rest as copilot), a duckbill cap, a slide rule, and a watch with seven hands."

Many of the pilots that Reeve hired quit and headed back for the States and "an easier route" after one trip out the Aleutians. There was a standing joke in the Alaskan aviation business which found its way, as truth, into *American Aviation* magazine. When Reeve hired a new pilot, so the story went, and the pilot got back to Anchorage from his first trip out the Chain, Reeve snatched his pants and shoes away from him—so he couldn't escape to the States! At the end of six months he got his pants back to wear around town—and his shoes at the end of a year.

Reeve kept a particularly close eye on his captains, rode as many flights with them as he could, watched their personal habits. One day, riding in an automobile with one of his men, Reeve noticed that the flyer handled his car in a rather absent-minded fashion. A few days later this same pilot forgot to put the control locks on his aircraft after returning from a trip. Reeve had one of his strong "hunches"—such as the one he'd had about the pilot who'd crashed the Hamilton out of Spokane. He made up his mind that he would let this man go—but let it slide, feeling he might be doing the man an injustice. He should not have waited. Reeve was at a dinner party one night, at a friend's house, when the phone rang. Merrill Field Tower had tracked him there to report, "One of your planes just crashed at the end of the runway, during take-off. That's all I can tell you now."

Reeve rushed to the field. The DC-3, with a full passenger load, had plowed through several feet of snow at the end of the runway and crashed into a half-dozen smaller planes. Miraculously, no one was injured, nor had the ship caught fire. But the plane was a total loss. The absent-minded pilot had yanked the partially iced-up plane off the runway during take-off, at the same time partially retracted the power so that it went into a prop-stall and crashed.

Reeve offered to settle the insurance claim for $19,500. The insurance company offered him $16,000. Reeve settled for $16,000 and signed a quitclaim. But Reeve's insurance broker Bob La Bow, went to the company and collected the other $3500 despite the quitclaim, since it was so obvious that the original claim had been legitimate.

Reeve Airlines was now down to three DC-3's. Reeve busted the careless pilot from captain to copilot—and the man quit. "He was a good flyer," says Bob, "but he had something on his mind beside flying, some sort of family troubles. I learned to hire only those men who had well-adjusted home lives. Any flyer with personal problems, or wife troubles, was sure to kill himself eventually."

Reeve added a Lockheed Electra 10-B and a twin-engine Beechcraft to his fleet, when he was able to get them on a surplus bid—but soon found them too small and short-ranged for Aleutian operations. By April, 1948, the hearings had been completed on Reeve's application for the Aleutian route, and he was awarded a temporary five-year certificate to run scheduled service from Anchorage west to Attu, and from Cold Bay north to the Pribilof Islands, which lie nine hundred miles west of Alaska in the Bering Sea. There are native villages on the Pribilofs, as well as a year-round Fish and Wildlife Service station, to control sealing operations. Reeve's 2500 miles of air routes constituted the longest twin-engine overseas certificate in the world. At the hearing, the attorney for Alaska Airlines asked that Reeve be barred from his certificate since he had been flying illegally, but Reeve's attorney, John Hellenthal, defended Reeve on the grounds that the demands for his services had forced him into a type of scheduled service before he had his certificate. Reeve was granted a temporary mail rate, of about forty-eight cents per mile, pending a hearing on the final mail rate, so that he could maintain a "breakeven" year-around business. (Alaskan airlines are still on mail subsidy; most of the large States lines have gone off mail pay as their ledgers have gone permanently into the black.)

Granted the certification he had been waiting for, Reeve suddenly found, to his dismay, that there were many ramifications to being placed in the class of scheduled carriers. "The old bush days were gone forever." The desk at his house was not an adequate substitute for a complete accounting department and an office staff to list tariffs, sell tickets, publish schedules. Reeve was now in the aviation business—with all its headaches.

"Wising up" to the need for top-drawer personnel with special training, Reeve hired Margaret Rutledge, formerly with Capital Airlines, to be his comptroller and treasurer—"one of the smartest things I ever did"—and rented office space downtown. "Maggie," as she is affectionately known by the Reeve family and other Reeve employees, took over the business operations and put them on a sound professional basis, ready for inspection at any time.

But when Bob went out with a CAA inspector on his first proving flight for an operating certificate, he was due for a "grim shock." "That inspector showed me a list of deficiencies that ran two pages long!" Reeve tried a month later, and failed again. By the third run, Reeve had "smartened up" and got his operations in shape so that the air line passed its test.

His pilots, Reeve found, so far as CAA regulations were concerned, had been running their own show in a casual style. Reeve began riding every flight, checking each man out for his deficiencies, indoctrinating his handful of unruly boys into the requirements of scheduled carrier operation—which were just about as new to former bush flyer Reeve as they were to the former fighter pilots.

"I never said anything during flight, but just kept a list, like an inspector, then showed it to the pilot at the end of the trip.

The second time a pilot repeated a deficiency, he got a warning. The third time, he was fired."

Reeve became obsessed with the importance to safe operations of the lengthy check list before each take-off and after each landing. In 1948, when he flew into Attu as copilot and caught himself muffing one of the items, Reeve fired himself as a pilot. "Those boys were a lot better on instruments than I was," he says, "and I'd found that there was too much worry and paper-shuffling to running an air line to do a good flying job." He let his own license expire—and has never renewed it.

Each time he went on a flight, Reeve watched for check-list items. From the outside of the plane he could see whether the tail wheel was locked at all times that the plane was on the ground, whether there were locks on the control surfaces. Inside, he checked to see if the master switch had been left on, the logbook completed. The pilots were all careful to go through the list when he had an eye on them—but he wasn't satisfied that they always did it so carefully when he wasn't around.

At a pilots' meeting in 1950, Reeve addressed his flock: "Gents, I've been pounding you on the head about your check list for the past three years, and this is the last time I'm going to do it. The next fellow I catch not using his check list is going to be in bad trouble."

"Why, Bob," one of the pilots protested, "we don't actually need a check list. We know this airplane by heart."

"All right, I'll tell you what I'll do," said Bob craftily. "If I can prove to you that you don't know the airplane by heart, will that be sufficient reason for you to never miss your check list again?"

The pilots considered that fair enough, and followed Reeve out to a plane on the field. Reeve called up Hank Orth and said, "Okay, Hank, now go through your pre-take-off and take-off without looking at the list."

Pilot Orth went through twenty-three of the twenty-four items on the check list from memory, then said, "I've taken off and I'm air-borne."

"No you're not," said Reeve. "You forgot to check your controls to see whether the control locks were still in. They were locked, and you crashed on take-off and killed twenty-three people including yourself. I feel sorry for all those widows and children."

The second man up, Pat Baker, went through eighteen of the list, then said frankly, "I give up."

Gene Strouse (who earlier had done some spectacular Polar reconnaissance flying) refused to enter the cockpit.

"From then on," says Bob, "that problem was licked." Only once after that did he have any trouble on check list. He suspended the guilty captain indefinitely, and the man eventually quit.

Reeve's personal knowledge of the tricks of Aleutian weather plays a great part in setting up safe operations. Although the weather moves fast, with constantly forming fronts, the wind shift and clearing weather that frequently succeed the passing front provide satisfactory flying conditions. Reeve's technique for slipping in and out of the precarious weather on schedule is principally based on flying through the fronts, then landing behind them. The instant the front has passed over "we dive out" to the next station. When the weather is at its worst, "we start to move." The planes take off when the wind shifts and the pressure rises—which enables them to land behind the front. "We beat through the front again on the return and overrun it all the way into Anchorage." Barring crosswinds, it is common for the Reeve Airways' DC-3's to land and take off in winds up to sixty-five miles per hour. "When we read about a seventy-five-mile wind labeled "hurricane" in the States," laughs big Bill Borland, "we wonder what they'd call the ones we got up here!"

In the Aleutians the weather on the ground and aloft are generally in great contrast. On the ground, the violent winds that roar through the passes between the cold Bering Sea on one side and the warm Japan Current of the northern Pacific on the other set up vicious gales, slanting sleet, sweeping rains. Aloft, however, at ten thousand feet the aircraft usually encounters broken clouds or clear on the tops. Despite the hazards, Reeve feels the tempestuous Aleutians furnish better flying conditions than the stormbound southeastern coast of Alaska where Bob Ellis and Shell Simmons (Alex Holden died in 1953) fight to maintain regular operations. "In southeastern," says Bob, "the storms build up solid, so you must fly on instruments for hours. Here, as a rule you can get above them. The Chain has severe ground conditions, but it's not so bad high up." On their long overwater routes, from Cold Bay on the Alaskan Peninsula up to the tiny fog-shrouded Pribilof Islands in the Bering Sea (Russian navigator Pribilof searched for these seal islands for years, finally found them only by hearing the noise of the seals on the rocks as his boat came near their shore), Reeve's planes as a rule do not encounter the dangerous cumulus build-up of storm that is found over land. Although they can never see the Pribilofs, and fly by charts, coming down blind with the aid of a loran navigational aid (there is no beam at the Saint Paul field), the Reeve pilots can usually get "on top" of the fog and storm for the overwater flight.

One of Reeve's biggest problems was the severe icing occurring between Anchorage and King Salmon during the winter months. Here the storm build-ups, as in southeastern Alaska, cannot be avoided, and where the warm air of the North Pacific hits the icy climate of the mountain area, the planes encounter some of the worst icing conditions in the world. On a flight in 1948, Captain Anse Tibbs and Bill Borland "almost got it." When they flew into a severe cold front the airplane became a solid sheet of ice. Although they applied full power, they sank from ten thousand feet to land level within one hundred miles, and just barely scraped into the field at Naknek. The DC-3's Pratt and Whitney 1830 engines were designed to operate for only a few minutes on maximum power, but had survived an hour wide open. It took Tibbs and Borland two days to knock the ice off the airplane; then they flew it back to Anchorage. On Reeve's orders, the engines were removed. It was discovered that the master rod assemblies on both engines had cracked beyond depair from the terrific strain of prolonged full power. At any moment they might have literally exploded.

"From then on," says Reeve, "I took a closer look at the engines." He began a careful study to determine what safety methods could be installed to prevent near-disaster such as had just occurred. With his precarious run, Reeve decided the one thing he could do was eliminate possibilities of premature engine failure by an accelerated system of overhaul and maintenance. After every flight, the oil screens were removed and examined for metal or foreign material, which would give a clue to impending engine failure. Reeve began replacing his engines at each 750 hours rather than waiting the 1500 hours of flying time allowed by the CAA. During overhaul, all the bearings were discarded and replaced with new ones. This ex-

tra mechanical caution quickly paid off. Today, Reeve enjoys
one of the lowest rates of engine failure between overhauls of
any carrier in the business.

Reeve quickly learned the value of devoted, able employees. Immediately following the war, as many people drifted
into Alaska looking for work, it was hard to sift down to the
"stable help" he needed. But eventually he was able to create
a skeleton staff upon whom he could rely to handle all major
problems. His five "key" employees are Treasurer Maggie
Rutledge; Bob Hanson, a former pilot and a born-and-bred
Alaskan, who became Reeve's superintendent of maintenance
and later a vice president and director of the company;
Thornton "Tex" Wheaton, former Aleutian fox-trapper and
expert radio technician, with air-line experience in both the
States and Alaska, who joined Reeve as superintendent of
communications and is in charge of maintaining the fields; and
big, friendly Bill Borland ("who has the most reassuring back
I've ever sat behind," as one nervous passenger remarked).
Bill, only twenty-two when he joined Reeve and easygoing by
nature, "came up too fast" and had to be busted back a time
or two before he finally developed into the mature and responsible pilot he is today. Bill is currently Reeve's chief pilot
and assistant superintendent of operations. (When I asked just
what his job was, Bill grinned. "Chief pilot, superintendent in
charge of operations, dispatcher—and if I turn my hat backwards, I handle baggage!") Jim Upson became Chief
Dispatcher, was later replaced, because of illness, by Frances
Ostendorf. ("50% of the women dispatchers in the scheduled
air carrier industry. Eddie Rickenbacker has the other one.")

In 1948 Reeve faced up to an auxiliary problem of service
rendered by his air line. All of his stops were at military fields,
with the exception of Atka and the Pribiloffs, with no provision for air connection to the canneries and villages that lay
along both sides of the Peninsula and the Chain. These areas
were so far removed from the airfields, by sea, that their only
access to the planes was by boat trip on the once-a-month
boat into Cold Bay. Assistant Postmaster General Paul Aiken,
aware of Reeve's problem, authorized a three-times-per-
month additional mail service, that would enable Reeve to
make some sort of connections to these outlying communities.
Bob contacted Aleutian boat man Mike Uttecht (who had
hauled Reeve in from the Boeing crash) and assisted Mike in

acquiring a sixty-foot motor vessel, the *Moby Dick*. The Coast Guard objected because of the nature of the open seas, so they spent three months converting the *Moby Dick* to conform with C.G. regulations. For a year the *Moby Dick* performed excellent service, hauling passengers, freight, and mail regularly into Cold Bay to meet the Reeve planes. But a year and a half later another boat was put on this run, and the *Moby Dick* was cut to one trip a month. Mike Uttecht gave up, since he found it impossible to operate on such a restricted basis. And Reeve was back where he started from, so far as serving the southern side of the Chain went.

Reeve decided the only thing he could do was work out some solution over which he had sole control. He traded the Electra and Beech aircraft he had bought on surplus for two Sikorsky S-43 amphibian planes. Two of his pilots, Gordon McKenzie and Slim Walters, were experienced with amphibians, and they provided the nucleus of trained personnel, equally adept on water and land.

Reeve bought a Link trainer for his pilots, to give them all additional training on instruments, and soon "every airline was using it".

He later added a Grumman Goose to his amphibian service, and although this water run along the southern side is operated at a substantial loss, it provides the connecting service Reeve needs and keeps his main-line planes full.

Inch by inch, Reeve was facing up to, and working out, the multitudinous, staggering problems of running a successful scheduled air line. But an unexpected blow for which he was totally unprepared turned up in March of 1949 when, with no previous warning, he received word that the Shemya airfield was to be closed within four days. Reeve got on the phone to friend Croil Hunter (then president, now chairman of the board, of Northwest Airlines), who was equally stricken by this decision, since Northwest had got their great-circle route to the Orient under way in 1947, and were currently using the Chain bases as refueling stations on their long overwater hop to Japan. The two men hastily caught planes for Washington.

# 17. Fight for the chain

Although the dramatic role played by the Aleutians in World War II, plus their singular position of being the only enemy-occupied American soil, would have seemed to have made their subsequent defense unquestionable, several factors contributed to a military withdrawal from the Chain. First, of course, was the inevitable postwar letdown when America historically, in its urge toward peace, hides its head in the sand of an illusion of peace—and pretends there will never be another conflict. Hand in hand with this unrealistic but typically American attitude is the equally inevitable demand to slash the military budget. Why, we conclude, should we dissipate our wealth in the maintenance of military might when we consider ourselves at peace?

It is a reasonable question, for everyone residing in the comparatively safe boundaries of the continental United States. But it is not so easy for our Alaskan cousins to relapse into this soothing lethargy, with Russia and Red China but a hand's breadth away.

An enemy task force left its grim footprints on Alaska in World War II. The threat of destruction of the population centers on the mainland was a constant fear then, and, for Alaskans, it was an equally grim possibility in the future. As American citizens, they felt entitled to a fighting chance, with something more potent than a dozen P-36's and a scattering of bombers. Of all on our continent, Alaskans are the most vulnerable to attack, the closest of all our people to the rest of the world, Europe as well as the Orient. Siberia may be seen from the Seward Peninsula. The Komandorskies are a short 250 miles from Attu. Only the Polar ice cap separates the Western Hemisphere from the land masses of Europe.

But a new concept of aerial warfare resulted from World War II. Wings and the jet engine shrunk the boundaries of the

242

world, and called for a drastic readjustment of the previous concepts of isolation and distance. With interim-range B-36's in operation and long-range intercontinental bombers coming off the drawing boards, the Air Force's strategy of global warfare underwent a radical change. With air-borne tankers capable of refueling fighter and bomber aircraft en route to the target, the costly upkeep of scattered air bases on the perimeter of our boundaries was questionable, especially in the face of the postwar limited budget.

When the Air Force was cut from seventy groups to forty-eight groups, after the war, drastic economies had to go in effect immediately.

The Aleutian bases, already a controversial item, were first on the list of expendables. Besides, as the Chain air bases became increasingly important in civil air operations, it had become a debatable question as to whether the Air Force or the Civil Aeronautics Administration was responsible for their upkeep. Chopped short of operating funds, the Air Force looked for a spot to economize and chose Shemya Airfield.

The blow, for Reeve, was staggering. Shemya, 1750 statute miles west of Anchorage and 35 miles from his terminal point, Attu, was his most important base in the North Pacific as an all-weather alterante to Adak, Amchika, and Attu. With its flat terrain and its all-weather ground-control approach system, it provided the one safe refuge for his comparatively short-ranged DC-3's for 1100 miles west of Cold Bay. Although Northwest Airlines operated long-range four-engine overseas aircraft, they were equally in trouble. They had just inaugurated scheduled overseas air carrier service to Japan, Hong Kong, and Manila on their recently certificated route from Seattle via the Aleutians to the Orient.

Aware of the controversy between the Civil Aeronautics Administration and the Air Force over the responsibility of operating Shemya, Reeve and Northwest's president, Croil Hunter, tramped the streets of Washington and the halls of Congress in a futile effort to plead the cause of retaining Shemya.

Every agency had its budget troubles, and the least of them all was Shemya. Shemya was strictly for the birds, "feathered, that is," as one department head told Reeve. Given the cold shoulder wherever they showed up, they eventually were referred to the Air Coordinating Committee. Reeve wangled its reluctant members into calling a meeting to hear his case. But these representatives, one each from the Navy, the Civil Aeronautics Administration, the Civil Aeronautics Board, and the Air Force, had a unanimous reaction. "We want no part of Shemya."

The conclave climaxed in a bitter row. Reeve, however, obtained one vital clue during the meeting. The key to a three-million-dollar appropriation to maintain Shemya was its natural death in the Bureau of the Budget for lack of two words, "militarily desirable," in the interest of the national defense. Reeve headed back to his hotel—at a dead end.

But his luck was turning. Leaving the government building, he bumped into Major General Sam Anderson, formerly a SAC commander and then in USAF operations on General Vandenberg's staff. Reeve had known Sam since 1927, when he was a second lieutenant with Reeve's brother Dick at Brooks Field.

"What are you doing here, Bob?" Sam inquired. Reeve told him, and knowing that Sam had heavy bombers deployed night and day over the North Pacific, added, "I'm sunk, and so are you too."

"I'll see General Vandenberg," Anderson promised Reeve. "I'll do what I can." Within an hour Reeve had a call from Anderson. "General Vandenberg," he reported, "has agreed to the change of two words in USAF's position on the Shemya budget matter which will clear the way for providing the funds." The three million dollars were forthcoming, and Shemya was saved.

Months later the Korean war exploded, and for three years Shemya became one of the hottest spots in the North Pacific Ocean. Its facilities, which had been slated to revert to the original muskeg and tundra, were in condition for the military's immediate use.

But Shemya was only the beginning of Reeve's troubles, as he was quickly to learn. In October of the same year (1949), Port Heiden Airfield was ordered deactivated by the Civil Aeronautics Administration, which had inherited it from the Air Force. "This time the jig was really up," says Reeve. "I was the only air line using Port Heiden, and I had to have it to run a safe air line." With Heiden's air navigational aids, it provided a necessary alternate when Cold Bay and Umnak were weathered in.

But running a full-fledged airfield with its maintenance and housekeeping was a costly enterprise, and Reeve had started his air line with two strikes against him. "There was some fine print in my temporary five-year Certificate of Convenience and Necessity from the Civil Aeronautics Board which let me in for all this hell. It stated that the certificate was issued under the stipulation that the federal government was not obliged to provide Reeve with any air navigational aids or en route weather or other field facilities in event that the war-built installations were deactivated or closed. Any agency could destroy or close any airfield whatsoever—and I had no recourse."

Determined to keep flying, Reeve filed an urgent application with the Civil Aeronautics Board for a hearing, to prove the feasibility of making his air line a success and to have the terms of his certificate modified in order to get the cost of operating the bases included in his pending mail rate hearing.

Dutch Harbor was the next field listed to be closed—and Attu was thrown at Reeve by the Navy at the same time. Reeve gave up Attu, but he had to have Dutch Harbor as a refueling stop. The Bureau of Yards and Docks obliged him with a long-term lease.

In December, 1949, the ax fell again. Cape Air Force Base on Umnak Island was ordered closed and deactivated in the near future.

"It was getting routine by then," says Reeve. "I squelched a protest and made plans to protect myself. But it was sure tough to stand by and see that fine field being dismantled and the installations cannibalized. I was helpless."

Awaiting his CAB hearing, Reeve sent a skeleton crew into Umnak to provide emergency weather and air navigational aids as a refuge for his iron birds. It took all his spare cash and much more he didn't have to keep his crippled air line flying. He went heavily in debt.

The upsets and losses of his landing facilities and air navigational aids, coupled with a persistent hunch that World War III was about to explode in or near the Bering Sea, had his nerves close to the breaking point. The simple fact was that he was fast becoming insolvent, with the strong possibility of losing his air line, as well as home and hardware business which he had mortgaged for operating capital.

His urgent plea to the Air Force to grant him use of the

Umnak air facilities met with a blank wall. The field was closed without warning; the range, weather, communications, and field lighting were shut off while Reeve's planes were in flight in the area. Fortunately, they were able to make it into Adak and Cold Bay on visual flight rules. "Within a day I had some emergency procedures going, and we were in the air again," says Reeve. "But I was in bad trouble ... I had friends and I had enemies, in the Air Coordinating Committee," he adds flatly. "When I was at the end of my rope, I sought out my friends."

The friend in this instance was Colonel (now Brigadier General) Jim Andrews, tall, lanky, friendly flyer (later the oldest active jet pilot), who was then commander of the 5039th Air Base Wing at Elmendorf Field. An expert flyer himself, Andrews was fully cognizant of what the loss of the Umnak facilities meant to Reeve. With nowhere else to turn, Reeve laid his cards on the table.

"I'm still theoretically commander of that base," mused Andrews. "I'll tell you what I'll do. I'm going to write you a permit, authorizing you to take over the whole air base and its facilities. Don't know whether it will hold water or not, but we can give it a try"—Jim smiled "—and the best of luck!"

With this "thinnest pretense of legal right" to take over a fifty-million-dollar air base, Reeve and a crew moved in and had the Umnak field functioning within forty-eight hours. The air base, which had formerly been run by several thousand military personnel, was now in the hands of two Reeve employees: John Taylor, maintenance man, and radio operator Morgan Richardson. "The most haywire outfit ever run!" says Reeve, "but it kept our planes in the air."

Record years for Reeve were 1949 and 1950, jam-packed with killing troubles. Along with his loss of fields, he was hit a haymaker by competition. With a big construction project going on out at Adak, the planeloads of construction personnel from the States to Adak and back should have been a healthy shot in the arm to Reeve's troubled line. Although entitled to transportation at no cost by NATS (Naval Air Transport Service) planes from the States and back if they completed their contract, the workers had to pay their own fares if they didn't complete it. There was a large turnover, a good source of revenue for a commercial air line. However, Bob found, NATS was selling air-line tickets just as he was—and copping the business. When he objected to the Navy commander at Adak, he was told, "Mister, this is a Navy base, and we are running it." Reeve's answer was to catch the next plane to Washington, D. C.

"For a quarter of a million dollars' worth of business a year, it was sure worth the trip." Bob had an audience with Defense Secretary Louis Johnson, who, with his background of legal training, recognized the incipient danger of government competition with private enterprise, and issued a directive to the Navy that all civilian commercial traffic in the Aleutians be turned over to Reeve as a commercial carrier. "For the first time in months," says Bob, "my planes were loaded again. Although," he adds with a twinkle, "there was quite a spell there where individually I was strictly *persona non grata* around the Navy bases!"

With his scant cash reserves poured into the maintenance of the fields, and deeply in debt, Bob fought with bush-pilot ferocity for business, and gave hell to all competitors. "A lot of competitors came out on the Chain—but usually one trip out and a good look at the weather and we never saw them again. However, there was one line that made repeated trips." Bob kept a shrewd eye on his competitor's operations, finally caught him in practices that warranted a CAB order to desist. With his lifelong ability at adaptation, Bob had learned the government can be a handy ally as well as a troublesome foe.

It saved his neck in 1950. When he finally was granted the hearing he had requested for maintaining fields on the Chain, Reeve appeared before CAB to appeal for a review of the terms of his certificate and some sort of financial support. Granted a special hearing by CAB in Washington, Reeve appeared before the board, whose chairman was then Donald Nyrop, former head of CAA and a lieutenant colonel in the Air Force during the war. With his background in both military and commercial aviation, Nyrop understood Reeve's predicament and felt his air line was entitled to aid, especially in view of his keeping the air facilities of the Aleutians available for the use of other air lines and the Navy, Air Force, and Coast Guard. It was a singular situation. Commercial air lines in general depended almost wholly on federal or municipal fields and facilities at a low individual user's charge. For Reeve's line the air was free, but there were no places to roost. To perpetuate the airfields for his own planes required expenses and fixed charges far in excess of ordinary air-line operation.

Despite the lack of obligation of the federal government to provide Reeve with any funds for the preservation of the facilities over his route, Nyrop felt that the Aleutian airfields were still of tremendous value as a national asset, and he and the Board agreed to assist Reeve to a certain extent. Asked what it would cost, Reeve estimated $130,000 a year, and offered to share half the sum if the Board would recognize the remaining $65,000 as part of his fixed charges in his pending mail rate proceeding. The Board agreed; the Aleutian bases and the North Pacific air route were back in business.

Five years later, when Nyrop was president of Northwest Airlines, this decision served to save Northwest Airlines as well as Reeve. But for NWA Captain "Skeeter" Johnson time didn't wait that long. In 1951, a Northwest DC-4, with fifty-two passengers and a crew of four aboard, en route to Korea, were zeroed out at Shemya. Anchorage was out, he was short of fuel. He next tried Umnak. It was marginal, and he didn't have the letdown procedure and was reluctant to accept verbal instructions from the Reeve employees so he decided to ditch. They then told him that Dutch Harbor was still open, and directions were given him for a letdown on the northwest leg of Reeve's range that would place him exactly north of Dutch Harbor. He could proceed VFR from then on. On his last hour's fuel, and in pitch darkness, Johnson followed instructions and headed for the hazardous 3700-foot Dutch Harbor field, which was literally carved out of the side of a mountain and had no field lighting.

Skeeter had his luck. By happy chance a transient Coast Guard cutter had just docked next to the unlighted field. Contacted by the Reeve station at Umnak, the cutter turned its searchlight on the edge of the airfield for Johnson to line up on his approach. He had to make it, since he was on his last fifteen minutes of gas. On his final approach, however, a sailor in a jeep dashed across the runway in front of him. Johnson pulled up to miss the jeep, then slammed the DC-4 down on the ground halfway down the field, pulled the air bottles on his emergency brakes, locked them tight, and came to a screeching halt in the same boulder patch in which Reeve had almost scattered his first scheduled commercial flight out to the Chain. By next noon a Reeve plane had flown Johnson in a new set of wheels and tires—and he was in Tokyo in thirty-six hours.

The Reeve-maintained fields provided a refuge for any planes in the area, either air carrier or military on patrol. A dozen aircraft in "mortal need" of an emergency field came to haven at Umnak within the next couple of years.

As each field fell, Reeve had his choice—either to give up his air line or take over, with his own funds and the Civil Aeronautics Board allotted participation.

Dutch Harbor, he discovered, cost him ten thousand dollars annually, Umnak fifty thousand. Port Heiden twenty-five thousand, and Cold Bay fifty thousand in direct costs. Indirect costs came to thousands more. Fields were run down and had to be rebuilt. At Umnak, Reeve converted the low-frequency loop range to a high-power beacon and installed a series of H markers adjacent to the runway that lowered his minima. During the July and August fog season, when Umnak was closed in for days at a time, Reeve reopened Berry Field on the north shore of the island which remained fog free, installed a homing device and communications—and his schedules went on uninterrupted.

At each field power plants had to be overhauled, antennae relocated, field lighting facilities rewired, buildings renovated, power lines rebuilt, and fuel flown in. Despite the terrific cost of these facilities, Reeve soon realized that his control of the airfields was a tremendous advantage over the stewardship of his former landlords. Selecting key personnel and sending out small, hard-working crews to each base, he was able to improve his communications by "1000 per cent." They speeded up his schedules and, most important, they contributed substantially to the safety of his operations.

But just as he began to see daylight in the insuperable problems of running a network of airfields as well as an air line, Reeve, in 1950, suddenly found himself in "double trouble." He had plowed several hundred thousand dollars into his fields, part of which he hoped would be returned to his air line in the final determination of his mail pay rate. When he ran out of cash, his bank, doubtful that the Civil Aeronautics Board would come through as Reeve represented, was reluctant to loan him further operating capital, even though he had kept his bank obligations on a current basis. "All they saw," says Bob, "was that I owed $148,000 and had no cash. They didn't care how much equipment or planes I had, they had already been stung by too many fast talking gyppos* in the flying business."

Without operating capital, Reeve had no alternative but to go into bankruptcy. The suggestion was made by several of his creditors. As a final resort, he flew to Seattle, hoping to get a new loan from the bank that had participated in his first loan. Their answer was a courteous but flat No.

"I walked out of the bank, and for the first time I didn't know which way to turn. The world had stopped for me."

Dazed, Reeve wandered over to his club to try to think over his next move. On the elevator he saw a friend, Alaskan banker Elmer Rasmuson, from Anchorage.

"What's the matter, Bob?" Elmer asked at Reeve's long face. Rasmuson knew Reeve's problems indirectly, and he joined Reeve in his room to hear the latest developments. Rasmuson was a born-and-bred Alaskan who also was a "Sunday flyer" who piloted his own plane over the Territory whenever free from his desk. He understood flying, and he also understood the ramifications of the Civil Aeronautics Administration and Civil Aeronautics Board and their aims to develop and support a healthy aviation enterprise.

"If the Civil Aeronautics Board has backed your efforts to keep the fields open despite their position in your original certificate," mused Rasmuson, "then they obviously feel that your air line is worth supporting."

Within an hour Bob's fortunes had experienced an abrupt shift. Rasmuson arranged a $125,000 participating short-term loan.

The day that Bob had been turned down by his Anchorage banker, he had also received the startling word that Pacific Airmotive, to whom he contracted all his aircraft maintenance work, was going out of business in Alaska. They had done all of Reeve's overhaul and maintenance, and, under the CAA requirements for air carrier operations, had provided him with hangar space and highly critical overhaul work on engines, accessories, and field equipment. Without this service, Bob knew his operating certificate would inevitably be canceled. When Rasmuson granted him the loan, the first thing Bob did was buy Pacific Airmotive, paying $50,000

* Gyppos is Alaskan for free-lance truckers and flyers who have a hard time paying bills.

down, with the remaining payments covered by a long-term note. He now had $75,000 operating capital. "The show was on the road again."

Or so he thought. When the CAB hearing on Reeve's permanent mail rate pay came up a few months later, Reeve happily appeared, having estimated that he was due to receive about $75,000 from the government in back mail pay. When the hearing was completed a CAB man said, "Mr. Reeve, there's one fact I'd like to get straight before you leave. Instead of our owing you $75,000, you owe us $65,000!"

"What?" howled Reeve incredulously.

"I am forced to disallow the ten years' supply of engines and accessories you have on hand. Our rules provide for yearly inventory only."

"Jesus!" screamed Reeve. "I'm ruined."

"You won't have to pay us in a lump sum, Mr. Reeve," said the examiner kindly. "We'll just take out so much per month of your mail pay during the coming year."

The series of year-long crises was too much for Reeve. Landing on crevassed glaciers, he discovered, had little of the nerve-wringing wear and tear of trying to keep a business afloat. In March, 1951, Reeve was walking along a street in Seattle on a Saturday afternoon when he experienced a sharp constriction in his chest. He went up to his room in the Washington Athletic Club, lay down—and the pain grew more intense. Hours later he called for a doctor. The medic took a look at him, said, "You're having a coronary. Don't move. I'll call the ambulance."

They carted him to a hospital, gave him a hypo, and put him under an oxygen tent. About two in the morning, Reeve came to, feeling fine again, and asked the nurse for some magazines to read.

The nurse told him she had strict orders for him not to move a hand. Then at noon the next day, "it really hit." A violent attack of virus pneumonia. The impending pneumonia had induced the heart attack by inflammation and constriction of the sac around the heart. Tillie was called, and flew to Seattle to join him. Numerous friends visited him. "They were," says Bob, "holding a living wake!" At the end of a week Bob's fever was down. But the prospects weren't good.

"You are to spend sixteen hours per day in bed for the next year," said the doctor.

Reeve went home and "was a good boy for two months." Then, restless about the progress of his business, he went down to the office to see how things were going—and was met by a delegation of new pilots who wanted faster promotions to captain. Reeve felt the special hazards of his route required extra experience and slower advancement than normal operations. A controversy ensued, and Reeve finally told them that if they struck, he'd fire them. The ringleader soon resigned, and the other men returned to work. One week later Reeve suffered another coronary attack.

"This one was really murder!" he says grimly. When he felt the pains, at three in the morning, he forced himself out of bed, staggered into the kitchen, and hung onto the kitchen sink for an hour till the seizure passed. By next morning his fever was soaring, the pneumonia was back—and he soon found himself again in a hospital. "Jesus, I was really sick!"

Doc Walkowski, the family doctor, pulled him through. The recurrence of virus pneumonia had induced the second heart attack. It meant an oxygen tent again, two weeks in the hospital, and then semi-invalidship for another year. When Reeve asked Walkowski earnestly if there was any chance of his ever feeling better, Doc shrugged, "Hell, you're not supposed to feel so good when you are old as you are!" Reeve was forty-nine.

Thinking back to the days when he had cured his crippled leg by the long hike to the country, Bob started going out as soon as he was able, sometimes for days at a time, on hunts, hiking expeditions. Anything that kept him away from business tension and strengthened his damaged heart. He went on trips into Canada and out on the Alaskan Pensinsula. He went everywhere—except to his office. He disciplined himself to ignore business—until he felt up to tackling it again. There was no use setting himself up for another attack. Besides, there was something spooky about a third time.

After nearly a year of recuperation, Bob decided he was ready to get back in the old grind. "I was really feeling better than I had in several years." When he came back to his office, he found what he had prepared himself to find—that the overall operation of the air line had deteriorated, the pilots had slumped back into some of their careless habits. The business, however, through the efforts of Reeve's central core of top-drawer employees, had survived.

"When each pilot was due to go on leave, I told him to think it over while he was gone. If he wanted to do things the right way, come back. If he didn't, then stay away. We were going to run a sharp, careful operation again, and anyone who didn't want to do it that way was free to leave."

"I'm glad to report," Reeve smiles, "that they didn't fail me. They all came back, loyal, efficient, and ready to get back to business."

# 18. Big Brownie

Reeve maintains that the day he dies, no one will say, "There goes old Reeve the glacier pilot, bush pilot, or Aleutian pilot." They'll just say, "Hey, wasn't that the guy that shot that bear?"

Reeve received more publicity and international attention for killing the world's record brown bear (his record held for five years) than for any flying he ever did. He got his picture (with trophy) in national magazines, in newspapers. Whenever Reeve was introduced on the streets of Washinton, Seattle, or Chicago, people inquired, "Aren't you the fellow that shot that bear?" When Tillie was on a shopping spree in San Francisco, a group of ladies converged on her. "You must be the wife of the man that shot that bear!"

As a matter of fact, it *was* a big bear. The hide, after shrinking, measured twelve feet four inches wide by ten feet four inches long; the official Boone and Crockett measurements of the skull were nineteen and three-sixteenths by eleven and one-half (including the lower jaw) which gave a total score of thirty and eleven-sixteenths inches. Stretched out on the floor of the Reeve house, the hide was plenty big enough for all five little Reeves to sprawl on—without touching each other. But it was not destined for such a prosaic position. The hide went to rest at the museum of the University of Alaska, and the skull was presented to the American Museum of Natural History.

Bob was so frequently asked (there are at least four published accounts in sporting magazines) just how he got his bear that he eventually wearied of the details and invented some interesting variations. One is that while flying the Chain he spotted a mother bear with four cubs and landed on the beach, with the idea of capturing one of the cubs. He managed to corner one, but the bear started chasing him—and he

254

just made it back to his plane. Resolving to get his revenge, he began dropping vitamins down to this bear to speed up its growth to record size. On each flight he dropped a row of vitamins from Port Moller to Cold Bay, and soon noticed that the cubs had beaten a trail all along that route, looking for their daily handouts. This trail, Reeve interjects with a sober face, became a "natural air navigational aid to follow in bad weather." One of the cubs was more adept at following the trail than the others and developed into an enormous bear. Reeve decided the time was right to bag him. But the thought occurred that it would be an even shrewder move to perpetuate a breed of trophy-sized animals—so that he would always have a spare world's record bear on hand.

He landed on the beach and started down the bear trail with a steel beer keg filled with vitamins and fixed with spikes in it, to hold the bear's head. He secured the barrel by a chain to a deadman log and buried it—and waited. The bear came along on schedule, stuck his head into the keg to get his vitamins—and was unable to withdraw his head, due to the spikes. Reeve ran up with a knife, slashed him from heel to heel, took the hide when the bear pulled out of his skin, and left him to get furred out again for the next year's record.

Another version of the story places the scene on Sitkilidak Island off Kodiak (there are no bears on any of the Aleutians except Unimak), where sourdough Jack McCord was trying to domesticate a herd of Longhorn cattle. A huge brown bear swam over from Kodiak to prey on the cattle, and McCord asked Reeve to kill the predator. Reeve cornered the bear in a box canyon, climbed on a boulder to get good aim, but, just as he was about to shoot, lost his footing and slipped off the boulder. He hurriedly climbed back up as the bear charged—and heard a terrible noise behind him. Looking round, he saw a Longhorn bull charging from the other side, thundering down on him like an express train.

"I had only one chance for a shot and I knew I couldn't get them both. But I gathered my wits, calmly raised the gun, and shot the bear." He pauses significantly, then adds, "I knew I could shoot the bull any day."

Actually, Reeve had been fascinated with bears since he first came to Alaska; and one of the few times in his life he admits to being thoroughly frightened was when he landed a pair of hunters on the Bering Glacier and three bears charged

Reeve, who was unarmed, cutting him off from his plane. He ran to a log and "tried to pull it over me, but I figured I'd have a hell of a time convincing three bears I was dead!" The hunters nearby heard Reeve yell, came to his rescue, shot the three bears as they charged. The last one dropped a few feet from where Reeve was trying to hide.

Reeve soon learned when he came to Alaska that there were two principal causes of violent death in the Territory: drowning in glacial streams and being killed by bears. There were also a few men who had survived an encounter with a bear—but bore the marks for the rest of their lives. Bob's old mining friend, Red Hirst, the one of the strange hairline, had been literally scalped by a bear. One of the Pinzon pals back at Valdez, sourdough Archie Parks, had been badly disfigured by a nearly fatal round with a bear. Attacked by the animal, Archie had had sense enough to realize his only chance lay in "playing dead," and he forced himself to lie quiet, despite the terrific pain of being mauled and chewed. The animal finally left him for dead, and Archie survived, although his head and face were badly mutilated and he was disfigured for life.

On a prospecting trip to Horsfeld on the Canadian border, Reeve decided, after landing, to take a nap in the sun. When he finally rose and walked into the cabin he was occupying, he happened to look back and saw a big grizzly sniffing the spot where he had just lain. Reeve shot the bear, and the animal's hide squared over nine feet, which he believes now might well have been a world's record grizzly.

Mort Moore, an Anchorage friend of Bob's, once brought a full-grown pet black bear into Bob's office, catching Bob at a time when he had just returned from a round of refreshments at Jimmy Carlson's Union Club and was "feeling no pain." In a playful mood, Bob was enchanted with the bear and had a wonderful idea. "Throw that bear in my pickup, Mort, and let's have some fun!"

Reeve drove out to his own house, had Mort stay in the car, and went in and told Tillie and the children, "I have a surprise for you. Go in the back room and don't come out till I yell." As soon as the family was hidden, Reeve and Mort trotted the bear up into the doorway of the house, went back outside, and yelled, "Okay, come out."

Seeing nothing in the living room, Tillie and the children started to go out the door—and stumbled into the bear.

"You should have seen them scatter!" chuckles Bob.

A housekeeper whom the Reeves were currently employing ran for her husband and a gun to shoot the beast, but Bob and Mort managed to rescue the bear first.

"We explained it was a joke, and then brought him back into the living room and he was really the life of the party."

The tame bear, the Reeves discovered, loved nothing so much as perfume. When Tillie put some on a handkerchief and gave it to him, he played with it, tossed it up in the air and caught it, and rolled round and round the room with his toy.

During World War II, Bob had become acquainted with the bears around Cold Bay on the Alaskan Peninsula. They were a real nuisance to the Air Force base, roaming ceaselessly up and down the alleys searching for garbage. Most prudent folk stayed inside, away from them, except for an ardent fisherman named Captain Manteuffel, whose bout with a bear became a favorite legend. Out trout-fishing in a nearby stream, he was catching some beauties when he turned around to find a bear eating his catch as fast as he pulled it in. Captain Manteuffel was so enraged that he kicked the bear on his south end, and the beast took the hint and lumbered off. According to Bob, this story is always tied in with the rumor that Manteuffel had a still nearby.

In the early days in Alaska, hunters, miners, and trappers ran into constant trouble with bears. At least a half-dozen men were killed each year. With only 30-30 calibre rifles—the standard arms of early days in Alaska—if they did not hit the bear in a vital area on the first shot, the bear generally got them. Stories of bears were legion. One classic Bob learned from the Aleuts.

An Aleut who was out fishing went ashore on a strip of beach, where he saw another Aleut astraddle of a live brown bear, hanging onto him by a death grip on the animal's ears. The bear had attacked the man, and the man was holding off his vicious jaws by a grip on the bear's ears. It was a ludicrous spectacle, and the fisherman laughed. The Aleut holding the bear said, "Do me a favor, will you. Hold him for a minute." The fisherman obligingly climbed on and took a hold on the bear, and the other man climbed in his boat and shoved off. "You think it's so funny," he shouted, "you try holding him yourself for a couple of days!"

Bob's record bear hunt occurred in 1948 on the Alaskan Peninsula, in the Cold Bay area. It was a hunt he had long planned with his friends and hunting partners, Lieutenant General Nathan Twining, Brigadier General Hank Everest, Bob's partner at Kennedy Hardware Ted Van Theil, Doc Bailey, official photographer and guide Mike Uttecht. Mike, a mixture of Aleut, Russian, and German, had been born and raised on the Chain and knew where the bears were. The quartet of hunters flew into Cold Bay, met Mike, then trekked overland from the airfield to Mike's trapping barabara* in Left Hand Valley.

As the hunters neared camp, they saw a bear sunning himself on top of a deserted barabara at their camp site. They chased him off and went inside, and two more bears that had been snoozing inside "made a hasty exit." It was a good omen for the hunt.

General Twining got the first bear, whose hide squared ten feet. Everest got the second bear. Then Van Thiel got his. Reeve hung around camp while the other men hunted, catching up on his sleep. (As with all bush flyers, sleep is a disease with Reeve; he would literally rather sleep than do anything else.) When the other hunters had bagged their bears, they started pestering Reeve about why he didn't climb out of the sack and go bear-hunting. "I was waiting for a big one," he says smugly. Stories were later circulated by his hunting pals that Bob happened to get his bear only when it came up to the camp after garbage and knocked over the can and woke him up. "This," says Reeve, "was not quite the truth!" One morning he woke up, slept out and feeling fit, and said, "Today I'm going hunting."

A mile from the camp, Reeve climbed on a small promontory, and about a mile off sighted a big animal which was cautiously passing through a patch of alders on the side of a mountain. Flying over this country regularly, Reeve had become familiar with the appearance of the bears, and knew pretty well how to judge their size. He realized this bear was exceptionally large, since even at that distance he could see a wide area of daylight between the bear's belly and the ground as the animal moved along the mountain side.

Reeve began to stalk the bear. Two hours passed before he

---

* Sod or earth hut used by the Aleuts, usually built wholly or partly underground.

got his first chance at a shot. Then when the bear finally moved into the clear, he was between two patches of alders, and Reeve realized if he didn't kill the animal with the first shot, the bear would escape into the alders before he could get another chance at him. He elected to continue the stalk instead of trying the one shot. An hour later the bear moved out into an open patch, and Reeve fired his .405 Winchester. The first shot was high. The second shot went into the stomach and lung section, and, although mortally wounded, the bear lunged off toward the alders. Reeve missed the third shot. His fourth broke both shoulders. The bear went down, dead before he stopped rolling. He was, as Reeve knew he must be, a "real trophy." The world's record Peninsula brown bear.

After riding the first SAS polar flight to Norway, Reeve was eating lunch in Oslo when a group of men came up and addressed him in Norwegian. Reeve asked his host what it was about. The host translated, "They just want to know if you are the fellow who shot that bear!"

Bob has had a lot of fun out of his bear. It has provided a subject to tease—and be teased—about during the hectic years of business tensions. In 1952, when someone persuaded Reeve he should run as Republican candidate for delegate to Congress, there were those who maintained that Bob's idea of a political speech was telling about his bear! He did find it a useful method to collect a crowd. Others felt if he'd just kept his mouth shut about political issues, as well as bears, he'd have won. Bob is good-natured about his defeat. "My pals told me they'd watched me in politics and in the air-line business—and I had better stay in the air-line business!"

He agrees. The whirlwind campaign against Democratic incumbent Bartlett, Reeve discovered, was expensive as well as hectic. He ended up feeling he'd better "skin his own skunk"—namely flying. One event, however, pleased him mightily. Several of his employees carried his campaign placard to the top of Mount McKinley and planted it on a tripod on the top of the mountain, so that his picture "rides the winds" six feet above the peak. "What is the highest point in North America?" asks Reeve. "Not McKinley—but my picture!" Although the Park Service objected, no one got around to taking it down, and so far as the last report went, Reeve's face is still "the highest point in North America!"

His intense patriotism for Alaska and his personal popularity in the Territory have made Reeve's a recurrent name on the political scene. In January, 1953, he was chosen by the Republican Central Committee for territorial governor of Alaska. However, realizing that a federal appointment, if it did go in his favor, would mean the loss of his air line, Reeve withdrew.

Politics are lively and personal in Alaska. Alaskans are eager to participate in the development of their region. Reeve's Valdez helper, Bill Egan, was elected United States Senator (on the Tennessee Plan) in 1956, on the Democratic ticket. Tillie Reeve has gone into politics as her children have grown past the toddler stage, and in 1955 was elected Republican National Committeewoman. Although Reeve maintains that his brief romance with politics is over, he serves as chairman of the Territorial Board of Police Commissioners, and his name is still actively mentioned for other posts. In the fast-developing Territory, anything can happen.

"You know," muses Bob with delightful honesty, "I'm mighty glad Tillie got interested in politics. It was getting to the point where the littlest fellows could pretty much look after themselves, and for the first time since we were married she began to have some time on her hands. She got to looking at me a little closer than she'd had time to before—and she began to notice a few things. Old Reeve was kinda careless; threw his socks and pants on the floor. Sometimes he dragged in late for dinner. If anybody was around to encourage him, he was apt to kick the gong and maybe have one too many. But now," Reeve's smile is cherubic, "now she's in politics, everything's great. She's too busy to notice those little things."

# 19. The air route nobody wanted

In September, 1953, the final deactivation of the Aleutian airfields Reeve was using occurred when the United States Air Force served notice they were going to deactivate Cold Bay, the most important refueling stop on the westward run. Reeve was not surprised at this decision. With the Korean armistice, the military need for the North Pacific air route had diminished in favor of the mid-Pacific route via Honolulu to the Orient. The Air Force took the position that the predominant use of the North Pacific route was by commercial air carriers, and the responsibility for the upkeep of the airfields belonged with CAA.

By now Reeve was accustomed to sudden crises and knew what to do. He realized that, in line with this present program by the military, Shemya also would soon be due for the ax, and Cold Bay would be "the Gander of the North Pacific." He moved fast, obtained a lease on Cold Bay from the Air Force ("I usually found the Air Force cooperative—in this case, Major General Bob Acheson of the Alaskan Air Command"), and took control of the Cold Bay facilities.

In June, 1954, the Air Force, as Reeve had predicted, ordered the sudden closure of Shemya airfield, stating, "We will operate it seven days more through our 1954 fiscal budget only." With Reeve running the Cold Bay field, both Northwest Airlines and Canadian Pacific were able to shift over to Cold Bay without missing a scheduled flight. The commercial lines were not the only ones that took advantage of the Reeve facilities. Navy, Army, and Coast Guard planes regularly dropped into Cold Bay, seeking refuge (three planes came in one day, one on fire, two with engine trouble). Recognizing the vital importance of the Cold Bay field, CAA in 1954 came to Reeve's rescue and took over the base. Reeve, however, retained the refueling concession, and all the lines using Cold

Bay deal with him. His cooperative friendship with Northwest Airlines dates many years back.* Many of his old Canadian bush-pilot friends are now the chiefs of Canadian Pacific Airlines, and, although arguments arise, Reeve and CPA always end up friends. Not so amicable are his relations with all-powerful Pan American Airways. Although personally friendly with Pan Am's chiefs, for several years Reeve waged a bitter feud with Pan Am over their depredations over his route in the form of cannery charter flights from Seattle. "I had plowed a million bucks into saving those Peninsula and Chain airfields. I flew empty all winter and felt entitled to the business during the seasonal activity. We aren't running a philanthropic organization."

Reeve's status as landlord of Cold Bay gave him one ace in the hole, a stiff landing fee. He next informed Pan Am that they must also pay him twenty-five dollars per head per passenger for loading, unloading, ground transportation, and use of his landing aids, and filed an agreement to that effect with the CAB, with the notice, "Your entry into Cold Bay will confirm acceptance and constitute a contract between Reeve Aleutian and Pan Am." Reeve made it stick, and collected his twenty-five dollars head tax. "I don't know who finally footed the bill in the long run, the canneries or Pan Am, but I got paid."

All the Alaska carriers nodded in gleeful agreement when Reeve took it upon himself to buck the powerful international air line's "chosen instrument" policies in the Far North. One member of CAB, reviewing the PAA vs. Reeve controversy, which eventually ended in PAA's discontinuing its service to the Aleutians, asserted admiringly, "By God, Pan Am finally met its match."

The next year Pan Am tried it again. This time Reeve told them bluntly, "We are most reluctant to become associated with any carrier with whom we do not engage in interline traffic exchanges in the Anchorage area. These carriers, Pacific Northern, Alaska Airlines Northwest and Reeve need this business. . . . Our lot is cast with these people and I am sticking by them. I am further opposed to becoming associated with Pan Am because of the damage your charters have accomplished against our rate structure. Were it not for your

_____
* In 1955 Northwest reactivated Shemya, and Reeve now uses it as an alternate.

charter pattern we would be able to reduce our Cold Bay rate substantially. . . ."

Bob spoke for all the local operators of Alaska. And some larger ones. After pioneering the great-circle route to the Orient, which they assert will not support more than one carrier, NWA discovered that Pan Am had filed for a parallel route from Seattle via the Chain to Tokyo. This would seriously affect NWA's entire operation by putting them back on subsidy due to loss of business. In 1954 Pan Am's charters, which they carried over Reeve's certificated routes, amounted to 10 per cent of Reeve's scheduled passenger revenues.

"In any event," philosophizes Reeve, "Pan Am is good for us in one way. They sure keep us sharpening our wits!"

Whether his stand is right or wrong, there is little doubt that Reeve is still a force to be reckoned with. As in his younger days, when he was an obvious bet for a fist fight at the drop of a hint, he is today always ready to take up the cudgel of protest. In 1952, when CAA decided to close the tower at Anchorage's Merrill Field (all of the scheduled carriers except Reeve had moved to the new Anchorage International Airport) for budget reasons, Reeve wrote the CAA administrator in hot protest, "What will you do with the hundreds of bush pilots and private planes based at Merrill?" If all these small craft were allowed unregulated flights in and out of the traffic patterns surrounding the busy International Airport, it would be, Reeve claimed, like "wild dogs in a slaughterhouse." They would "clobber the military jet and scheduled air carrier traffic patterns all over the area. . . . We are not going to have blood on our hands, our planes. You had better think twice. . . ." CAA revoked the order for the closure of Merrill tower. With the private plane serving as the "family car" of Alaska, little Merrill Field is still today one of the busiest ports in North America. When Reeve converts to DC-4's† in 1957, as is already planned, he will move over to the International Airport with these longer-range planes, and leave Merrill for the private flyers and bush pilots.

Reeve wages his battles openly, with great vigor and bullheaded obstinacy. His emotions are transparent. There is never any doubt where he stands. He creates admirers and enemies with equal ease. "The trouble with Bob," mused one of

† Reeve bought his first DC-4 in November, 1956.

his associates, "is that when he's an SOB he makes sure the whole world knows it. When he's a good guy, he keeps it mighty quiet!"

The people that Reeve and his pilots serve out on the Chain and up at the Pribilof Islands will attest to the "good guy" phase of Reeve's character. "Bob Reeve," said one woman out on Umnak Island, "is the only person who ever gave a damn about the folks that live on the Aleutians!"

In 1950, when Reeve made an application to service additional communities, by amphibian planes, a resident of King Cove was called in before the examiner to describe life on the southern side of the Chain. He explained that when he first moved there in 1936 two boats per month came in during the summer. Now they received but one boat every two months. There were no medical facilities.

"Is there any form of recreation during the winter months?" asked the examiner.

"Nope," the man shook his head. "We all just sit home and drink beer."

It is greatly reassuring to the 7500 inhabitants of this isolated area to know that, in an emergency, they can call a plane. In the old days the saying along the islands was, "When we get sick, we die."

Although Reeve is a shrewd business operator and, as his business friends say, "knows how to charge," he is keenly sympathetic to the people he serves and inevitably a "soft touch" in emergency. The Reeve pilots (who have filtered down to a hard-flying, responsible corps of men) are in a sense a projection of their boss's independent, salty, and warm personality. Due to the vagaries of the violent weather they fly and the enforced responsibility for plane and life, the Reeve pilots to a great extent resemble the bush pilots of a generation past. When they head down the 1783-mile stretch over the fog-shrouded Chain, they are literally "on their own." "Use your own judgment," are Reeve's orders, "and we'll hash it over later." "That," as one pilot explained it, "is what makes this job different from just drivin' an airplane." Although Reeve finally yielded to the pressure of convention and bought his pilots uniforms in 1955, they still help load and unload the freight (which includes baby chicks, crated fur seals for zoos, mail, eggs, milk, vegetables), handle passengers, serve boxed lunches, answer tourists' questions. "The least we do," joked one, "is fly the plane!"

Since there are no civilian hospital or doctor (and only one nurse, at Saint Paul) along their 2500 miles of air routes, mercy flights are routine. With their boss's knowledge and approval, the Reeve pilots are always "on call" for any emergency. They have the experience and knowledge of the area, and they are the only help available.

Quiet, gentle-eyed, Catholic "Pat" Kelly has become a specialist at emergencies and manages to be on the scene when they occur more often than other pilots, although they all regularly haul emergencies. The father of four, Kelly recently made an unscheduled landing at Dutch Harbor to pick up an eighteen-month-old Aleut child, ill with pneumonia, and hauled the sick baby in to the native hospital at Anchorage, changing its diapers and administering penicillin while gassing up his plane at Cold Bay.

A few days earlier, a Reeve plane at Port Heiden, cleared into Anchorage, reversed its flight plan to go back to Cold Bay and fetch a boy who had been carried in from a nearby village, stricken with acute appendicitis. One winter a Reeve plane circled for more than an hour in a swirling snow storm over Saint Paul, awaiting sufficient ceiling to fight its way down and remove a woman who needed emergency hospitalization. In December, 1951, Bill Borland circled over Unalaska in a blizzard for three hours before he could land to bring out a man who was critically ill. It was a job of flying that the mayor of the city called "nothing short of heroic."

When word was sent to RAA that the wife of a Unalaska man was dying in Seattle hospital and he should come at once, Captain Kelly went to get him—but he was off fishing "somewhere in the Bering Sea." Kelly took off in his DC-3 from Umnak and scouted the Bering Sea for two hours, making a grid-pattern search. He finally located the man's boat, wrote a message, wrapped it in an inflated life vest, flew over the boat, and tossed out the jacket—which landed on the deck of the small boat! Robinson read it, headed his boat in for Umnak where Kelly awaited for him, boarded the plane, and was at his wife's bedside in Seattle in eighteen hours.

In the spring of 1956, when a Canadian Pacific plane crashed at Cold Bay, Bill Borland was at the scene of the wreck within seven minutes, and personally dragged the only survivors out of the burning plane.

Although Reeve sometimes has trouble making out acceptable reports to explain these "deviations from schedule for the purpose of saving human life," he sincerely feels that his line is "the public servant, under obligation to the people in our area—because we are the only ones out there." During the summer of 1956, five stretcher cases were hauled in at one time from the Pribilofs. Specialists in the area, Reeve pilots have an advantage over military personnel and are able to render service to the Army, Navy, and Coast Guard as well as to civilians. When a Navy plane failed to return to its base at Adak from an Atka flight, Pat Kelly and his copilot Hank Orth volunteered to fly the hundred miles over "to take a look," discovered the Navy PBY crashed and lying across the abandoned runway. Kelly managed to bring his DC-3 down just short of the wreck (a job the Navy commandant hadn't the heart to order his own men to do), removed the injured survivors, and made a second trip to get the body of the dead pilot, completing a mercy mission which the Secretary of the Navy called a "superb achievement." Called on the carpet by air-carrier officials for his decision to take his commercially scheduled flight into the abandoned field, Kelly's explanation to the inspector was simple: "No one else could have gotten in there."

This sort of on-call emergency service has become as much an expected part of Reeve service to the ranchers, trappers, fishermen, and military who live on the Chain as the mail, freight, and passenger run. Reeve's files bulge with letters of appreciation. "We no longer feel like outcasts on these dismal little islands." "We, who at times feel a sense of isolation, are grateful and imbued with hope to know that in time of real need and emergency we can depend on you and your pilots."

Such personalized, informal, bush-style service makes difficulty for Reeve's office staff. "We must keep our records straight," moans Maggie Rutledge, "but Bob lets any broke Aleut or old-time Alaskan climb on his planes on credit."

When he sees "office shy" old-timers hovering outside his window, Reeve goes out and collars them and leads them in. A broke Eskimo recently approached Reeve, wanting passage back home to Nome. Bob let him work out his ticket money by cleaning the warehouse, which hadn't been cleaned in years. The Eskimo worked a while, then called to another Reeve employee and showed him a machine part that he had uncovered, which contained copper coils. "Bob don't want me to throw out his still, does he?" he asked.

When "Tex" Wheaton hired Aleut workers to help set up Reeve installations on the Chain, many turned down their pay checks, saying, "Just put it against my account to Bob."

Reeve is hardly a philanthropist. He is a shrewd business-man who follows the bush flyers' dictum that good business comes out of the good will of the people he serves. That Reeve's customers are in turn loyal to him shows in the fact that Reeve Aleutian Airways has one of the highest pay-load factors of any Alaskan carrier—averaging three thousand pounds of mail alone on each trip. In 1956, Reeve grossed over a million dollars. In communities where there are no landing fields, Reeve planes supply regular mail service by carrying mail sacks strapped to the belly of the plane in a bomb-release device (which Reeve salvaged from junked bombers) and dropping them on the isolated villages.

Islanders take a possessive interest in the Reeve pilots, whom they refer to as "our boys." They have their radio sets equipped with bands that will cover the Reeve frequencies, "wish" the planes down through swirling fog and blinding blizzard, and listen in on all the pilots' reports. "Just like talkin' on a party line," grinned slender, dark-eyed Captain Grant Forsythe. "They know everything about our flight before we get on the ground."

When, fresh from travel on Stateside lines, you first check in for a Reeve flight, it is at first difficult to realize just how far Bob Reeve has come, how many changes he was forced to make to achieve the status of a scheduled commercial carrier. Reeve operations, to a Stateside eye, still look like "overgrown bush." There is no nonsense about the little frame passenger office at Merrill Field with its giant urn of coffee and its Chick Sale plumbing. Reeve prowls restlessly around barking affectionately at passengers and pilots alike, helps load baggage, loans an outsider a parka or a pair of boots for protection against the penetrating Chain winds. Contrasted to the plushy interiors of most commercial aircraft, the Reeve DC-3 cabins are paint-shy and work-horse. There are no shiny chrome fixtures, no hostesses. (A mechanic is usually cabin attendant.) Half the cabin is piled high with well-roped mail and freight.

But when the plane revs up for take-off, the engines, as a CAA inspector once remarked, "purr like kittens." After he took over Pacific Airmotive, Reeve hired "the best mechanics in the Territory" and now boasts the finest engine and maintenance shop north of Seattle. Other lines farm out work to him, as does the Army. Reeve's preoccupation with engine care as a safety factor has paid off. In his eight years of operation as a certificated overseas carrier, he has consistently won the National Safety Award. Despite its rigorous route, Reeve Aleutian is generally conceded to be the "safest air line in Alaska."

But the responsibility never ceases to haunt Reeve. "If I ever lost a man or a plane I don't know what I'd do," he confesses. "Quit, I guess." When he pleads for extra caution and severe checks, he reminds his pilots, "I'm the one on the telephone. I'm the one who would have to tell the widows and kids. So—you do as I say!"

Reeve planes never take off without safe alternates; it is not certain that they will reach their destination on schedule or, if a flight is interrupted by weather en route, how long they will be delayed. Reeve Aleutian is laughingly referred to by Bob's rivals as the "most unscheduled scheduled air line in the business." Although his printed schedules list departure time from Anchorage, all intermediate stops and arrival times are marked "variable." "You can't be in a hurry and fly the Aleutians," commented Bill Borland. "Once last winter I was laid over in Cold Bay for seven days." To facilitate the inevitable layovers, Reeve has RON facilities for both passengers and crew at all regular stops. Despite the unpredictability of flying conditions, Reeve has a record of 98 per cent completion of schedules since 1946.

At the main Reeve stop at Cold Bay, even in mid-August passengers are greeted by a cold, slanting rain. It is difficult for station agent "Cal" Reeve (a distant cousin of Bob's) to keep the steps from blowing back up into the plane. Before your eyes stretches a treeless, colorless, storm-sodden land. Remarked Captain Forsythe, "A fellow can be feeling pretty cheerful out here—until he looks up and sees those seagulls flying backwards!"

When they head out over the three hundred miles of open ocean northwest from Cold Bay to the Pribilofs, Reeve pilots have no beam to go by. If they overshoot, they will end up in the Soviet Union. They fly by chart, listen for the loran station on Saint Paul which they use as a homing beacon, and descend through the inevitable dense fog that completely obscures the islands. It is only within the last few hundred feet that the sodden green land and doll-size runway of crushed volcanic rock become visible.

As he did with the mines back of Valdez, Reeve is trying to prove that the Chain is no longer "isolated" and unavailable. Airpower ties the communities together. People who formerly migrated back to the mainland after a short try at fishing, ranching or trapping, because of the lack of mail and medical service, now remain within the communities. The Aleutians, Reeve would like to inform the world, are not barren of wild life although barren of trees. There are reindeer herds on Umnak, Atka, and up at the Pribilofs. There are blue and red fox on most of the islands. In the fall, Cold Bay boasts the largest concentration of migratory birds under the American flag. The fishing industry, accelerated because of fast airplane transportation, has now expanded from concentration on only salmon to the commercial catching of giant king crab, halibut, and herring. With their natural resources only partially developed, the Aleutians show promise of mineral wealth in iron, gold, lead, zinc, and copper.

A few years ago Reeve made a bid for tourist trade, now hauls planeloads of tourists into the Pribilofs for the seals' mating season, when the wet, rocky, fogbound shores witness an indescribable roaring, fighting multitude of do-or-die love affairs.

In 1953, when the DEW line activity moved into the Territory, Reeve as well as other operators participated in government supply contracts. In one sixty-day period the Reeve line moved one thousand tons of strategic material to DEW line sites, in addition to carrying on their normal schedule. In March of 1955 Reeve got an urgent call from the DEW line contractors in Edmonton, Canada, who wanted five hundred construction workers hauled from Edmonton to the Amundsen Gulf in the Arctic Ocean (two thousand miles north). Within forty-eight hours Bill Borland, copilots Grant Forsythe and Carl McArthur, and mechanic Leo Slama, were en route from Edmonton with the first planeload. For the next two months, in weather ranging from twenty to fifty below zero, with blasting winter winds, they flew 458 men up to the Arctic

Ocean, made wheel landings on the Arctic ice, unloaded, and flew back for more. Each trip was twenty-four hours long; they made three per week. "That engine never cooled off." They flew all day, did their maintenance at night; one plane and one crew took care of the total job. When the Air Force was ready to move in, Bill Borland flew their personnel in to set up communications and facilities for the Air Force planes.

When Reeve went out to check his flight blackboard, he found his operations excitingly widespread. "I had a plane at Attu, one in the Pribilofs, one at Kotzebue, one in Churchill on Hudson Bay. Then in forty-eight hours they were all back in the nest. Within a few more hours they were spread out again." With the DEW line now being extended out the Alaskan Peninsula and the Aleutians, Reeve is in line for more busy days.

Until recently the Reeve family owned 100 per cent of the Airline, "probably the tightest ownership outside of Howard Hughes!" Several years ago, Reeve passed control of 10 per cent of the stock to his superintendent of maintenance, Bob Hanson, and eventually plans to "slice in" some of his other key employees. Although he hangs on tightly to the ownership, Bob denies that he runs a "one-man line." "Each department head is free to run his operations as he sees fit, so long as he doesn't deviate from my safety standards," claims Reeve. His pilots admit they have much more freedom of decision than they would on a big air line. "Don't know as I'd like to work for Bob," commented an acquaintance, "but his operations are tops in the Territory. He won't tolerate faulty work—or faulty flying. And he just doesn't have any!" Reeve is a hard taskmaster, but it is a hard route he serves. And his biggest concern is somewhat unarguable: safety. He prowls around his shop and office, inspects planes and pilots and mechanics with a critical eye that knows what it sees. "I can walk around an airplane and usually know if anything's wrong with it," he boasts.

Reeve feels that he pays above the average, points out that in 1955 his employees' average annual salaries were the highest among America's forty-eight scheduled air carriers.

Ever alert for safety, in 1953 Reeve became greatly concerned over the cause of a rash of accidents in the Alaska theater involving large multiengine aircraft of both military C-47 and commercial DC-3 types. Studying the accident reports, Reeve concluded that most of the accidents were caused by the flight crews lack of training in or inattention to the critical air speed of the aircraft (known as VI) at take-off prior to becoming air-borne. The pilot either had pulled the airplane that would carry it through the stall stage, or had experienced an engine failure during the critical period and had attempted off the ground before it had attained the safe ground speed to become air-borne on a single engine and encountered a stall.

Reeve made a complete examination of his crews' technique in order to prevent any such incident on RAA. Due to the short fields Reeve operated in and out of with his DC-3's, he found that the pilots' current technique was to get the craft air-borne as soon as possible, the lesser of two evils. Due to these field conditions, Reeve allowed the pilots a "spot deviation" from the basic rule. "I knew the pilots and knew they'd make the right decision." But on fields of normal length, passing through the critical phase before becoming air-borne became an ironbound rule. "If an engine quits before V2 [V2 safe flying speed is 78.9 miles per hour on a DC-3], cut the throttles and slam on the brakes. If you can't stop, then ground-loop or dump the landing gear. Parts are cheap compared to human life."

Reeve figures that violation of the V2 rule and collision in flight are the only factors that will cause him to lose an aircraft. He had gone to all lengths possible to eliminate engine failure, and pilot error is at a minimum. He hammers the use of the check list, sometimes to the point of being repetitious. "We've got an out for every emergency except one that results from disobeying the rules."

Reeve is a better passenger on his own than on other air lines. Twice he has climbed off air liners in the States and refused to go on with the trip when he was suspicious of the pilot's judgement. Before 1942, when he became personally indoctrinated with instrument letdown procedures, Reeve distrusted any but visual flying, and habitually climbed off flights where the ceiling was low and he couldn't "see where we were going." On a flight between Madison, Wisconsin, and Saint Paul, Reeve went up front to chat with an old barnstorming pal, Captain Eddie La Parle of Northwest Airlines, saw a huge black cloud looming up ahead, "a real thunderhead," said "See you later, Eddie," and beat it back for his seat to get into his seat belt. "I didn't quite make it before we hit. First thing I knew I was lying against the top of the ceiling of that airplane and then I came crashing down onto the stewardess's lap." Reeve smiled reminiscently. "She hung onto me—and it turned out not to be such a bad bump after all."

Passenger Reeve always sits near an emergency exit, keeps his seat belt tight, is on the lookout for trouble. After one Stateside visit, in 1954, he boarded a Northwest Stratocruiser in Seattle for his return flight home in a blinding snowstorm. They taxied down to the ramp ready to take off, and Reeve noticed uneasily that the wings were covered with snow. Then he reminded himself that "the skipper knows his business," and made himself relax—closed his eyes and fell sound asleep. A little while later he woke. The first thing he noticed was that all four engines had quit. He looked out of the window. "We were on top of clouds with the moon shining in. I thought, Oh golly, here we go again!" Reeve unbuckled his belt, jumped up, and grabbed the life vest, ordering all the other passengers to do likewise, then sat back and buckled himself in—for the ditching. Another glance out the window revealed to his amazement "a half-dozen men walking around on the clouds, brushing snow off the wings!" The "moon" was the big floodlight inside the hangar. They had pulled the airplane into the hangar to get it cleaned off before taking off. Reeve sat down sheepishly—and the planeload of passengers had a good laugh.

High-strung as ever, Reeve is constantly prowling around his office, shop, hangar, or house. Always in a hurry, he is forever exhorting his children and friends to "get a move on," "let's put the show on the road." No snob, Reeve enjoys relaxing with the young fighter pilots out at Elmendorf (the Sixty-Sixth Fighter Squadron made him an honorary member) as well as the Air Force brass he has known so long. His pleasures, these days, are handsome suits, Borsalino hats (which he throws away when they get dirty), and Scotch whisky. If you offer him a drink, Reeve is apt to wiggle his thick black eyebrows and growl happily, "I know a command when I hear one!"

A devoted family man, Reeve is playful with his children, gets a kick out of their various activities, likes to roar at them once in a while and to see them jump (which they do to please him). He's always threatening to throw out some of the thirty-seven-odd menagerie members (dogs, cats, canaries, flying squirrels, hamster, banty chicks, pigeons and one Peruvian cavy with pink eyes), but recently chased someone else's puppy for six blocks, thinking it was his kids' mutt, Marvin, strayed from home.

Reeve has made the transition from "star" to audience with pretty good grace. He is proud of his pilots, tries to restrain himself from being overcritical when they do something differently than the way pilot Reeve would have done it. Even closer to home is Reeve's role as the worried parent to son Richard's flying. The first time Richard made a cross-country flight alone, Bob paced the floor all day long. When Richard hadn't arrived home on exact schedule, Bob said tensely, "He's probably down on a beach somewhere with a busted landing gear." A few weeks later, however, when stable, conscientious flyer Richard was running late, "the old man" shrugged indifferently. "Oh, he'll be along." Although still a student at the University of Alaska, nineteen-year-old Richard is checking out as copilot on Reeve Aleutian and served as watch dispatcher. Twelve-year-old David and seven-year-old Whitty expect to start flying lessons as soon as they are old enough, hop every ferry flight they can get, and help Captain Borland "get the wheels down" on landing. The Reeve girls, pretty, snapping-eyed, sixteen-year-old Roberta and witty, brunette, thirteen-year-old Janice, are more interested in boys and gardens respectively, have no desire to learn to fly. (The Reeve children, by the way, were heartbroken when a family motor trip was supplanted by a flight to the Yukon. "Heck, we never get to ride in a car!")

In 1956 Reeve Aleutian Airways, along with other Alaskan and Hawaiian carriers, was at last granted a permanent certificate by a special act of Congress. "After twenty-five years in business," commented Bob wryly, "they finally got around to giving us permanent certificates!"

When CAB reviewed the case for permanent certifications of Alaskan carriers, their report found that by 1955 Alaskans were flying thirty times as much as other American citizens‡, and boasted nine major scheduled air lines. Although it was only in 1925 that the Alaskan legislature authorized the con-

‡ During 1955 Ray Petersen's Northern Consolidated line carried over four thousand passengers in and out of the town of Bethel, which has a permanent population of one thousand!

struction of its first dirt airstrips, by 1955 Alaska had over three hundred modern airports. The report stessed the need for granting permanent certification to the long-neglected Alaskan carriers (States carriers had received theirs in 1946), so that they might proceed with long-range plans. Banks refused to put up the necessary loans to Alaskan aviation business so long as the carriers could show only temporary certification. As a final historical reminder of the value of Alaska to the world, the report stated that the gross volume of business in the Territory had increased 86 per cent from 1951 to 1954. The 1954 volume equaled *seventy times* the original purchase price of Alaska!

Alaska, through the loud urgings of its loyal citizens and the proddings of a few wars, has come into its own. It was a great gain for the Territory, Reeve feels, when General J. H. "Hamp" Atkinson became commander of the Alaskan Air Command in 1947 (he left to take command of the Air Defense Command at ENT Air Force Base, Colorado, in October, 1956). A brilliant combat leader in Europe and Africa, Atkinson draws from his experience and knowledge of aerial warfare a deep insight into Alaska's needs. "Today," says Reeve proudly, "due to Atkinson's leadership and General Twining's master strategy, Alaska has become a real armed fortress."

On his frequent trips to the States, when people ask Reeve, "Aren't you afraid of the Russians?" he roars:

"Hell, no. If we don't knock 'em down like pigeons before they get across the Alaskan Range, we Alaskans, each with a half-dozen guns and ammunition, will just kick their teeth out!"

Reeve speaks for the big, bellicose, vigorous Paul Bunyan spirit of our last frontier. He is, as his Stateside friends remark when they introduce him, "Mr. Alaska."